The Needle is Threaded

The Needle is Threaded

'The History of an Industry' by *Margaret Stewart & Leslie Hunter*

HEINEMANN/NEWMAN NEAME

First published for the National Union of Tailors and Garment Workers by
William Heinemann Ltd in co-operation with Newman Neame Ltd
© 1964 The National Union of Tailors and Garment Workers' Union
Printed in Great Britain by The Millbrook Press Ltd, Southampton

Foreword

BY JOHN E. NEWTON, GENERAL SECRETARY OF THE
NATIONAL UNION OF TAILORS AND GARMENT WORKERS

When we decided to produce a history of our union, we invited as joint authors Margaret Stewart and the late Leslie Hunter, both well-established writers with a particular knowledge of the trade union and labour movement. All our relevant records were placed at their disposal and we gave them all the help we could from our own experience. We asked them to write a comprehensive and readable account of the development of the union as we know it today from the multiplicity of small societies which attended its growth.

The Needle is Threaded is, however, more than a straightforward account of the union's growth. It sets the story against the background of the wider union struggle and shows how the tailors were ever in the van of social progress. They played a vital part in the fight to improve wages and conditions and eliminate the vicious exploitation and 'slum' conditions of earlier years. We believe that the success of the garment workers in forging a single national union may be both helpful and instructive at the present time. We are an industrial union, but we still retain a strong craft basis, as our insistence on the need for systematic training amply demonstrates.

These pages show how the obstacles to unity were overcome, thanks to the vision of some of the earlier leaders and to the devoted and unselfish support of countless men and women in the ranks of the union.

It is to these men and women that this book is dedicated.

Contents

Contents (continued)

Illustrations

Illustrations (continued)

Author's Note

Leslie Hunter, my former husband, died before this book was completed, but it is in every sense a joint effort. In writing it, we sought to tell the story of the Tailors and Garment Workers' Union in such a way as to appeal to the general reader, as well as to the more serious student of trade union affairs – to write about the men and women who made the union and avoid overloading the pages with procedural detail and statistical references. The result, we hoped, would be readable even if deficient in 'academic' terms and different from many of the more orthodox trade union 'histories'.

Thanks are particularly due to Mr John Newton, and others at union headquarters for generous help in supplying material and in checking the work at various stages. Many union 'veterans' provided vivid recollections of past events and personalities, and the *News Chronicle* library provided a wealth of information about the *Daily News* anti-sweating exhibition. Notes collected by the late Herbert Tracey and the records of the late Dr J. J. Mallon were especially helpful in the early stages of writing.

The main sources of information were the union's own journals, from the *Tailor* of the 1860s to the present-day *Garment Worker*. The Webbs' *History of Trade Unionism* (Longmans, 1920) provided indispensable general background. Considering its importance and interest, surprisingly little has been written about the clothing industry, but we found useful material in R. G. Tawney's *Minimum Rates in the Tailoring Trade* (London

School of Economics, 1915), Dorothy Sells' *The British Trade Boards System* (P. S. King & Son, 1923), S. P. Dobbs' *The Clothing Workers of Great Britain* (Routledge & Sons, 1928), Mrs Joan Thomas's *A History of the Leeds Clothing Industry* (Yorkshire Bulletin of Economic and Social Research, 1955), Rt Hon C. Booth's *Life and Labour of the People in London* (Macmillan & Co, 1902, 1903), and F. W. Galton's *The Tailoring Trade* (Longmans Green & Co, 1896). Margaret Cole's *Makers of the British Labour Movement* (Longmans Green Ltd, 1948), and Shirley W. Lerner's *Breakaway Unions and the Small Trade Union* (Allen & Unwin Ltd, 1961), are authoritative works, and we owe them a considerable debt. For more recent history, the Working Party reports on the clothing industry and Margaret Wray's *The Women's Outerwear Industry* (Gerald Duckworth Ltd, 1957), were useful reading. Recourse was had, as appropriate, to Hansard, the Board of Trade *Journal*, the Ministry of Labour *Gazette* and the trade press.

All these are essential reading for serious students of the clothing trade and the union's development and for those who wish to delve more deeply into the fascinating story of the tailors of Britain.

The authors were conscious of doing less than justice to the many individuals who contributed so much to the formation of the union and are active in its ranks today, but it was clearly impossible, in covering such a wide sweep of time, to name all those who make up the union's roll of honour.

One major difficulty was to know where to end. The authors were tempted to stop at 1932, year of the big amalgamation when the needle was finally threaded. In the end, 1960 was chosen, as a purely arbitrary date. But the present leadership, under difficult conditions and building on the foundations laid in earlier years, is now putting into effect many of the plans conceived earlier for building up and strengthening the organisation. The union will continue to provide fascinating material for the chroniclers of the future.

Chapter One/'Men Must Needs Have Clothing'

JOURNEYMEN TAILORS IN THE MIDDLE AGES; 'FLOGGING THE CAT'; THE
BLACK DEATH; PERSECUTION OF JOHN BADBY; DISCIPLINING THE TAILORS;
THE GARLYKHYTHE HOUSE; PURPOSE OF COMBINATION; THE GUILDS; BROTHER
BERTHOLD'S ADVICE

A full history of the tailors would embrace the whole story of
civilisation. There is no older craft. The most primitive peoples
show a nice discrimination in the choice of skins and the manner of wearing them. Eve, no doubt, found satisfaction in the
stylish arrangement of her fig leaves, both for cover and
adornment.

Once society rises above the brutish level, clothing replaces
mere covering and the demand for the craft of tailoring arises.
The thonging of pelts with a bone needle and animal gut is
the genesis of a skilled trade, painstakingly learned. For the
very poorest, the method of clothing the family remained much
the same from the stone age to the earliest years of the twentieth
century. The materials changed, and different implements
were used, but the great majority of people wore clothes that
had been made at home. The idea of buying one's clothes is
comparatively recent.

Long before Shakespeare's day the wealthier members of
society were seeking to be 'the glass of fashion and the mould
of form', and the tailor's place in the community was assured.
In the earlier civilisations, the best tailors were bought, inherited or seized by the richest and most powerful as household
slaves. When slavery had given place to serfdom, and serfdom

I

to the nominally free society of the middle ages, a new pattern of organisation emerged which still exists today side by side with the mass production factories.

The successful tailor needed the eye of an artist for colour and design, the skill of a craftsman in manipulating his tools and material, and the business acumen of a trader in selling his goods and services. The least difficult parts of the process of turning a piece of cloth into clothing are readily taught, and the busy tailor could increase his output by handing over this part of his work to semi-skilled labour. In return for such work as he was able to do, a young man could gradually learn the whole of the trade. Not all of those who had passed through such a training had the financial resources and the combination of diverse capacities needed to succeed as master tailors on their own. They could seek work for wages, or work by themselves as individual one-man businesses.

In a sparsely populated country with poor communications, the self-employed tailor could find work by journeying from place to place offering his services at farms and homesteads throughout the land. Tailors were still 'flogging the cat'[1] within living memory, arriving with goose iron, sleeve board and the rest of the tools of their trade to set up in the parlour of a farmhouse and remaining until all the family had been clothed before passing on to the next customers.

The division into masters, journeymen and apprentices is discernible early in the middle ages, but at first their social and economic relations were ill-defined both as between themselves and with the rest of the community. The Black Death wiped out one-third of the working population and put an end to the ramshackle pretensions of the feudal system, but no generally acceptable alternative was at once perceived. The change to a wage economy was slow, unsettling and the cause of bitter hardship.

The work of the tailors called for above average skill and intelligence, and the elements at least of figuring and lettering.

---

[1] *The origin of the phrase 'flogging the cat' is obscure. It is just one of those phrases which grew up with the trade, some of which are still in use, though most have disappeared. An article in* The Garment Worker *1950 listed some of the more picturesque language used by tailors – his wife is his 'hipstay'; getting drunk is to 'go on the cod'; 'striking a bright' is being in financial or other trouble; when a man dies he is 'carrying sand'. A man who starts an independent business 'puts up a cat's face'.*

They had time to philosophise as they stitched, and opportunities for seeing at first hand how the other half lived. It is
not surprising to find tailors playing a sometimes quite considerable part in progressive movements throughout the ages.

The horror of the Black Death came at a time when the
church, bloated with wealth, was sunk in corruption. It was
against this background that Englishmen began to read the
Bible newly translated into their native language for the first
time by Wyclif. The Lollards related its story to the society in
which they found themselves with devastating results.

> 'When Adam delved and Eve span,
> Who was then the gentleman?'

In this fourteenth-century couplet lay a challenge to all
constituted authority, whether lay or ecclesiastic; there were
those who were ready to make the challenge not only by
preaching but by armed rebellion. Denounced by the church
as blasphemers and heretics and by the state as recreants and
traitors, they were persecuted with a savagery notable even for
those rude times.

One such was John Badby, a tailor of Worcester, who was
brought to the stake in the presence of Henry, Prince of Wales,
in 1410. The faggots were lit, put out and lit again as the prince
tried, first with an offer of a pardon and finally with the bribe
of a life pension as well, to get him to recant. He died un-
repentant, guilty of having been born before his time.

The Lollard vision of a Christian society based on brotherhood and equality was too grandiose to be attainable either by
persuasion or by force in the context of the times. While the
Lollards were being suppressed, less visionary but more endur-
ing historical processes were unfolding.

Five years after watching John Badby burn to death, the
Prince of Wales, now crowned as King Henry V, was preparing
to invade France. Later in the year the campaign would be
brought to a brilliant military conclusion at the battle of
Agincourt, a victory that was to prove one of the emptiest in
the history of war. While the king was preparing for war overseas, the mayor and aldermen were seeking to establish and
maintain his peace in the city of London.

On the morning of 19th April 1415, Thomas Fauconer,
mayor of London (the title of lord mayor did not come into

3

general use for another 130 years) presided over his court of aldermen in Guildhall. It was intimated to them, says the record, in a relation not unattended with alarm, 'that some serving men and journeymen of the tailors of the said City, called yo-men taillours, dwelling with one another in companies by themselves, did hold and inhabit divers dwelling houses in the City against the will of their superiors in the said City and of the masters of that trade'.

The phrase 'yo-men taillours' has been interpreted as young men, meaning apprentices and also as yeomen, in analogy with, for example, yeomen farmers. In the latter sense they would be hired journeymen or possibly self-employed. In fact, too much can be read into this and similar documents, written in crabbed and abbreviated Norman French or Latin at a time when the apprenticeship system was neither universal nor fully organised. This case seems to be one in which the city authorities and the masters of the trade were seeking to elucidate and clarify their own control over all those working in the trade who were not full members of the masters' guild.

Whatever their precise station in life, these tailors were said to have behaved in a way that was bound to shock the susceptibilities of the worthy mayor and aldermen. They had, 'in past times, like unruly and insolent men without head or governance, oftentimes assembled in great numbers and had held divers assemblies and conventicles in various places, both within the said City and without; and now of late had grievously and of their malice and imagining aforethought, wounded, beaten and maltreated many lieges of our lord the king, and especially one Thomas Trepenelle, one of the masters of the trade aforesaid'. Among the many other evils and enormities laid at their door was the crime of rescuing people under arrest by the city serjeants and officers. One suspects that the beating-up of Thomas Trepenelle was the occasion of a decision to discipline the junior members of the trade.

After careful deliberation, the magistrates decided they must suppress such malignity, but their first move was against the masters of the trade rather than the authors of the trouble. They summoned Thomas Whityngham, the then master of the tailors' guild, and his wardens to appear before them six days later 'to speak to them on the matters aforementioned; why that whereas they, under the mayor and aldermen and other governors of the said City, had especial governance in the trade aforesaid, they allowed their servingmen and journeymen to occupy such dwelling houses, so as to live together in companies by themselves, without any superior to rule them and to commit and perpetrate so harmfully such evils and misdeeds'.

When they appeared at Guildhall on 25th April, Thomas Whityngham and his companions expressed themselves as being exceedingly sorrowful at there being such offenders and such misdeeds. The masters and reputable members of the trade were suffering from the many scandals and inconveniences of this inconsiderate conduct, but the men had refused, after frequent warnings, to vacate their dwelling houses.

The mayor and aldermen found the complaints to be 'just and consonant with reason' and ordered Otho Bris, their serjeant, to bring David Brekenhok and John Stanbury, who were living with others in a dwelling house in Garlykhythe, before them on 29th April. When they appeared and were questioned, they 'could not gainsay or well deny the same' and were ordered to appear for judgment on 2nd May.

At this, the fourth hearing, the city fathers held further careful council and conference on the problem before making their decision. They found that by wearing a livery at their annual assemblies and living together without proper supervision – like a race at once youthful and unstable – the men's conduct 'did expressly imply a breach of the peace of our lord the king'. They 'did therefore award and judge that the servingmen of the trade should in future be under the governance and rule of the masters and wardens of the trade, the same as other servingmen of other trades of the said City are, and are bound to be'. They were forbidden to wear livery or hold assemblies in the future and told to quit the house at Garlykhythe by Sunday 6th May.

Two years after being put firmly under the discipline and control of the masters, the servingmen again appeared before the mayor and aldermen of London. They asked permission to assemble in the church of St John of Jerusalem, near Smithfield, on the feast of the Decollation of St John the Baptist (29th August) and yearly thereafter 'to make offering for brethren and sisters of their fraternity who had departed this life and to do other things which theretofore they had been wont to do'. A marginal note in the brief record suggests that the application was refused after reference to the judgment of 2nd May 1415.

It has been suggested that these events show that the workers in the tailoring industry attempted as early as the fourteenth and fifteenth centuries to combine together in associations which were the forerunners of modern trade unions, and that the masters suppressed these demonstrations of working class militancy. Such evidence as there is does little to support the theory that they combined for economic purposes. There does, however, appear to have been some degree of combination for social reasons.

It is not to be supposed that when any group of men working in the same trade met together for any purpose, they would not sooner or later discuss among themselves the conditions and rewards of their occupation. In times of hardship the idea of a joint demand or even joint action in an effort to improve their lot would naturally occur to them. There is evidence that in various trades sporadic activity of this kind occurred from time to time in the early middle ages, but that is not to say that the 'fraternities' were associations formed with the object of furthering the economic interests of their members against the masters.

The magistrates in the towns and cities were charged with the responsibility for maintaining law and order at a time when they had neither a police force nor any other part of the apparatus of a modern state at their disposal. It was in their own interest as leading tradesmen that their communities should be well governed, and there was the added incentive that the king's hand could fall heavily on those who failed to keep his peace on his behalf.

The companies and guilds of masters which had grown up in the medieval towns provided a natural authority to which the magistrates could delegate their responsibility. In this, the great age of restrictive practices, the masters were able to establish their own privileges and prevent others from sharing them. With their own distinctive liveries and corporate activities, they were recognisable as the modern equivalent of a feudal household. It was natural for the magistrates, drawn from their ranks, to look to them to control the whole of their trade and to be responsible for the good behaviour of all engaged in it.

The growth of the towns brought with it an increase in the working population who could not themselves hope to enter the guilds. Their tendency to form themselves into liveried companies with their own mystiques in imitation of the masters was seen as a dangerous threat to law and order. It was because, by living apart and engaging in rowdy conduct the serving men of the tailors were considered to threaten a breach of the peace, that they were told to submit to the control of the masters.

The religious aspect of the fraternities must not be underestimated. It was a pious duty laid on all Christians to pray for the soul of the dead and for the well-being of their neighbours. To those who, a generation before, had been countrymen, and who were now congregated together round the headquarters of their trade in London and other towns, it was an easy translation from the village parish to a fraternity of those engaged in the same trade. Communal religious observance and the giving of alms to the poor of the parish found this counterpart in the towns. The fraternity alms box was used solely for charity, and there is no suggestion anywhere of its being used to finance strike action or for other trade union activity.

Since holy days were holidays, the establishment of a peculiar interest in a particular church feast had the added advantage that when religious observance had ended, the jollification could begin. Why the tailors chose to celebrate the commemoration of the decapitation of St John the Baptist is not clear, but had they succeeded in their application they would have been assured of one extra annual day's holiday, apart from the universally accepted feasts in the calendar. The borderline between the enjoyment of an outing and the beginning of a riot was ill-defined in this age of boisterous energy. The magistrates were acting on hard-won experience when they sought to ban these gatherings which they had not the means to control.

The case heard by the city justices in 1415 was only one of a whole series dealing with various trades. Nineteen years before the same court had dealt with similar complaints against the servingmen of the saddlers, and here was one of the rarer cases in which the men were said to have combined to demand higher wages. This last point does not seem to have concerned the court very seriously and the question turned on the claim of the men to have assembled on the feast of the Assumption, dressed alike, to go to Mass in the Church of St Vedast in Foster Lane, Cheapside, next the Saddlers' Hall, 'time out of mind'. The court heard that the custom for which such venerable antiquity was claimed had in fact been started thirteen years before and was now being revived after a lapse of several years.

These cases involving the saddlers and the tailors and those dealing with other trades, together with the fact that nowhere did any of these associations develop further, suggest that the fraternities were looked on as means to secure new social privileges rather than economic advance, and that they were resisted in the name of law and order.

The appeals to immemorial custom put forward on all sides do not mean that the workers were really being robbed of ancient privileges they had enjoyed in the past. No one, from the king down to the lowliest peasant, dreamed of asserting a right to a new privilege. There were conceived to be certain rules which had always governed the conduct of Englishmen to each other. All that could be done was to find out and establish these rules with the help of the chronicles of the past or the witness of those most likely to know. The courts decided, in the light of the evidence and of a growing body of case law, how the half-remembered customs of Viking pirates and Norman fiefs applied to the quite different life of trading and manufacturing towns.

To this elegant use of the art of hypocrisy, the country owes the foundation of the common law and all that flows from it. The saddlers in 1396 and the tailors in 1417 were merely attempting the same technique as those who had written Magna Carta in 1215 when the first claimed their assemblies had been held 'time out of mind' and the second asked to be allowed to do as 'they had been wont to do'.

In rejecting these claims, the magistrates themselves appealed to the past. When they denied the right of the saddlers to free association and put them under the control of the masters, they told the masters that the men must be properly treated 'in such manner as the servingmen in like trades in the city have been wont to be properly treated and governed'. That the mayor did not regard himself merely as the voice and creature of the masters is shown by his further invitation to the men to complain at once of any grievance unduly inflicted on them, with a promise of speedy justice against the masters should it be required.

The tailors, in 1417, were similarly told to treat their servingmen 'the same as other servingmen of other trades of the said city are, and are bound to be'. There was no Act of Parliament or other legislative device laying down rules by which the men of any trade should be governed by their 'superiors'. The magistrates established the system of control by working from precedent to precedent. The system survived for many centuries. In 1755 James Watt, the inventor of the steam engine, spent a year in London not daring to leave the house of the instrument maker to whom he had paid twenty guineas to teach him the trade. Being neither a regular apprentice nor a 'creditable tradesman' he would have been scooped up by the press gangs in search of men for the Royal Navy if he had been caught on the streets. Not for many centuries did the system finally vanish to be replaced by control through joint negotiation between the employers and trade unions.

Even if they had been allowed to continue to associate together for social and charitable purposes it is doubtful if the fraternities would have developed into militant organisations. The masters were themselves working tailors belonging to the same social grade as the handful of journeymen and apprentices working for them. The more able among the latter could expect to become masters or at least self-employed. Few, if any, of the young men in the trade saw themselves remaining as wage-earners for the rest of their lives. The ardent spirits who led the occasional movements which might have been the foundation of a permanent organisation soon lost interest when they gained their own economic independence.

The restrictions imposed on entry to its ranks by the Merchant Tailors' Company might well have led to a revolt against its authority by the growing number of comparatively well-to-do traders and journeymen who could not obtain admission. They were bought off by the formation of a company of 'Bachelors' or 'Yeomen Tailors' subordinate to the parent company but with their own livery and privileges. Though there were probably some journeymen in the Bachelor Company, for the most part it was composed of quite wealthy merchants who could hope for eventual election to the parent company.

9

With that deep reverence for the past, whether real or imaginary, which illuminates the thought of modern Britons no less than it did the Anglo-Saxons, attempts have been made to show that the yeomen companies or even the guilds themselves were the forerunners of trade unions. The theory cannot be sustained unless we accept a definition of trade unionism so wide as to be meaningless.

In their origins the guilds were combinations of craftsmen whose one or two assistants were members of their own family or household, rather than employees. With the growth of the towns the guilds became the organisations of employers and the instruments of law and order. They adapted and developed the usages of the feudal household to medieval town life and commerce so far as they found these useful and applicable. These outward forms served to give an appearance of continuity at a time when new and radical changes were taking place. Centuries later they were copied and developed further by the infant workers' organisations with their ceremonials, oath taking and the like. The superficial resemblances cannot hide the totally different content and purpose of the new organisations when contrasted with the old.

We catch a glimpse of the state of the craft in the thirteenth century from the sermons of Brother Berthold, a friar who wandered about Europe preaching. 'In order that ye may compass men's praise,' he told the women in his open-air congregation about 1250, 'ye spend all your labour on your garments, your veils and your kirtles. Many of you pay as much to the sempstress as the cost of the cloth itself; it must have shields on the shoulders, it must be flounced and tucked all round the hem; it is not enough for you to show pride in your very buttonholes, but you must also send your feet to hell by special torments.'

History shows that the friar's warnings against fashion as an artifice of the devil fell on deaf ears; men and women continued to patronise the tailors and sempstresses despite the danger to their immortal souls. But in another sermon he struck a note which appealed to the self-interest of customer and tailor alike. 'Men must needs have clothing,' he said, addressing the trade direct, 'therefore should ye so serve them as to do your work truly; not to steal half the cloth, or to use other guile, mixing hair with your wool or stretching it out longer, whereby man thinketh to have gotten good cloth, yet thou hast stretched it longer than it should be and makest good cloth into useless stuff.'

Lest it should be thought that tailors were particularly venal, it is fair to note that the same sermon castigated smiths, carpenters, butchers, wine merchants and traders in general, together with agricultural workers and quack doctors in far stronger terms.

In this second sermon, so far from preaching against habits no one intended to change, the friar was voicing a growing public opinion. Among the many other rights against arbitrary and unjust treatment, the Englishman felt he had the right to be protected against cheating. Nothing so sophisticated as a Consumers' Protection Association or even an Act of Parliament dealing with false pretences occurred to the medieval mind. The masters, in their endeavours to make themselves at once respectable and respected, took a larger view of their own self-interest than that of concentrating solely on restrictive combination. The guilds assumed the right to set standards below which no one could fall without incurring penalties. In doing so, they were not only enhancing their own reputation and status, but were acting in a very real sense as protectors of the buying public.

This was a function which could not be carried out except by controlling the entry and practice of the craft. Thus, the tailors came to lay down the terms and duration of apprenticeship, the wages of journeymen and the ethical standards of the craft. In the end, as we have seen, they were made responsible for the general good behaviour of the young men in the trade.

While the masters were able, with the help of the magistrates, to establish their own privileges and responsibilities, the employees, inexperienced and leaderless and lacking a common economic aim, remained for centuries unorganised. On a broad front they could, like John Badby, join in any of the series of ineffective rebellions which marked the age. On the narrow front where they did temporarily combine on a specific issue, they were easily defeated by the masters who were themselves an integral part of the evolving state apparatus.

Chapter Two/Early Attempts at Combination

BREAKDOWN OF THE GUILD SYSTEM; PARLIAMENT INTERESTS ITSELF IN WAGES AND CONDITIONS; THE SHOPKEEPING TAILORS; HOUSES OF CALL; LONDON AND WESTMINSTER TAILORS COMBINE; ILLEGAL ORGANISATIONS; COMBINATION ACTS; THE STRUGGLE IN SCOTLAND AND IRELAND; FERMENT OF FRENCH REVOLUTION

In their heyday the craft guilds performed functions which have now been assumed by a wide variety of public and private organisations. They were the ancestor of the friendly society, the factory inspector, the police force, the school attendance officer, the assistance board, the inspector of weights and measures far more truly than they were the ancestor of either the employers' association or the trade union. The system failed to solve the problems posed by the runaway inflation of the later Tudors, the growth of capitalist competition and the first rumblings of the industrial revolution. The underlying idea of a regulating authority dealing fairly between the different interests within a trade and between the trade and the rest of the community survived. It was to Parliament rather than the guilds that men began to look for the redress of their grievances in the sixteenth century.

New methods and new machinery resulted in hardship for the growing class of workers who could now hope for nothing more than to be wage earners for the rest of their lives. When they found their earnings dwindling, they appealed to Parliament and found a sympathetic hearing. Their right to a 'convenient proportion of wages' was fully recognised.

From the middle of the sixteenth to the middle of the eighteenth centuries, Parliament attempted with diminishing success to enforce this policy. The Statute of Artificers in 1563 gave legal force on a national scale to the ordinances of the medieval guilds. The justices in each locality were bidden to consult with 'discreet and grave' persons and fix wages yearly in the light of circumstances. This was a flexible system more suited to an age of inflation than the old one of attempting to standardise maximum wages. Strict rules were laid down governing the terms and duration of apprenticeship and the number who could be employed at one time.

In the course of the next two hundred years, this statute was amended by other general ones on the same lines and by numerous particular acts dealing with specific trades and industries. The latter were the result of petitions from workers complaining of breaches and abuses of the general statutes in their own industries. Though Parliament was still sympathetic in intention, it was engaged in the long struggle with the crown, and there were frequent and prolonged periods when it was not in being at all.

A change in the methods of the tailors began to emerge in the latter half of the seventeenth century. Hitherto, the customer had bought his own cloth and taken it to a working craftsman who made it up. The business consisted of the tailor himself with perhaps members of his own family, one or two trained journeymen and an apprentice or two. Now there appeared the shopkeeping tailor, catering for the growing number of wealthy patrons. The traditional craftsmen looked askance at these new symbols of capitalist enterprise, with their expensive shops in fashionable neighbourhoods who were at once skimming off the rich cream from the market and debasing the ancient craft.

The shopkeeping tailor carried the division of labour between the skilled craftsman and his less skilled helpers to its logical conclusion. Where the apprentice or journeyman could in former times hope to set up on his own and enjoy a reasonable standard of living, the most lucrative part of the trade now fell into the hands of those who could command the capital resources needed to rent an expensive establishment, to stock it with costly materials and to grant extended credit to their highborn customers. Working in a seasonal trade and with sudden changes in the pressure of demand, the shopkeeping tailor took on hands as he needed them and ruthlessly cast them off when he had no further work to offer.

A convenient method of keeping in touch, in the days before labour exchanges had been invented, was developed in the house of call. Men in search of work would arrange to call at certain times at a particular public house. When a sudden spate of work, such as a number of orders for a court ball, came the way of a tailor, he could rapidly recruit the necessary staff by sending a message to one of these inns. It no longer suited the employer to have his 'yo-men' living in as it had done the master tailors of the early fifteenth century. He could now use them when it was profitable and abandon all responsibility for their welfare when he had exhausted the current orders.

So long as there was plenty of work to be done, the call-houses were a convenient way of obtaining labour at the cheapest price. When work was short they became meeting houses where men thrown into idleness gathered together to discuss their problems and grievances. With that charitable neighbourliness which springs from real poverty, provision was made for a fund to help the sick, the most needy and those who could no longer work. Travel money could be obtained by those journeying about the country in search of employment. In this the men were doing no more than interpret in modern terms the ancient practice of almsgiving and mutual help. In their other activities they came nearer to illegality. Agreements were made whereby each man entered his name in a book and those first on the list had first refusal of any work. It was agreed that none should work overtime or overwork while any brother remained unemployed. These rules might well have been held to be conspiracies in restraint of trade, but there is no record of any prosecution.

Indeed the common law provisions against conspiracy even though reinforced by such statutes as that of Edward I – 'Who be conspirators and who be champertors'[1] – were not invoked at this stage. When the journeymen tailors in the various houses of call in London and Westminster linked up to present de-

---

[1] '*Champerty*' *defined in* Oxford English Dictionary *as 'the illegal proceeding, whereby a party not naturally concerned in a suit engages to help one of the litigants to prosecute it, on condition that in the event of success, he is to receive a share of the property in dispute.'*

mands for shorter hours and higher wages, they were clearly offending against the law of conspiracy, yet the master tailors appealed, not to the law courts, but to Parliament. It was not always felt that ancient laws could be applied to new circumstances with any certainty; old customs still existed side by side with new and contrary statutes. The confusion was neatly illustrated as recently as 1818 when a litigant confounded the judges by demanding the right to trial by battle, and only then was this primitive method of deciding the law abolished!

It was to Parliament, then, that the Master Tailors of London and Westminster went with their complaint in 1721 that their journeymen had formed an association to demand more money and shorter hours. This association was something quite different from the rowdy fraternity at Garlykhythe which had been broken up over three hundred years earlier.

The journeymen who for many years had provided themselves with club benefits at the call-houses now levied themselves to establish a fighting fund to be used for trade union activities. A prolonged agitation in the early years of the eighteenth century resulted in a reduction of the working day from fifteen to fourteen hours, and an increase in the weekly wage from 10s 9d to 12s 9d. This success in 1710 put the tailors in the van of the new working class movement which was now emerging. Despite increasingly repressive legislation, the call-houses provided a skeletal organisation which remained in being until the formal establishment of trade unions superseded it.

The London and Westminster tailors were the first working men in the capital to make an organised effort to improve their conditions. With one possible exception, they were the first in the country to do so. Journeymen in this and other trades had hitherto combined to protect themselves against abuses of existing customs, or breaches of the law. They were frequently joined and supported by employers, for example in agitations against the use of 'illegal men'. The better type of employer saw his own position threatened by those who used cheap unindentured and unskilled labour to undercut him in the market. His interests were identical with those of the men whose standards were being undermined by such practices.

Combinations of this sort were not regarded as conspiracies, for they existed to enforce the law, not to change it. Parliament frequently heard petitions from them and passed new laws to correct the abuses. The combination of journeymen tailors was of a different sort. The men were now using their combined strength to force the masters to make new concessions. By doing so, they were introducing a new, revolutionary idea. In accepting the right to a 'convenient proportion of wages', Parliament had left the fixing of wage rates to representatives of the community at large and the consumers, acting in consultation with the masters of the trade and others of like mind. Now the workers in a particular trade were seeking to fix wages and conditions in relation to their own needs irrespective of the effect on profits, the price to the consumer, the general level of wages in other trades or such questions of interest to the whole community as the effect on the export trade.

The masters were as quick to see the dangers to their own position as the men were to see the advantages of strengthening their association. They complained to Parliament that more than seven thousand of their men in London and Westminster had joined the association and had subscribed considerable sums to the fighting fund. The fund was used to present the men's own memorial to Parliament and to reply clause by clause to the bill submitted by the masters.

The masters succeeded in their main strategic objective, for the association was declared illegal and suppressed. It was an empty victory, for the call-houses were an essential part of the economic apparatus of the trade and the masters could not do without them. So long as they existed for legitimate purposes there was no means of preventing the men continuing to fall under the spell of 'agitators', and entering into unofficial but effective agreements about not working overtime and sharing out the available work.

All such associations for advancing wages or lessening hours of work were declared 'illegal, null and void *to all intents and purposes*'. The italicised words meant a comprehensive ban in legal language. By their actions the journeymen reduced the impact of the phrase to the modern usage of 'roughly speaking'.

For the rest, the men obtained legal backing for the concessions they had already won from the masters ten years earlier. The masters sought to fix a working day of fifteen hours at a rate of 1s 8d a day, which the men claimed meant working long hours by candlelight in ill-ventilated workshops to the detriment of their health. They demanded a fourteen-hour day with one and a half hours off for meals, which they pointed out was two hours longer than the legal maximum for labourers. The Act passed in 1721 conceded the fourteen-hour day and fixed maximum wages at 2s a day from March to June and 1s 8d for the rest of the year.

While forbidding the men to combine to fight for themselves, Parliament was thus willing to afford them what it considered to be reasonable protection. Unfortunately the law could not be strictly enforced, for the tight control of the craft exercised by the guild was no longer possible and nothing had replaced it. The whole idea of regulating trade was now coming under attack, and the new capitalist employers of labour on a larger scale than ever before were beginning to claim the right to conduct their businesses as they thought fit. The 'two sides' of industry were now emerging, and an uneasy Parliament was attempting to maintain old traditions in circumstances to which they were no longer applicable.

The masters flouted the laws governing the number of apprentices and the terms of their service. The fixing of a maximum wage meant that real wages were constantly falling as the cost of living rose. Young green labour was drafted in to replace experienced journeymen who attempted to maintain the legal standards, and work was organised so as to use the minimum number of highly skilled workers and to work these as hard as possible.

The process of decay in the system of legal safeguards for the workers in the older crafts was hastened by the development of the new engineering and other industries and the growth of mechanisation. The employers could fairly claim that laws deriving from medieval customs could not be applied to factories using power looms and the like.

The workers were faced with a situation in which new techniques and new machines were resulting in great increases in their individual productivity, yet this was accompanied by a steadily falling real wage, longer hours and long spells of unemployment. Their solution was to ask Parliament to limit the use of machinery and to enforce the old laws and customs limiting the number of apprentices and regulating wages. However willing Parliament was in theory to support and protect them, its select committees found it increasingly difficult to reject the well-argued case of the employers that to do so would be ruinous to trade and to the country. Nor was the direct action of the machine-wrecking Luddites more successful in stemming the tide of industrialisation.

The machine and not the sun was now beginning to dominate the lives of working people. A predominantly agricultural country had been used to work to the rhythm of the seasons. A prolonged fine spell meant intense hard work from sunrise to sunset to be followed by spells of comparative idleness and jollification. The more continuously and evenly it was worked the more profitable a machine was to its owner; he demanded longer and longer hours with fewer and fewer holidays. In trades like tailoring where the machine was not yet introduced, the beginnings of a factory system had been started by the shopkeeping tailor.

The age which saw the early flowering of inventive genius was also one of war, revolution, pestilence and near-famine. The revolution of 1688 was followed by the war with France, by the two Jacobite rebellions at home, the loss of the American colonies and the extension of British power in India, while on the Continent the French revolutionaries were proclaiming a new doctrine of the rights of man under the banner of liberty, equality and fraternity.

It was against this turbulent background that the tailors in common with other workers sought a decent life and their fair proportion of wages. The lessons of the earlier agitations were not forgotten when their combination was explicitly made illegal by the Act of 1721 but their organisation remained in being. It has been described by Francis Place.

'Each house of call has a deputy, who on particular occasions is chosen by a kind of tacit consent, frequently without its being known to a very large majority who is chosen. The deputies form a committee, in whom, on every particular occasion, all power resides, from whom all orders proceed and whose commands are implicitly obeyed; and on no occasion has it ever been known that their commands have exceeded the necessity of the occasion, or that they have wandered the least from the purpose for which it was understood they were appointed. So perfect indeed is the organisation and so well has it been carried into effect that no complaint has ever been heard; with so much simplicity and with so great certainty does the whole

business appear to be conducted that the great body of journeymen rather acquiesce than assist in any way in it.'

This formidable organisation, working in semi-secrecy, was
able to organise strikes, overtime bans and prosecutions against
employers who failed to pay the legal wage or sought to extend
hours of work. The travelling journeymen roaming the country
in search of work were able to keep groups of call-houses in one
town in touch with what was being done elsewhere.

It is impossible to uncover the full extent of the activities of
these illegal organisations. Their orders were whispered by
word of mouth and passed from man to man, few records
survive and the evidence is based on hearsay. The masters
were quick to prosecute on the flimsiest evidence that the men
were combining and wherever possible the leaders tried to give
an air of spontaneity to the action of the men.

A description of a tailoring shop in 1752 tells of the men
'sitting so many hours in such a position, almost double on the
shopboard, with their legs under them, and poring so long
over their work by candlelight, their spirits exhausted, nature
wearied out and their health and sight soon impaired'. If, in
such conditions, all or most of the workmen left with their work
unfinished after fourteen hours' work, who was to say they
had left in unison as part of an overtime ban organised by their
call-house? The masters certainly did, and were on many
occasions successful in proving their case to the appropriate
court, but on others the men were able to argue successfully
that it was ill-health and not ill-will that had compelled them
to stop work.

Again, if a notoriously bad employer found no response from
his usual house of call for labour to meet a rush job, and none
from the neighbouring houses either, he could not be certain
the court would accept this as a strike and not listen to the
men's excuses that they had been elsewhere or had never
received the message. If he was compelled to mend his ways
many worthy burghers on the bench would welcome this reform of a tradesman indulging in what they themselves regarded
as reprehensible practices, such as price cutting, to the detriment of the standards and profits of their own businesses.

The journeymen tailors were thus organised and engaged in
militant action to a far greater extent than a list of the acknowledged successes and defeats would make it appear. Even an

exhaustive search through every record which has survived – a task not yet undertaken – would leave out of account the far greater number of successes which were only achieved because they did not appear at the time to be organised at all.

The master tailors found their men so well able to resist the lowering of their standard of life that towards the eighteenth century they began to tap a more amenable and less obstructive source of labour. For the first time, apart from the women-folk of the old craftsmen working at home, women were now employed in large numbers by the shopkeeping tailors. The status of the apprentice-journeyman who might one day aspire to be his own master had been steadily reduced to that of a wage-slave; his position was now further undermined by the recruitment of a new lower layer of workers with no status at all and no relation to any earlier group of workers in the craft. There was no need to pretend that these women were apprentices or journeymen and no one, least of all the journeymen themselves, sought to apply to them the legal wage. They were employed at half the rates for men, or even less.

In Ireland and Scotland, the journeymen tailors were no less active and militant than their brothers in London and England. In Ireland, with its special problems of religion and race, the division between masters and men was sharper and developed earlier than in the rest of the kingdom.

Combinations in all trades were forbidden by an Act of the Irish Parliament as early as 1729, and unlike the English Act of 1721 dealing with the regulation of journeymen tailors in London and Westminster, this general Act made no provision for the protection of the workers. It was not until the latter half of the century that the Irish Parliament began to copy the English statutes in laying down fixed wages.

In Scotland where conditions were even worse than in London, the struggle was also sharper. In 1721, when the London journeymen were consolidating their own earlier gains, the Aberdeen tailors were paid 4d for a thirteen-hour day. Fourteen years later their hours had increased to sixteen and they remained at this level for another thirty years. A strike to obtain a 2d a day increase in wages (which had now risen to 8d a day) was defeated in 1764, and the masters drew up a black list of rebels to whom all employment was refused. A new strike in 1797 was met with even harsher measures. The

Francis Place (1771-1854)

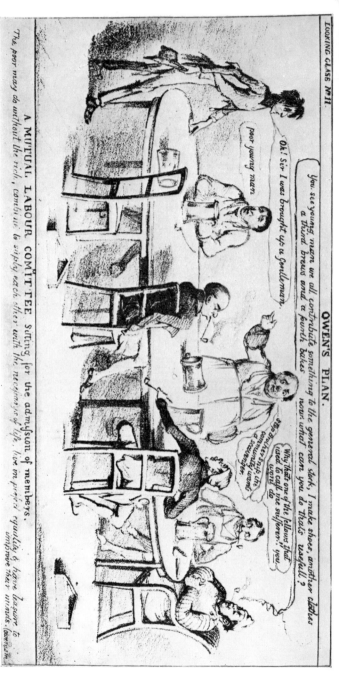

'Owen's plan' for a labour exchange : a cartoon of 1830

men were prosecuted for illegal combination and twelve of them were fined 10s with eight days' imprisonment. The strike leaders were impressed into the armed forces.

Similar action was taken in Edinburgh. Striking journeymen were prosecuted in 1748 and imprisoned for forty-eight hours. They were not released until they had paid damages to the master tailors and promised not to strike again. This was effective in keeping the Edinburgh organisation completely underground for the rest of the century.

So the flame of revolt flickered across the country, here to burst into brilliant flame for a moment and there to be quenched almost before it had been kindled. The Privy Council was invoked in 1744 against the London and Westminster journeymen for combining in defiance of the 1721 Act; their combination was behind a successful appeal to the Middlesex justices in 1751 to order the masters to pay the legal rates. Strikes became a commonplace; their repression ever more ruthless.

The whole trend was against the workers. The ferment of ideas produced by the American Declaration of Independence and the French Revolution could not be kept out by the Atlantic or the Channel. *The Rights of Man* by Thomas Paine was widely read despite the outlawry of its author. A frightened ruling class plunged the country once more into war with France and used all the arts of chauvinism to concentrate attention on the foreign enemy. The patriotic appeal, which was not lacking in success, was reinforced by the passage of new Treason and Sedition Acts and the suspension of habeas corpus in 1795. It was in this atmosphere that the ever-increasing strikes led by combinations formed in defiance of the law were seen as dangerous portents of a possible revolution. A strike by the millwrights against the London engineering employers led the Commons to pass a bill banning combinations in the trade. It was dropped in the Lords in favour of a wider measure forbidding all combinations whatsoever which was passed in 1799 and reinforced by an even more stringent Act in 1800.

The advocates of *laissez-faire* had at last persuaded Parliament to abandon the responsibilities it had inherited from the guilds to offer some protection to the workers. The wage-fixing Acts had been dead letters for more than fifty years, and

C

attempts to invoke them were met by their repeal. The judges were increasingly ruling against all forms of united action on grounds of common law quite apart from the specific statutes. Not only was the pretence that Parliament could protect the workers abandoned, but they were now expressly forbidden to act in protection of themselves.

The general Acts were no more successful in suppressing the journeymen tailors' organisation than the specific Act against them passed four score years earlier. Organised in small units round the call-houses, it presented no vulnerable nerve-centre which could be attacked and destroyed. While this loose, fractional system of organisation was admirably suited to the situation of the times when neither the employers nor the forces of law were much better equipped for battle, it was the beginning of a tradition which was to prove a source of weakness in the future. There were to be many years of painful and bitter struggle before a single amalgamated union covering almost the whole of the industry could be built up from the innumerable small societies born of the call-house system.

Chapter Three/Francis Place

APPRENTICESHIP AND MARRIAGE; JOINS BREECHES-MAKERS' BENEFIT SOCIETY;
FIRST STRIKE AND BLACKLISTING; BECOMES SECRETARY OF SOCIETY; IMMEDIATE
AIMS ACHIEVED; CAMPAIGN AGAINST COMBINATION ACTS; HIS CONTRIBUTION
TO TRADE UNION MOVEMENT; ASSOCIATION WITH JOSEPH HUME; SELECT
COMMITTEE ON COMBINATION ACT; ACTS OF 1824-5 CONCEDE RIGHT TO
ORGANISE

The picture at the end of the eighteenth century was not one
of complete gloom and universal oppression. There were those,
like the playwright Sheridan, who resisted the passage of the
Combination Acts and made every effort to lessen their severity
when they were debated in the Commons. Even when passed,
they could not be applied in their full rigour. Not only was
the will to enforce them lacking in many enlightened minds,
but there was no efficient state apparatus for the purpose.

The law was invoked when the activities of unions were felt
by employers to be seriously inconveniencing them, but at
other times the unions were not only tolerated but even asked
to co-operate with the masters. Thus, in the period of greatest
tension, between 1794 and 1810, we find the masters and men
of the tailoring trade in the villages round Nottingham meeting
regularly to discuss all aspects of their business. So little was
the law regarded, that these meetings were convened by public
advertisement in the columns of the *Nottingham Journal*.

This was only one example of the way in which common
sense prevailed when ordinary men came down to deal in
practical terms with real-life problems. Nobody had yet

advocated collective bargaining and joint consultation. These eighteenth-century tailors, both masters and men, arrived at them empirically, without the help of economists and practised them openly in direct contravention of the law. They were not alone, either in their own trade or in others.

In this period a young man was growing up in surroundings of squalid brutality in the London slums. Francis Place, who was born in 1771, was the son of a drunken gambler who had graduated from being a working baker to running a private debtors' prison before setting up as a tavern keeper. Apprenticed at the age of fourteen to a leather breeches maker, he spent his spare time haunting the vice-spots of Westminster, leading gang fights in the streets and hunting bullocks down the Strand. (The problem of juvenile delinquency does not seem to be as modern as some suppose.)

At the age of nineteen, when he had finished his apprenticeship, he married seventeen-year-old Elizabeth Chadd and obtained a job as a journeyman at 14s a week. Trade was bad, and he supplemented his intermittent earnings by making stuff breeches in his spare time. He had now settled down to a respectable hard-working life, and joined the Breeches-makers' Benefit Society as an insurance against sickness and other adversities. He had taken no part in the life of the society, and had never even attended a meeting, when the word came that they were all on strike for higher wages. They were promptly discharged, Place among them.

A born organiser, the twenty-two-year-old family man – his first child was a year old – now came face to face with problems which called forth his highest virtues. Attending his first meeting of the society, he learned for the first time some of its secret life. Some two hundred and fifty members were now dependent on the communal chest, and it contained £250. These were the sole reserves, and to Place it seemed self-evident that they must be conserved as far as possible and, better still, augmented.

At his suggestion, it was agreed that all those whose personal responsibilities permitted should leave London. With one week's strike pay and a 'tramp certificate' they set off for the provinces to seek work. The certificate would entitle them to a night's lodging and information about any work available in any town where there was a call-house used by their fellow workers. There they would report on the situation in London and seek financial support for those on strike. It was frequently forthcoming.

Apart from this, Place suggested that the men left behind should themselves take the economic offensive. One idea was to open a shop for the sale of cheap breeches made from spoilt material by the men on strike. Another was to print and circulate leaflets explaining why the men were on strike and appealing to the public for moral and financial support. All these suggestions were adopted, and Place became the secretary of the strike committee by that process of 'tacit understanding' which he was later to describe in the excerpt quoted in the previous chapter.

Despite this energetic leadership, the strike collapsed after two months. The leather breeches trade was in decline and the men were not only fighting the masters but an economic trend as well. Place and the other leaders were blacklisted. He and his wife were compelled to pawn all their possessions and live on the charity of their neighbours before he once more found brief employment at his trade.

All this took place while the 1721 Act forbidding journeymen tailors to combine was still in force and on the eve of the general Combination Acts. The story illuminates the whole system then in being. Place was called out on strike by a society whose meetings he had never attended, and on the authority of some unknown leader or leaders. Yet he and those in a similar position unhesitatingly obeyed the order. As soon as he demonstrated his capacity he moved by tacit agreement into the key position. The suggestions he put forward, which were adopted by his fellows, demonstrate the masterly skill with which the men fought their employers.

The losses suffered in this battle were severe. The strike defeated, not only were the leaders penalised, but the funds of the society were exhausted and its membership thinned by those who had disappeared into the provinces. All seemed lost, but with characteristic resilience, the men decided to reopen the struggle within twelve months. The Breeches-makers' Union was reorganised and Place was appointed its paid secretary. Within a year he had won by negotiation the rise in wages which the men had failed to obtain by strike action. This, be it remembered, was in a year when the country was at war with France, new Sedition and Treason Acts were being passed and habeas corpus was suspended with the avowed object of putting away militant leaders of workers' combinations without recourse to trial. The breeches-makers met and negotiated with a man they refused to employ, who represented an illegal body which had recently engaged in illegal action, and in doing so had openly flaunted its existence in published leaflets. Here was another chink of light in the general gloom cast by the ever-worsening relations between masters and men. Faced with the need to save what they could of a dying trade, the breeches-makers chose to enter into a conspiracy with their conspiratorial men, and reached a compromise which gave the men all that had been so lately refused to them.

Pitchforked into the strike without being consulted or represented, Place had laid down the only strategy by which it might have succeeded. Now he had achieved all the aims of the strike by peaceful negotiation. Had he been allowed to build on this experience, Place might well have put his organising genius to the task of establishing a stronger and wider union which could have followed the same path. Alas, having obtained their victory, the Breeches-makers' Union decided it had no further need of a paid secretary. Place was once more out of work.

This was the end of Place's brief career as a trade union official, but not of his interest in social reform. While struggling to earn a living by casual work for private customers, he played an active part in the radical movement with its programme of manhood suffrage, annual Parliaments and salaried M Ps. In 1801 he had saved enough to open his own tailor's shop in Charing Cross with, as he claimed, the largest plate glass window in London. He was so successful that he was able to retire sixteen years later, handing over a business earning £3,000 a year to his son's control.

This success as a master tailor did nothing to alter his radical ideas, and he threw himself with great energy into politics. While some argued that nothing could be done until Parliament was reformed, he accepted this longer-term objective but still sought to wring concessions from the existing Parliamentary system. His house became the recognised meeting place of all the agitators and from there he organised the wire-pulling, lobbying, article writing, drafting of resolutions, petitions and Parliamentary bills inseparable from his campaign.

He was invited by his fellow masters to join them in promot-

ing a bill in the Commons in a final effort to outlaw the combinations of journeymen in the trade. Not only did he refuse,
but it was his evidence based on experience on both sides of
the trade which persuaded a select committee in 1810 to reject
the bill. It seemed to him monstrous that the masters should
thus openly combine in a fresh attempt to prevent their
journeymen doing likewise. The existing laws, designed to
regulate the trade, had failed in their purpose and he now began
to collect evidence to back a campaign for their repeal.

Conditions in the new textile factories, the mining industry,
shipbuilding and other heavy industry were far worse than
they were in the tailoring trade. The heartless cruelty and des-
potic tyranny with which men, women and children were
treated, particularly in the textile factories, provoked counter
action which bore the same brutal stamp. Secret societies, with
oathtaking ceremonies that it was sometimes death to refuse,
and nearly always death to break, organised machine wrecking,
arson and the murder of blacklisted employers, were the retort
of brutes to those who had brutalised them.

Great power was falling into the hands of a few men working
in secret, who showed themselves willing to prey on workers as
well as masters when it suited them to use their terrorist
organisations for the purpose. These evils seemed to Place to
flow from the repressive laws which forbade the men to combine and negotiate freely on their wages and conditions.

'Combinations will soon cease to exist', he wrote after the
triumphant conclusions of the campaign. 'Men have been kept
together for long periods only by the oppressions of the laws;
these being repealed, combinations will lose the matter which
cements them into masses, and they will fall to pieces.

'He knows nothing of the working people who can suppose
that, when left at liberty to act for themselves without being
driven into permanent associations by the oppression of the
laws, they will continue to contribute money for distant and
doubtful experiments, for uncertain and precarious benefits.
If let alone, combinations – excepting now and then, and for
particular purposes under peculiar circumstances – will cease
to exist.'

That he was so completely wrong in his forecast of the effects
of repeal does nothing to detract from the debt owed by the
trade union movement to Francis Place nor from the admira-

tion evoked by the skill and pertinacity with which he organised the campaign. Harsh and contemptuous in his opinion of almost all with whom he came into contact, forgetful of the shortcomings of his own wild youth in his judgment of those who fell short of the respectable and abstemious standards of his later life, he saw himself as the most important and capable person in any enterprise with which he was associated. He was not a lovable man. It can be argued that William Cobbett with his propaganda network of fifty thousand groups reading the *Political Register* did as much as or even more than Place, but it was Place's genius that he could leave other more original minds to play their part while he remained in the background, supplementing their efforts and ceaselessly burrowing beneath the surface to knit the whole campaign together. He gave it coherence and a steady, unswerving direction.

Despite his wide reading, his outlook remained as narrow as his own experience. Within these limits he was a warm-hearted sympathiser with the workers whose life and struggles he had shared in his youth and whose cause he still embraced when he had himself become a master. It is perhaps significant that at the height of his wealth and influence he was excluded from a Commons committee room on the grounds that 'he was neither an MP nor a gentleman'.

He was a master of some thirty-odd years' standing when he burst out against those who complained of the congenital idleness of the British worker. (Yes, this one too has a venerable history!)

'A labouring man should have no fits of idleness,' he wrote; 'so says pride, wilfulness and ignorance. He who of all men, the negro slave excepted, has the fewest inducements to constant, unremitting toil, should be free from idle feelings. I know not how to describe the sickening aversion which at times steals over the working-man, and utterly disables him from following his usual occupation, and *compels* him to indulge in idleness. I have felt it, resisted it to the utmost of my power, but have been so completely subdued by it that, in spite of very pressing circumstances, I have been obliged to submit and run away from my work. This is the case with every workman I have ever known; and in proportion as a man's case is hopeless will such fits more frequently occur and be of longer duration.'

It needed rare warmth of heart and depth of understanding

for a master who owed everything to his own efforts thus to excuse and sympathise with the feelings of his own idle apprentices, and to remember not only the diligence which had brought him success but the backslidings of his earlier days as an employee.

This humane outlook was combined in Place with a genius for intrigue and management of affairs. He found his principal ally in Joseph Hume, one of the leading members of the growing group of radicals in the Commons. By intervening in every trade dispute which came to his notice, Place accumulated a mass of evidence to demonstrate the evils and unworkability of the Combination Acts. He found it hard to win the confidence of workers who were often suspicious of a master-tailor attempting to inquire closely into the workings of their illegal unions. He fostered an educational programme through press and pamphlets which built up an informed public opinion on the subject. This was so successful that one member was moved to introduce a complicated bill which would certainly have been lost and thus set back the campaign for many years.

Its sponsor was adroitly sidetracked and recruited as an auxiliary by Hume on the advice of Place. The government was persuaded to appoint a select committee to inquire into the export of machinery, the emigration of artisans and combinations of workmen, under Hume's chairmanship. The government thought the main purpose of the committee was to discuss the export of machinery, but Place and Hume meant it to come to a favourable conclusion on one specific point: the repeal of the combination laws.

The committee was packed with friendly MPs and Hume used his position as chairman to arrange the calling of witnesses so that while none was denied a hearing, the impression left was of an overwhelming wish among masters and men for repeal. The opposition were unorganised, and appearing as individuals were subjected to searching cross-examination by the chairman. The favourable witnesses were carefully groomed by Place at his Charing Cross home before they appeared. Though he had by years of ceaseless activity succeeded in allaying the suspicions of the workers, this proved the most arduous part of his task.

From all over the country men from widely different trades and industries were brought to London and each had his own ideas about what was wrong with industrial life and what should be done to right it. Had they appeared before the committee it would have assembled a mass of conflicting evidence and a profusion of nostrums which would have made any single conclusion impossible. Place set himself the delicate task of interviewing each one, persuading him to forget his own pre-judices and his dearly-held beliefs that the level of taxation, the use of machinery, the selection of magistrates or perhaps the irreligion of the masters was at the root of the trouble, and that his evidence should not stray beyond the brief with which Place would supply him. For three months Place did nothing else but organise in the background.

His witnesses were thoroughly drilled, and Hume was sup-plied with a copy of all briefs so that he could bring out all the relevant points and head off any dangerous discursiveness. The daily proceedings of the committee, which met in private, were printed and circulated to its members and a copy was sent daily to Charing Cross by Hume. It was returned carefully annotated, so that the chairman was able to keep the whole campaign under his eye while examining the witnesses.

This meticulous handling of every detail of the work of the committee resulted in a report in favour of the repeal of the combination laws and those hindering emigration. The government's own objective, removal of the ban on the export of machinery in order to help foreign trade, was left over until the following session. A bill implementing the committee's report was passed through both Houses within a week, at the tail end of the session.

To observers of modern Parliamentary affairs, it is astonish-ing that so momentous an Act should have passed through Parliament without debate and without a division. Some of the masters were clear-sighted enough to see the fundamental danger to their own interests of allowing the workers the right to combine. To them the Act was a nightmare plunge into a future filled with prospects of disaster. So skilfully were they outmanoeuvred that they had no time to make their voices heard between the sudden publication of the report of a com-mittee they had largely ignored as unimportant and the passage of the Act itself. So lax was the machinery of government that Lord Liverpool, the Prime Minister, and Lord Eldon, the Lord Chancellor, were to confess in the next session that they had known nothing of the bill and would never have allowed it to pass if they had. So quietly and speedily had the work been done that weeks after the passing of the Act, Lancashire magistrates imprisoned cotton weavers for the crime of combination, unaware that the law had been changed.

Those workers who had been illegally organised for years, like the tailors, now came into the open, and their example was quickly followed by the formation of new unions all over the country. The prophecies of the gloomier masters were quickly fulfilled. The Act was seen as an admission that for years the workers had been wrongfully denied the right to compel their proper share of their own production. So far from fulfilling the expectations of Francis Place that combinations would wither away, they not only became more numerous but more militant.

In Dublin, the tailors led the move to form the 'Board of Green Cloth', which passed its own bylaws regulating all the industries represented on this joint committee of workers' representatives. The masters found themselves temporarily powerless before this council of workers as it assumed wider and wider powers.

In Sheffield tailors were in the van of a similar movement whose aim was to double wages and halve the working week. Strikes were met with lockouts throughout the country, and in many places wrecking and rioting were symptoms of the intolerable tension between employers who thought themselves faced with immediate ruin and workers who had been filled with a sudden hope that all their troubles were over.

The shipping employers led the move for a reimposition of the ban on combinations. This time it was the government which packed the select committee where Hume had to fight alone. Place organised countless demonstrations, kept the corridors of the House constantly thronged with workers demanding to be heard by the committee or buttonholing MPs, and poured a stream of information and petitions into the committee via Hume. These defensive measures led to the abandonment of the shipowners' draft bill. Though the common law prohibition on combinations was reaffirmed, the new amending Act expressly allowed the right to combine for purposes of regulating wages and hours of work and to withdraw labour by concerted action. The fundamental right to strike thus conceded for the first time has never since been successfully challenged.

These two acts of 1824 and 1825 transformed a secret and illegal struggle into an open one. At first it looked as though the unions having won their freedom might well go down in defeat. In the aftermath of the Napoleonic wars, a financial panic resulted in commercial chaos. Unemployment rose and the workless were dependent on charity to avoid actual starvation. All-round wage reductions were ruthlessly imposed and the resulting strikes were almost uniformly defeated, frequently with the break-up of the union which had organised them. The employers, who had failed to get Parliament to suppress the unions now took every possible step to do the work for themselves. Known membership of a union, trade society or even friendly societies became a bar to employment wherever employers felt themselves strong enough to enforce the ban.

Despite this inauspicious beginning and the many setbacks which were to follow, the rights which were reluctantly conceded in these Acts were never lost and proved the foundation stone for vast new developments in the future.

The journeymen tailors had played a conspicuous and important part in the struggle which led up to this landmark on the road to emancipation. They were among the small minority of workers who consistently defied the law and over the years presented to the rest of the workers an example of the advantages of unity in action. To them goes the honour of having produced Francis Place without whom the Combination Acts would have remained in force for many more years.

Chapter Four/Robert Owen's Big Ideas

PLANS FOR GRAND NATIONAL CONSOLIDATED TRADES UNION; FIRST LODGE OF
OPERATIVE TAILORS; ORGANISATION OF WOMEN; ULTIMATUM TO EMPLOYERS;
ATTACK ON *The Times*; MASTER TAILORS' COUNTER-OFFENSIVE; THE 'ACCURSED
DOCUMENT'; COLLAPSE OF STRIKE AND GRAND NATIONAL; INTERNAL DIVISIONS;
ASSOCIATION OF UNITED TRADES FOR PROTECTION OF LABOUR

The tailors entered the new era of open combination with
enthusiasm. They had built up strong traditions of loyalty
and discipline during their many years of illegal activity. They
had felt their way towards a nationwide union in their efforts
to establish and maintain the tenuous links between groups of
call-houses in the various towns. Robert Owen found them
ready listeners when he began to preach the organisation of all
workers into one huge national union.

The Reform Act of 1832 was a bitter disappointment to those
who had imagined it would usher in the millennium. In those
rare constituencies like Westminster where numbers of workers
already had the vote, it was taken away from them. The new
House of Commons was reluctant to look beyond the interests
of the middle class. The fight for political democracy having
brought little but disillusion, Robert Owen's plans for industrial democracy seemed all the more attractive.

A successful manufacturer in his earlier years, Owen was
fertile in ideas for destroying capitalism which grew more
grandiose and less practical as the years went by. Having
failed in his attempt to set up a model community, New Harmony, in the United States, he returned to Britain and threw

himself into his self-appointed task of bringing to the workers the whole fruits of industry. The result was the foundation of the Grand National Consolidated Trades Union early in 1834. This was to bring the whole working class into one body which would control strikes, start co-operative stores and engage in manufacture. In each industry a Grand Lodge would take over control, thus abolishing competition and socialising the means of production.

This is not the place to analyse the impracticability of the movement; the brevity of its history is the most telling answer to its pretensions.

The First Grand Lodge of Operative Tailors was formed in London at the end of 1833, embracing nearly all the small societies already in existence. It was this union which summoned the delegates from other unions in February 1834 to a conference at which the Grand National Consolidated was formed. Its officers organised the conference and John Browne, its secretary, became a co-secretary of the Consolidated. Within weeks some half a million workers were enrolled under the banner of the 'Grand National', in their appropriate lodges. These included lodges for women workers among which was the Lodge of Female Tailors. This is the first record of organisation among the women workers in the tailoring trade. The men had made the entry of women into the trade as difficult as they could and remained hostile. It is indicative of the mutual suspicion that one of the first things the Lodge of Female Tailors did was to ask if the Grand Lodge really intended to prohibit women from making waistcoats. The answer was probably: yes, if they could.

The authorities were alarmed at this startling growth in trade unionism. In March the seven Tolpuddle martyrs were arrested for oathtaking under an act never before applied to the trade unions. Like most unions at that time the lodges had complicated initiation ceremonies, and these simple countrymen were following normal precedent when they founded their own Grand Lodge, to the accompaniment of solemn oaths and mysterious rites. The sentence of seven years' transportation aroused the anger of the workers, and those unions which had remained outside the Consolidated joined in a massive protest.

Troops were brought in to London and special constables were sworn in when the unions announced they would march through the streets to present a petition to the Home Office. The fears of the authorities that the demonstration would end in rioting proved groundless. A vacant plot of ground was rented for the occasion so that the procession could form up on private property unmolested by the police. Each man, wearing a scarlet ribbon, formed up behind one or other of the thirty-three banners. By far the largest contingent was provided by the tailors. They accounted for more than a fifth of an orderly crowd of some 30,000.

For the tailors, this demonstration was not only a protest against the savage treatment of the Tolpuddle victims. It was also a rally of their own Lodge on the eve of the biggest strike so far organised in their industry. That they fully intended to take over the whole of the trade and control it themselves is shown by the curt authority with which they announced the decision of the Grand Lodge to the masters:

'In order to stay the ruinous effects which a destructive commercial competition has so long been inflicting on the trade, they have resolved to introduce certain new regulations of labour into the trade, which regulations they intend shall come into force on Monday next.'

These regulations fixed the working day at ten hours from the third Monday in April to the last Saturday in July, and at eight hours for the rest of the year. The ten-hour day would be worked from 7 am to 6 pm at 6s a day, and during the rest of the year hours would be from 8 am to 5 pm at 5s a day. There would be an hour off, in which the employee could leave the premises for meals, all the year round. Work would only be done in 'healthy and convenient' premises and at daily or hourly rates.

These demands were so reasonable, said John Browne, secretary to the Grand Lodge in his letter to the employers, that he was sure they would be agreed and thus contribute to mutual confidence between masters and men. He did not seem quite confident that the demands would be received in this enlightened spirit for he went on: 'It only remains for me to add that your workmen, members of this Society, will cease to be employed by you should you decline to act upon the new regulations.'

This was not the language of negotiation for a wage claim but an announcement of a decision by men who imagined they were on the eve of changing the whole social order. Through the haze of easy optimism with which he clouded his own mind, Owen had assured them that this could be brought about in a matter of months. The awakening was rude and salutary. The resulting strike broke the Grand Lodge of the Tailors, and since this was perhaps the most important branch of the Consolidated, was largely responsible for its demise.

The tailors may be criticised for accepting Owen at his own valuation, but at least they were in good company, for something like a million other trade unionists were following the same lead. They cannot be held responsible for the crash. Under the rules of the Consolidated, its executive had to sanction any strike for an increase in wages. Owen's influence was supreme on the executive and the decision to sanction the strike must have had his full approval. The result is one of the many sad and equally painful commentaries on his judgment.

Some 20,000 workers[1] were thrown on the resources of the Consolidated when the strike began. It had no funds of its own, but had the authority to impose a levy on all union members to support action taken with executive approval. There had been too many of these levies for the liking of the members, and despite the support they had given, none of the strikes so far had succeeded. There was considerable dissatisfaction when another 8d per member was demanded on behalf of the London tailors and the response was far from good. Instead of the maximum 10s a week strike pay, the tailors were reduced to 4s. The strike began to crumble as the men drifted back on the employers' terms. Inefficient though the capitalist system and the state apparatus may have been on any absolute scale, they none the less presented a formidable obstacle to a revolution of the kind envisaged by Robert Owen. To oppose these forces the workers had nothing but an idea. As the tailors quickly learned, men cannot even live on an idea, much less take over the industry of what was already the most advanced country in the world.

The government needed to do no more than give a nod of approval for the venemous treatment meted out at Tolpuddle. The employers were taking their own steps. A meeting, attended by nearly 450 masters covering practically all the trade in London, unanimously decided that the new regula-

[1] *This estimate was made by* The Times. *Other sources give a lower figure.*

THE CHEAP TAILOR AND HIS WORKMEN.

'*The cheap tailor and his workmen*': *a Leech cartoon from* Punch (*1845*)

The Mansell Collection

'Room occupied by a military tailor and his family, at No 10, Hollybush-place': a drawing of 1863

tions were unreasonable and should be rejected. They called on the 'nobility, gentry and public' to go without new clothes until the men had been brought to heel, and decided to set up their own call-houses to recruit non-union labour at the old rates. A strong committee was formed which immediately published the masters' case by way of an advertisement in *The Times*.

The journeymen replied with a tremendous philippic which is too long to be given in full, but which is well worth quoting. It was printed in the *Pioneer* of 10th May 1834. They felt called upon, they said, 'to make an honest appeal to the public and their friends in vindication of the measures they have adopted, and to expose and refute some of the gross errors, falsehoods and prejudices which the masters and that infamous tool of a pampered aristocracy, *The Times*, have so unjustly, cruelly and maliciously attempted to foist upon the public mind'.

The Times, which had long been thundering against the menace of the union (the GNCTU) had enraged John Browne and the executive of the Grand Lodge. Its editor was castigated in terms which are refreshingly forceful and contemptuous.

'Does that idle and useless part of Society, the aristocracy, know from whence they spring? Do they know whom they threaten with starvation?

'To whom do they owe all the necessaries, comforts and luxuries of life they so ungratefully enjoy, but those whom they unite against? Does the poor mercenary, time-serving tool of tyranny and oppression, the editor of *The Times*, think the unions, or any branch of them, regard the names or silly epithets with which he is pleased to assail the honest, industrious artisan, with his usual fraudulent meanness? In order to justify a barbarous conclusion, he has been compelled to advance a villainously false position.'

The statement goes on to give a lengthy and cogently argued reply to the suggestion that 6s a day is too high a wage. As the trade was organised, few journeymen could hope to reach this level of earnings. The masters had introduced a piece work system under which one man no longer did one job, but as many as six might be engaged on making a single coat. Fixing a price of 15s for the work and allotting thirty hours for its completion appeared to give 6d an hour to the men, but in fact the job could never be completed in the time. Moreover there was continuous employment in only one month of the year; for

the rest there were hours and days to be spent in idleness waiting the word from some insolent employer or his more insolent
foreman.

'Men are kept in the fear of poverty, insulted and oppressed,
ever and anon threatened with immediate dismissal for the
most trifling, the most trivial mistake or mishap; loitering and
crippling away their valuable time one part of the day or week
about the workshops – are hurried, oppressed or desponding
the other: this, with a few exceptions, is the lot of the favoured
part of the trade, the fortunate few; what is the lot of the many?

'Let the man of feeling, in whose breast the milk of human
kindness has not been curdled or dried up by the wretched
circumstances in which a great portion of society has been
placed; let him visit the branch lodges and see the pale haggard
countenances of the starving many; let him follow the married
man home to his almost unfurnished garret, and see the deplorable condition in which is the famished partner of his
misery, with him in the like deplorable condition, and then
let him say, with the dastardly *Times*, that the proposed regulation is uncalled for.

'Contrast these sufferings and misery with the stately man-
sions, the splendid halls, the costly furniture and the princely
fortunes of the masters, and with your hand on your heart, say
whether the regulation is, or is not called for.'

The highflown language was not exaggerating the misery
and squalor in which the journeyman lived. More than a
hundred years earlier a writer had described them as 'wretched
emblems of death and hunger' and since then their condition
had grown worse, not better.

The statement went on to deal with the 'lies' of *The Times*
when it said they were, among other things, striking against
the tailoresses. These had been unfeelingly torn from the
maternal duties of a parent, and unjustly encouraged to compete with men in ruining the money value of labour. That some
masters took more than an economic advantage of women
seeking work was openly hinted: 'The terms under which they
obtain employment are of a nature too gross for the public ear.'

Worst off of all among the journeymen were those increasing
numbers who were being employed as outworkers. They had
to provide their own trimmings, pay for extra candles and
heating for their irons, and journey in their own time to and

from their employers. These extra costs reduced their earnings to 3s 6d or 4s a day – when they could get work.

In accordance with Robert Owen's ideas, the men announced they had bought large quantities of the best materials and were about to open shops which would undersell the masters.

This wordy document which makes three attempts to bring itself to a conclusion before it succeeds, is nevertheless fired by a passionate sense of injustice which gives it in places a dignity and sincerity which are lacking in many a more polished polemic. It was followed a week later by the publication of a series of resolutions carrying the counter-argument a few steps further and opening an appeal fund which the public is asked to support.

A body calling itself the Operative Master Tailors of London called a meeting which sided with the journeymen. It may have been, as the masters alleged, that this was a 'front' organisation of the journeymen themselves, but at all events it had no influence on the struggle. The committee of Master Tailors which had been set up to break the strike was able to issue a jubilant circular telling of 'reports from all quarters of the metropolis of the most gratifying description'. The committee unanimously urged every master to make it a condition of employment that no one should be given work who refused to sign a declaration:

'We, the undersigned foremen, journeymen tailors and others, in the employment of .... do declare that we are not members of the trades' union, that it is not our intention to become members of any such association, nor do we now, nor will we in any way, directly or indirectly, contribute towards the support of any such associations; in attestation of which, we hereunto subscribe our names, this .... day of .... 1834.'

The committee at the same time urged that the utmost protection, kindness and consideration should be given to those who had blacklegged during the strike. The masters were well aware of the financial difficulties into which the Consolidated was running through the failure of the general levy. They heard that this had forced a change of policy. Owen's easy optimism was proving unjustified, and so far from the capitalist system crumbling before their very eyes, the workers were meeting a determined opposition which put them on the defensive at once. The executive council of the Consolidated therefore decided to try to build up a central fund and meanwhile advised workers to keep in employment on what terms they could get until the Consolidated had sufficient funds to fight for the liberation of 'all the producing classes from the slavery and degradation in which they have hitherto been and now are'.

This excellent plan needed only one thing for success – the docile co-operation of the masters. They were not prepared to give it. Knowing that the men had been told to accept temporary defeat while preparations were made for ultimate victory, they decided to prevent those preparations ever being made. The attestation paper was the means they employed. It was all very well for the Consolidated, having told the men to get work on what terms they could, to greet this 'accursed document'[1] with a manifesto saying that no man or woman in the kingdom should sign it, and to declare 'It would be far better to resolve to die, rather than thus be compelled to be the lowest of such slaves to ignorance and presumption'. The tailors reacted in the only way possible to this plethora of advice which in sum meant they must at once die of starvation while they continued on strike and at the same time find means to support the 'workers' bank' which would one day finance their liberation. They crept back to such work as they could find.

The journeymen tailors had provided the largest and most influential section of the workers engaged in this forlorn attempt to change the whole structure of society. They had thus thrust their employers, who represented an insignificant element in capitalist society, into a position in which they alone were called upon to defeat the whole working-class movement. They proved equal to the task, not so much because of the solidarity and ruthlessness with which they faced the problem as the woolly idealism and utter incapacity of the leaders on the other side.

It is interesting to note that a mass meeting called by the newborn Grand Lodge in December 1833 decided to campaign

---

[1] *The 'document' technique has not been abandoned in post-war years: examples exist of decisions of managements to demand from employees their signature to a good conduct pledge following strike.*

for an eight-hour day and an increase in wages to 9d an hour and at the same meeting refused by an overwhelming majority to hear Robert Owen because he was 'so wound up with plans and projects'. This earthy but practical attitude of the rank and file was unfortunately not taken to heart either by Robert Owen or the executive of the Grand Lodge.

It is sad, but necessary, to admit that this defeat owed something to jealousy among the different trades. Robert Owen had laid down the grand strategy with telling simplicity. If all the workers were prepared to subscribe in order to support their fellows, then industry by industry the workers could gain improvement in their conditions and ultimate control. Two things were missing. Who was to decide in which industries the advance should first be made, and secondly what were the possible reactions among the employers as the grand design unfolded? No answers were provided. Inevitably there was competition among different groups of workers to be in the van of such a movement. People who had recognised Owen for the windbag he had become were not slow to draw the conclusion that it was best to get in while the going was still good. The tailors pressed their leaders for action, having read correctly the lessons provided by the lockout of some 1,500 men, women and children in Derby which demonstrated the shaky financial structure on which they were asked to rely.

It would seem that the Grand Lodge executive used the advantage of John Brown's dual role to influence the Consolidated executive to give permission for a tailors' strike in advance of the claims of the shoemakers of London.

Unwilling to accept this decision as a majority one, democratically arrived at (they suspected, probably rightly, that wire-pulling had played its part) the shoemakers left the Consolidated. The incident throws up into sharp relief the whole weakness of the Consolidated. To be successful a revolution – and no less was on the agenda – needs meticulously careful planning. In its place were offered wild generalisations and hopeless optimism.

In a report to a general meeting of the master tailors, their own committee showed they had grasped the central facts of the situation. They said, barely a month after the tailors had astonished their fellow unionists with the announcement of their strike:

'1 The journeymen tailors are the moving power of the trades' union (the GNCTU).
'2 The executive council of the union ordered the tailors to strike.
'3 When the funds fail, the executive of the trades' union order the operatives into employment upon the best terms they can obtain, and require them to subscribe a fixed sum weekly to form a fund for future purposes.'

Not even Field-Marshal Montgomery could have demanded a clearer and more succinct 'appreciation of the situation' from his general staff. It was scarcely necessary to add an appeal to all employers to insist on signature of the 'accursed document' as a condition of re-employment. Some 4,000 strikers had already capitulated.

This display of force was not necessary to break the Grand National Consolidated Trades Union. Its inherent weakness had already been shown in the débâcle of the Derby lockout, but this had been masked by the new wave of fervour engendered by the Tolpuddle judgment. This culminated in the tremendous enthusiasm of the London demonstration of 21st April. The complete failure to support the tailors' strike followed. By midsummer the Consolidated had ceased to be able to pretend it was an effective force. It was wound up before the end of the year. The effects of the strike were not confined to London. In Lewes and Cambridge it sparked off the formation of local lodges; they were broken by a lockout with comparative ease. In Hull, 1,000 men were recruited to a local lodge in a single night; the lodge did not long survive.

The First Grand Lodge of Operative Tailors which had been formed in December 1833 with such high hopes of a new dawn breaking was itself broken and in ruins six brief months later. Those who had so confidently moved forward under the slogan 'We are the masters now', faced the bitter humiliation of unconditional surrender.

Not all the masters were evilly disposed; not all the men and women inspired solely by idealism. There were masters who had learned the same secret as Francis Place, that sympathy and understanding for workers who enjoy good conditions can produce better work (and better profits) than a slave-driving attitude in slum workshops. Among the workers there were men to whom the humanity of those like Place meant nothing but who were bent on following his rise from poverty to wealth at whatever cost to their fellows.

The declaration of war on the established order had been made at a time when the country was prosperous and trade was expanding. The collapse left the tailors, like other workers, embittered and divided with a standard of living even lower than before.

Inevitably there were large numbers who lost heart for the struggle and drew the lesson that trade unionism had been tried and found useless. The very structure of the tailoring trade encouraged divisions. The highly skilled journeymen saw themselves as the aristocrats whose economic interests had nothing in common with those of the rest of the tailors. On the contrary, seeing themselves as potential masters, they were frequently antagonistic to their fellows. In an increasingly specialised trade the breeches - makers, the coat makers and the rest saw themselves as having special rights to consideration. We have seen how the women workers feared they would be banned from specialised work like waistcoat making even in a world freed from competition and full of fraternal love that Owen had taught them was about to be created. The gulf between all who could make the slightest claim to craftsmanship and the mere stitchers was wide and deep.

The centrifugal force generated by these divisions among the workers was to remain in being for many years to come, leading to fruitless internal struggles which the masters would be more than willing to encourage and exploit.

Even among those engaged on similar work there were divisions. The first attempts of the masters in the eighteenth century to introduce piece-work instead of hourly or daily wages had been resisted strenuously, in particular by those who had served their apprenticeship and considered themselves 'real' tailors. These excluded from their call-houses men who accepted lower wages or who worked by the piece. A second, though at first smaller, group of call-houses grew up to serve the interests of these outcasts. The first called themselves the 'Flints' – presumably with some reference to their willingness and capacity to strike. They named the second group the 'Dungs'. This term of opprobrium came to be applied to non-unionists and blacklegs long after piece-work had come to be accepted as the general system of payment.

The determination of the majority of the masters to stamp out unionism altogether was more effective than the laws passed by Parliament had ever been. The tailors fell back to their traditional defences against poverty and ultimate degradation. Such unions as began to re-emerge were small, devoted to special and sectional interests and were at first almost wholly friendly benefit societies. Even greater secrecy had to be observed than in the days when such combinations were merely illegal. There was no need to invoke the cumbrous and chancy machinery of the law against combinations; now the masters held the 'document' with its clear and penal provisions against any trade union activity.

As the boom turned once more to slump, the Chartist movement grew in strength during the Hungry Forties. Just as John Badby had played his manful part with the Lollards more than four hundred years earlier, so individual tailors joined this new insurrectionary movement. But their unions were too weak and too preoccupied to play any corporate part. Indeed even those unions which had survived in much stronger and more militant forms on the whole ignored the Chartists.

Among these other unions the idea of a united working class survived, and in 1845 the National Association of United Trades for the Protection of Labour was formed. The association posed two self-evident facts; that the workers were not getting a fair day's pay for a fair day's work, and that almost all their efforts to get it had failed. The cause was their isolation in different sections. The association did not attempt, as Owen had done, to form a single national union, but rather to establish with the consent of existing unions, an authoritative voice which could put the interests of the workers before Parliament, the law courts or the employers. Its aims were conciliatory and its methods peaceful. Mediation, arbitration and legal proceedings were seen as the best means of protecting the workers and the promotion of political, social and educational activities the most effective way of improving their lot.

In its cautious and carefully worded report the committee which recommended the formation of the association called the attention of those trades which were sectionally organised to the benefits of wider organisation. It called upon those who had secured higher wages for themselves to support the claims of the less fortunate in their industry.

This appeal reawakened the dormant spirit of the tailors. Discussions were begun on the formation of a national union soon after the association was formed. In 1846 the National Association of Tailors came into being and joined the work of the larger organisation.

The National Association of United Trades was already running into difficulties when the tailors formed their union under its inspiration. Though it had appealed to the employers to recognise that no more was intended than an organisation which could speak on something approaching level terms with their associations in rational discussion of wages and conditions, the masters disdained the conciliatory offer. They quickly re-introduced the 'document' as a weapon against the association and the unions, whether long-established or newly-formed, like that of the tailors. A new trade depression had begun, and it was accompanied by the usual wage-cutting and lockouts.

The response of the workers was a wave of strikes which the association was powerless to prevent and not rich enough to support. Faced with the militant hostility of the employers and undermined by the mistrust of workers who had asked in vain for help, its influence waned. Despite all the difficulties, it did some useful work by way of conciliation, and much more effective work in organising pressure on Parliament. The Ten Hour Act of 1847 was one result of its activities. The withdrawal owing to ill-health of Thomas Slingsby Duncombe from active work in 1848 was followed in 1849 by a disastrous strike of the Wolverhampton tinplate workers. This bankrupted the association. Duncombe, a fashionable man of the world who had devoted himself in Parliament to the causes of the Chartists and the trades unions, had been the guide and mentor of the association. Money was its life-blood. Both were now gone and the organisation limped towards its ultimate dissolution.

Chapter Five/Manchester Leads the Way

INVENTION OF SINGER SEWING MACHINE; RUSSIAN JEWISH EMIGRES; NUMBER OF SMALL SOCIETIES; REPUTATION FOR INTEMPERANCE; MANCHESTER CONFERENCE IN 1866 FORMS AMALGAMATED SOCIETY OF JOURNEYMEN TAILORS; CAMPAIGN FOR UNIFORM TIME LOG; EMPLOYERS IMPORT FOREIGN LABOUR TO BREAK STRIKE

Engineers, carpenters and ironfounders were among those who set the pace about the middle of the nineteenth century. They provided examples of national unions which were strong enough to support their own workers on strike and even to offer financial help to others. The tailors lagged behind in the development of the new unionism. They had been illegally organised for well over 100 years when they played their not insignificant part in the repeal of the Combination Acts. They had been prominent in the first attempt to form a national union and had staged the largest of the first legal strikes. The continuous evolution of their industry denied to the workers that unity of interest and purpose essential to the formation of national unions of the new kind.

New stresses were now to be imposed on them. In 1851, Isaac Merrit Singer patented the first successful sewing machine.[1] In 1854 the tailors of Glasgow passed a resolution: 'That those employers who have pit-shops at present receive notice

[1] *The sewing machine had been invented some twenty years before by a French tailor, Barthélemy Thomonnier, in the village of Arbresle, Rhône valley. It was first manufactured in Paris. Patents for prototype sewing machines had previously been taken ou in 1753, and in 1790.*

to get proper shops, otherwise the men will be obliged to refuse to work in all shops, the same not being above ground.' In that year the Crimean war broke out, adding to the distress of the Russian government which would later seek to solve its insoluble problems with new pogroms against the Jews.

The effect of the invention of the sewing machine was not to be felt fully for some years. The protest of the Glasgow workers was against a system which had already manifested its evil possibilities but which waited on the development of the machine before it was revealed in its total ugliness. This was the sweating system. The acute competition which had given rise to the shopkeeping tailor had been carried a stage further. Journeymen who failed to set up on their own as master tailors settled on the next lower rung of the ladder to fortune. They accepted the position of sub-contractor to their more successful fellows. Bargaining keenly against each other, they obtained their work by offering the lowest possible price. Their narrow margin of profit depended entirely on the savagery with which they could exploit those whom they called to their aid.

By 1850 two-thirds of the tailors in Glasgow were working for these middlemen.

Glasgow tailors were not alone in facing this evil. An even worse development was taking place, equally rapidly, in England. This was the practice of out-working, which was sufficiently well developed to be worthy of special mention in the manifesto of 1834 and continued to increase. Just as women had been exploited by the shopkeeping tailors to depress standards, so they were now used to depress even further the standards of the journeymen compelled to work at home.

The situation was further complicated by the injection of a stream of poverty-stricken Jews, fleeing from the Tsarist oppression. Bereft of all but life itself, those who survived the pogroms arrived in Britain with little more than the will to survive. In the second half of the nineteenth century, they provided a new reservoir of cheap labour which could be, and was, used to lower the standards of even the lowest-paid workers in this jungle of exploitation. The refugees brought with them not only poverty but ideas and imagination, and among them were many who were to play an honourable part in the struggle against the employers.

There were as yet no foundations sufficiently stable on which

47

to build a national union as the engineers and others were doing. Yet the will remained strong and the fighting spirit high. The 'accursed document' had proved a stronger weapon in the hands of the employers than the old Combination Acts, yet it was a threat which the tailors showed themselves willing to defy as soon as they recovered their breath after each succesive defeat. The masters had intended to end trade unionism for ever when they broke the London strike in 1834. In the provinces other masters had joined the assault. An eighteen-week lockout in Manchester later the same year ended in the apparent destruction of the local societies. Six years later a large body of organised tailors were taking a prominent part in a great demonstration of the Manchester Political Union.

In 1843 a committee was formed to draw up rules for a new London union, but it had little immediate effect. It paved the way for the abortive National Association of Tailors which began its brief existence in 1846. If the grand objective of a national union still remained beyond grasp, the local societies continued their fitful activity.

In Liverpool the journeymen revived their old established society in 1853 to combat, with partial success, the growing evils of the slop system. By 1859 the London tailors had again combined to form the United Society of Tailors, London; this was one of twelve societies of London tailors which are on record as contributing some £90 to the strike fund of the builders. A directory of all the known unions published in 1861 lists forty-eight different tailors' societies in forty-four of the larger towns throughout the United Kingdom.

These small societies could never be suppressed for long, but they were never strong enough to combat the steadily declining standards of their members. Where they were able to extort concessions which slowed rather than reversed the decline, more often than not they would be locked out as soon as trade fell off and received back when the alternative to new humiliating conditions was starvation.

The small society based on the call-house had served its purpose; its weaknesses were now apparent to all. The traditions of the call-houses lived on long after they themselves disappeared from the scene.

For a century and a half the small societies had managed their own affairs and controlled their own finances. These were to remain features of the constituent branches of the larger unions formed from them. This local autonomy, particularly in financial affairs, was to prove a source of grave weakness and it was not finally eradicated until the twentieth century.

A second tradition was that of drunken rowdyism. The inn-keeper who allowed his premises to be used as a call-house expected them to be used as a place of refreshment as well. Part of the dues paid went to a 'house fund' to be spent on drink. In bad times the landlord subsidised his customers and their future earnings were thus mortgaged in advance. Money came only after a period of long and exhausting work; settlement with the landlord took much if not all of it; then a new period of short-time or unemployment began. The ritual of 'wetting the bargain' too often proved the beginning of another 'jag'. This was a time when drink offered a temporary amnesiac to millions of workers.

An article by an anonymous journeyman in the *People's Magazine* of March 1867 shows how the tradition survived. He describes the journeyman working up to sixteen hours a day and perhaps all night in the busy season, and then being told that things are slacking off and he need no longer hurry over the next job.

'He allows himself then to be enticed away to have a glass, which leads on to another, and then another, until at last he becomes quite "muddled", and finds himself the next morning in his bed without knowing how he got there, and his head aching so badly that he feels utterly unable to work at all. Then he goes out just to get a "reviver". This, of course brings him into the same company in which he got drunk the night before. He finds a dozen men just reviving, then others. Then a shopmate comes in who has often stood treat to him when he was short; of course he must do the same for his mate, so he finds himself fairly in the stream again, sailing along towards an empty pocket and another headache. It is seldom when a man has got so far as this that he leaves off as long as he has a penny in his pocket; nay he will often run up a score with the landlord and sometimes even pawn his coat in order to get a drink.'

By 1865 Manchester, though it had less than one-tenth the number of tailors working in London, was the second largest centre of the trade in England. The Manchester tailors were in the heart of the northern industrial ferment where the lessons of the class struggle were posed in their starkest and most brutal forms. From them came a new appeal for the formation of a national union on the lines of the engineers and carpenters. The Manchester secretary, Peter Shorrocks, summoned a conference of delegates from all the known societies. This met in Manchester on 12th March 1866, and was attended by some seventy delegates from sixty-seven societies, representing about 6,000 members. Thirty-one other societies in England and Ireland sent messages of support. At this conference, after a debate lasting six days, the Amalgamated Society of Journeymen Tailors was founded. Within three months it could claim a membership of 7,272 members belonging to 118 societies in England. Within six months every town with nine or more journeymen had formed its branch. At first the London and Irish societies kept out of the amalgamation, but they too were amalgamating among themselves. The London Operative Tailors' Association was formed in 1865, and Peter Shorrocks, now secretary of the Amalgamated Society, was given a warm welcome when he addressed its first annual meeting on 13th November 1866.

In Ireland an amalgamation based on Dublin had collapsed with the death of Cosgrave, its inspirer and leading figure. The Drogheda and Limerick societies joined the English Amalgamated. An argument broke out between those who felt the other Irish societies should follow suit and those who, doubting the ability of an organisation based on Manchester to serve their interests, thought it would be better to form an all-Irish amalgamation which would work autonomously but in harmony with the English, Scottish and London amalgamations. Religious differences played their part in continuing the argument, but eventually the Irish societies were to join the English amalgamation.

In Scotland a federal union had collapsed fifteen years before, but it now proved possible to form an amalgamation similar to the English one and covering the whole of Scotland. Wages in Glasgow and Edinburgh were 18s a week and the working week was eighty hours. Putting in a demand for a rise to 23s 9d and a fifty-seven hour week, the union ordered a strike when it was refused.

The wage claim was based on a time log. There were two

different systems of arriving at the wage packet. One was the money log in which the price of a task was set out irrespective of how long it took to complete. The other was the time log in which the time taken to do the task was set out and earnings depended on the hourly rate of wages. To take one example, in one time log, dress and frock coats, 'single breast, raw bluff, stoated, or felled edges, two plait pockets, round cuffs, when no cuff short, vent if required, five rows in stand and eight rows in fall of collar, lapels to correspond, side linings or plain cloth under arm, silk, lustre, or cloth skirt facings, shoulder padding basted on canvas', were rated at twenty-nine hours. Every possible variant on this work, or part of the work, was listed in the log. If 'bound threequarters round the bottom,' for instance, an extra one and a quarter hours was allowed. A time log of this kind, once agreed, left the earnings to be decided by further negotiations on the hourly rate. At 5d an hour on this log the above work on a dress or frock coat would bring the journeyman 12s 1d. At 6d an hour on the log he would get 14s 6d.

The money log was a different way of expressing the same thing. Payment of 13s 3d for a dress coat was equivalent, but for a halfpenny, to a time of twenty-nine hours at a rate of 5½d an hour.

Wide variations in conditions in the United Kingdom led to considerable differences in the logs of different towns and districts. In places so near as Croydon and the West End of London, there was a difference, in Croydon's favour, of ten hours for a shooting jacket and of five and a half hours on a frock coat. The rates were lower in Croydon, but this wide difference led to trouble in border areas. Men in a place like Bromley, Kent, would claim the London rate for the Croydon log.

Employers and workers were both suffering needless vexation as a result of this chaotic system. The more thoughtful on both sides were moving towards the idea of a uniform time log as the best solution to the difficulty. If a generally accepted average time could be fixed for each job, local variations could be dealt with by different hourly rates. The better employer was not averse to his men having time to breathe at their work; the less scrupulous had other ways of doing business open to them – the sub-contractor and the outworker.

The first national conference of the Scottish Amalgamated

Society approved a uniform time log for the whole of Scotland, and this was the basis of the wage and hours demand put to the employers. When the employers rejected the log outright, the union executive ordered a strike and the employers retorted with a lockout. The timing of the strike was excellent. Trade was brisk, and the masters were hard put to it to fulfil the orders on their books. They spent £400 on shipping foreign journeymen from Denmark and Germany to fill the gaps left by the strikers. They found the Scottish journeymen would not work alongside them.

The device of importing foreign workers had been used in the London strike of 1834, though the weakness of the union made it superfluous on that occasion. In Scotland, thirty-two years later, there was a very different state of affairs. The union, though newborn and still suffering from serious organisational defects, was stronger than anything known before. There were more powerful unions in other trades and these, with fraternal generosity, poured money into the strike fund. The union had its own organ the weekly *Operative Tailors' National Appeal*, ably edited by John Williamson. There could be no question of crushing this powerful force with the aid of lockout and 'the document'. The employers realised they must negotiate.

In the third week of the strike, a conference between the two sides discussed the union log and one drawn up by the employers. The conference broke down when the union refused to negotiate except on the basis of their own log. The employers by the end of the third week realised they would have to capitulate. They sent a single emissary named M'Leod to call on the union executive. His first offer was to accept the London log which, he understood, had recently been negotiated, but which he could not produce. The union refused. He then offered an immediate advance of fifteen per cent in wages over the next twelve months in return for an immediate resumption of work. This would be superseded by a rate of $5\frac{1}{2}$d on the London log when a copy could be obtained. Since the union had asked for only 5d on its own log, the executive accepted the bargain and the strike was called off.

It was then discovered that no more than a start had been made in preparing a London log. A joint meeting agreed to accept what there was of the log and that a deputation drawn from both sides should visit London to collect evidence from a number of different shops about the time allowed for all remaining items. An average of these figures would be accepted as the Scottish log.

This amicable and reasonable end to the dispute was by no means to the taste of all the employers. The foreign workers remained in the neighbourhood – the employers who had brought them over at such expense did not see their way to paying for their repatriation – and thought they might provide a useful reserve if opportunity arose for a counter-attack. But the new spirit was not so easily killed. The agreement survived even the return of mass unemployment in the depression of 1867.

Chapter Six/'Respectable and Formidable'

PETER SHORROCKS AND MATTHEW LAWRENCE ADVOCATE CONCILIATION AND
CONSOLIDATION; CAMPAIGN FOR SINGLE UNION; OPPOSITION BY 'MILITANTS';
SECTIONAL DIFFERENCES; CONDITIONS IN GOVERNMENT UNIFORM FACTORIES;
EARLY 'SWEATING DENS' VISITED

The manner in which the Scottish settlement had been reached
was wholly in tune with the thinking of those who had formed
the English Amalgamated Society and the London Association.
The thirty-first of the forty-six draft rules laid before the conference at which the Amalgamated Society was formed laid
down that 'recourse to a strike should only be an extreme
measure' and the rule went on to approve the setting up of
arbitration machinery. The first aim of both unions was to gain
strength from which to negotiate. Scotland had proved the con-
tention of the union founders that it was possible to sit down
and argue out a reasonable compromise. They wished to arrive
at this point without the preliminaries of strike and lockout.

Matthew Lawrence, retiring president of the London Association, was loudly cheered when he told the first annual meeting of the London Association on 13th November 1866 that in
future negotiations with the employers 'everything must be
done to conciliate, and everything must be both tried and done
before a strike on the one hand or a lockout on the other may
be thought necessary . . . If a good and friendly feeling can
only be brought to exist between us, I see no reason why an
end should not be put to those wranglings and petty disputes
which have so long unhappily distinguished our trade.'

Peter Shorrocks, general secretary of the Amalgamated Society, while underlining the benefits of goodwill on both sides, stressed the need for closer unity. When the men were disunited, the masters dictated any terms, but when they were united the masters consulted them as to terms. In this simple sentence he drew the lessons of more than 150 years of struggle which had left the journeymen no better off than at the beginning.

Both Shorrocks and Lawrence, who now became secretary of the London Association, were keen advocates of a single union. Negotiations had been opened between their organisations and the Scottish union, but the Scots had deferred a decision. The two decided to go ahead together. At the beginning of January 1867 a joint meeting was held in Manchester which for practical purposes joined the London Association and the Amalgamated Society into one union with 20,000 members. The agreement provided for the closest mutual assistance and cooperation; membership cards of the one were valid in the area of the other and subscriptions were paid to whichever society was responsible for the locality in which a man was working, irrespective of which union he had joined.

Hitherto men had been able to dodge paying their dues by claiming to have paid elsewhere. The two general secretaries were convinced that numbers were not enough; they must be backed by as efficient an administration as the members would accept. The task of providing it was not easy. One of the weakest links lay in the strong local feelings of the branches. Insisting on controlling their own finances, they tended to resent being called upon to contribute to the central organ. In London this was one-quarter of the branch collections. Through mismanagement and misplaced loyalty, some branches voted such salaries to their officers, and for other purposes, that nothing was left for the central fund. Elsewhere untrustworthy people were voted into office. Within the first year of their formation, the Holborn and Paddington branches had disintegrated – the secretaries had decamped with the cash box. It proved difficult to revive these branches. The members who had seen their money disappear did not wish to subscribe if it was going to vanish again.

The leaders wished to perfect the organisation as far as possible before embarking on national negotiations for the first time. The branches, seeing they had a larger reserve than ever before (owing to the big increase in membership) and thinking a sudden rush of work provided a good opportunity to squeeze the employers, would start an unofficial strike. To demonstrate the benefits of unity they had to be supported once their funds ran out, but all this was a drain on the reserves the leaders were trying to build.

Matthew Lawrence campaigned ceaselessly for a pause in industrial action while the unions gathered strength. Speaking to the Woolwich branch in December 1866, he noted that Middlesbrough, Darlington, Rawtenstall, Burnley and Knutsford were all locked out on what both masters and men considered a matter of principle. News had just come that the men in Lincoln had put in a claim for a rise. Lawrence showed considerable courage in declaring his own point of view. Since negotiations were about to begin on a national scale, it was unwise for masters or men to hold out any longer. There should be a resumption of work. Since he had no influence with the masters, this was tantamount to a call to the workers to accept the masters' terms. He went further and said it was 'undoubtedly wrong' for any branch to make any move for advancement at that stage, and advised the men in the north to make what compromise they could.

'The men may, at the beginning of a busy season, compel the masters to yield an advance, but as soon as that season is gone the masters will embrace their opportunity, and neither have any principle to act upon. But let every branch remain still for the present and let both masters and men bear for a little longer what they may consider oppressions, let the men bear a little tyranny, and the masters a little robbery (laughter) until an agreement shall be come to between the representatives of the masters and the men's association and we shall then have a principle to act upon.'

Here was the kernel of the policy being pursued by the union leaders. The temporary victories in local struggles had seldom if ever been made permanent; they had left the local masters full of ill-feeling towards their own men. If a national agreement could be negotiated with representatives of the better employers throughout the country, the whole force of the union could be brought to bear on any locality where the masters sought to pay less.

In the north, said Lawrence, both masters and men were afraid of creating precedents: the masters of establishing too high a price, the men of establishing too low a payment. 'Whatever party may be successful at present, whether it be the men of Darlington getting what they want for their edges, or the masters in reducing the prices they have hitherto paid, each must be stripped of what they have gained when the new log comes to be introduced.'

This was the voice of one who was trying to see the problem whole. He was speaking to the men; he knew he was overheard by the masters. The path of steady and progressive reform to which he was committed could only be opened by establishing a clear point of departure. This was a national agreement. Given that, all else would follow. Those workers who were in a good position to extract even better terms would extract them the more readily if they had already obtained a generally agreed minimum on which to argue their case. Those in the weakest positions could more easily defend themselves if they could point to a basic agreement which had a nationwide status.

This approach was by no means to the liking of those 'militants' who felt that willingness to fight was the first essential of union activity. Lawrence was followed at this meeting by a fellow member of the central executive, Blissert, who said he would not like any misunderstanding about the position of the men in the north. Some of these men had been asked to submit to a reduction of twenty-five per cent, and 'it is no time to whip a child when it is rode over.'

Here was a sentiment much more to the liking of men newly converted to the idea of joint action. Some degree of demagogy and an over-simplification of the problem is inseparable from any programme of rapid recruitment to a mass movement. It is the task of statesmanship to channel the resulting wave of enthusiasm and to provide the dams by which it can be converted into a disciplined and irresistible force. Thus the engineer converts the scattered raindrops into an artificial lake to drive turbines which produce electricity – and power. It was to men like Lawrence that the tailors owed the fact that their enthusiasm was not dispersed like water running away in sand but guided and directed towards the production of power.

There were other problems facing the leadership. Self-respecting, they wished to be respected. They saw themselves as the equals of the masters, fit to engage in rational discussion with them on the best means of bettering conditions in the trade in which all were engaged. Not all the men felt likewise. Meanness on the part of employers engendered meanness in those who were employed. Men would arrive in town and get advance payment for work, 'shooting the moon' before it was completed. Worse, they would prey on their fellows. John Ellis, secretary of the Hitchin Society wrote to the official journal in February 1867 to complain of the activities of one Robert Kinder who had arrived very badly off, with a wife and child, seeking help and work. His family were found lodgings, and he work. He repaid this kindness by selling the iron he had been lent and the trimmings given to him to do the job before decamping.

Anxious as they were to increase their numerical membership, the leaders made every effort to encourage local secretaries to withdraw the cards of those guilty of cheating either the employers or their fellow workers. By exerting discipline over their own weaker brethren, they would be on stronger ground in attacking the practices of the worst of the masters.

There remained the problem of the division of interest between the different grades of workers. What had the top grade journeyman employed in a West End house as a cutter in common with the girls employed in the Woolwich factory making army uniforms or the immigrant Jew in his hovel off Petticoat Lane? To the first, enjoying comparative affluence in his regular work based on a reasonable time log, the foreigner working at piece rates and with his whole family impressed into service appeared as an obvious enemy rather than as a brother in distress. This was the wide gap that the union sought to bridge.

In that same speech to the Woolwich branch which we have already quoted, Matthew Lawrence spoke in the spirit which inspired the writers of the preamble to the rules of the sister Amalgamated Society when they wrote: 'Ours is no partial movement calculated to benefit a few; we embrace all, act for all. Let all then join with us, and help to win and keep the reforms we propose to accomplish.'

An apt text was provided by the government factories in Woolwich, where army clothing was made, which were 'a disgrace to the government of any country,' and where starvation prices were paid for the making of uniforms. A week before, some 2,000 of the London tailors had taken part in a great reform demonstration and their leaders had played a prominent part on the platforms along with such nationally known figures as Bright and the rest. Even the odious *Times* had to admit that the tailors were distinguished by 'the superior appearance of the men who represented them.' The *Telegraph* said they came in for a large share of the popular enthusiasm, with their clean and neat appearance and light jaunty step. The *Star* was even more impressed. 'One of the largest, if not the largest, body of men connected with any society taking part in the procession were the tailors, who presented a most respectable and formidable appearance. It is said that there is scarcely a branch of industry in England the members of which take so great an interest in politics as do the tailors, and certainly judging from the manner in which they turned out in the demonstration yesterday, there must be some ground for the saying.'

Respectable and formidable. It was thus that Matthew Lawrence wished to see the tailors. 'Our appearance last Monday showed that we are quite equal in any point to our fellow artisans and mechanics. I cannot see why journeymen tailors should be treated differently from the rest of humanity.' Yet there in Woolwich were 'Her Majesty's Establishments' where girls worked in wretched hovels at prices barely sufficient to keep body and soul together. They were 'sweating dens, the abodes of destitution and misery'. Lawrence calculated that though they bore their equal share of taxation, the tailors were through these low prices being called upon to clothe half the army as well.

Their mission was something higher than merely increasing wages. 'We want to elevate our poor fallen brethren who are at present wallowing in the mire, and that, gentlemen, is the one object of our Association. We want to raise the whole tone of being of every grade and class of workmen in our trade.'

Lawrence called on the members of the Woolwich branch to become apostles preaching the doctrine of the unity of every tailor and tailoress in one united body. With a determined recruiting drive all the workers in the government factories could be organised within a month. If only one half, or even a third joined, the union could well afford to withdraw them and pay them full wages, so pitiful were the prices they received.

Girls such as these, working in a government factory, were recognisably doing parallel work to the journeymen in a west end shop. Even the most snobbish anti-feminist could be brought to see the basic identity of economic interest and the benefits of combining to raise the level of the lowest as part of a process of improvement for all. It was otherwise with that growing body of outworkers, many of whom were as hostile to the working journeymen as the latter were to them. If it was difficult to persuade the journeymen they had a duty to welcome these outworkers into their ranks, it was no less difficult to persuade the outworkers they had everything to gain by joining the union.

John Williamson, the editor of the union journal, has left a description of a visit he made with union officials to outworkers in and around Petticoat Lane in the east end of London. He tells of a nauseating journey through evil-smelling hovels where Jewish immigrants from central Europe and Russia worked and slept cheek by jowl, without sanitary arrangements, washing facilities, light or air; in these conditions of dirt and disease, they were making fashionable garments at a price which meant that every moment not actually spent in sleep was spent at work.

Approaching by a dark narrow stair, they came to a room where a 'sickly and emaciated' German Jew was working in one corner while a woman worked a sewing machine in another. They explained that the union was trying to get a higher price for his work, but he answered that when he had himself raised the question with his employer he had been told there were plenty of others who were willing to do it for less. He was making a black Whitney Chesterfield coat, with a fly, three outside pockets and bound edges. He was to get 4s, out of which he had to buy his own trimmings. He averaged about eighteen hours' work a day.

'By this time we were nearly stifled through inhaling the atmosphere of the apartment. We told them there was to be a meeting on Monday to consider what could be done for him and his class, and we made a hasty retreat.'

At the next place, when they asked for the householder, a group of three or four ringed them round and tried to prevent them getting in. It needed diplomacy and persuasion to get past this barrier, through a bedroom and a kitchen to the workshop where a number of people were sitting round working. The head of the household was making a fashionable light Melton Chesterfield, with double stitched seams, edges turned in and double stitched, three outside pockets and silk facings. This was for a private customer and would bring in 5s, but would cost at least 6d for sewing materials.

'Our attention was directed to a man at work over in a corner, whose look was quite in keeping with the dilapidated state of everything around him. By his side was a loaf which appeared to be torn in two and some butter in a newspaper. "Would you believe it," said our companion who had frequently visited them, "he sits there as long as his poor body will endure it, and when the feeling of hunger comes upon him he makes a dive at that loaf and butter!" ' Finished work was lying about: a highland cloak, double stitched all round and with a fly, for which 2s 6d would be paid. Women at machines were making a heavy brown Melton overcoat with lapped and double sewn seams, edges double stitched, four outside pockets with flaps and a velvet collar. All the trimmings would be paid for out of the 3s 6d for this garment.

In places like these they 'received us as criminals would a magistrate, conscious that they were doing wrong, and both they and their homes bore all the marks of the low and degraded position into which they had sunk'. There was one bright spot, with a workroom 'as tidy and clean as a respectable workshop could be.' There were two men and seven or eight girls at work, and the head of the household showed an immediate and keen interest in the visit. But his wife joined them and took up the argument. Supposing they did get 200 to unite, and 800 were left, what would be the result of any effort to raise prices? It would be to give the 800 a larger supply of work.

' "It don't pay us or these girls to work for such prices, but our children want bread and what can we do?" ' The deputation pointed out they were not proposing to call a strike, but that if they could only get enough of the outworkers to join the union they would be in a stronger position to negotiate higher prices. Without unity they were completely helpless. The visit ended with a promise that the son would attend the meeting the following night. The son was working about sixteen hours a day preparing work for the girls who normally did a twelve-hour day.

The writer was told he had seen only the best and the bad; he refused to be taken to see the worst. 'We had seen quite enough for one day.'

Summing up this first hand experience of sweating, he made these comments. 'First, in regard to the prices, how is it done? It is done by their working all the hours God sends, except the few deducted for sleep. It is done by their employing as many girls as they can get hold of, who augment the small pittance they receive by prostitution; that is how it is done.

'What end does it serve? It enables Messrs Parnell, Lynch, Moses and Son, Samuel Brothers, Nicolls and others, to under-sell honest and respectable tradesmen, and supply garments in a style and at a figure which no employer with a conscience could approach. It enables the engineer, the builder and the clerk who have from 30s to £3 a week for eight to ten hours a day, to sport their figure in stylish garments at two-thirds of their value, at the expense of poor wretches who work eighteen hours a day for a bare existence. It, more than anything else, serves to perpetuate an amount of evil, misery and wretchedness, for which the above respectable and philanthropic tradesmen ought to be held responsible.' The tale was the same in Manchester, Birmingham, Glasgow, or Edinburgh. It was a national evil and nothing short of a great national effort could cure it. But it was to take another fifty years before such a national anti-sweating effort became effective.

Chapter Seven/A Journalist's 'Scoop'

JOHN WILLIAMSON, EDITOR OF *The Tailor*; 'A POWERFUL AUXILIARY'; THE LUTON MANIFESTO; MANCHESTER LOCKOUT; EMPLOYERS FORM MASTER TAILORS' ASSOCIATION; WILLIAMSON'S REPORT OF LONDON MEETING; GOOD AND BAD EMPLOYERS

One of the most useful and important developments in this latest attempt to build a national union was the start of publication of *The Tailor* on 6th October 1866. John Williamson, who had edited the Scottish *Operative Tailors' National Appeal*, had spread its circulation into England and Ireland when it was closed down. There are hints of asperity in Williamson's later writings about the Scottish comrades which may indicate some obscure quarrel. Since the Scottish union was to pursue a slightly different policy from the rest of the kingdom in the important years, it was perhaps fortunate that Williamson's great abilities were put at the service of the larger body of workers.

His new paper aimed at a national circulation among all tailors in the kingdom, and had offices in London, Manchester, Birmingham, Glasgow and Edinburgh. Both the Amalgamated Society and the London Association gave it their blessing and helped in its distribution. So too did unions in Scotland and Ireland. From its inception *The Tailor* played a vital part in the struggle for steady, progressive reform.

It is easy to pick holes in his style of writing – he was over-fond of those dangerous weapons, irony and sarcasm, and his humour was more pawky than sophisticated. His powers of

63

description did not always measure up to the occasion; he could be windy and verbose. Yet these criticisms are themselves a form of praise. He did so well, one could wish he had had the capacity to do superlatively. At least he had the heart of the matter constantly in mind. He was, in his own way, and in the context of his times, a great journalist. He sought to *inform* and did his best to entertain. His columns were open to the official pronouncements of the union leaders and to the ramblings of the least literate of the rank and file. The weekly leading articles he wrote covered the widest possible field and never once deviated from the central message: closer unity, embracing all, in well-administered organisations, with the strike weapon used only as a last resort when all honest attempts at negotiation had demonstrably failed. He was not over-estimating the role *The Tailor* was to play when he wrote in its first number that he hoped it would be 'a powerful auxiliary' in the fight for improvement.

Its columns provide a graphic picture of the struggle in all its aspects. The Luton branch writes asking the editor 'to insert the following Requisition . . . as we are desirous the whole of the trade should have it in their power to judge how far we are in the right in this our first combined attempt to obtain something like justice from our employers.' The enclosure was printed in full:

'TO THE MASTER TAILORS OF LUTON AND NEIGHBOURHOOD

'Gentlemen, – We have chosen this as a fit time to lay before you the following request, viz: For an alteration in the affairs of our trade, the present system being unsatisfactory and injurious to both parties. First – That the time for labour be ten hours per day for five days and seven hours on Saturdays. Second – That you pay by the enclosed Log for all work done at the rate of 4d per hour. "For Overtime," Time and a quarter. Should you find anything that you think wants altering in the Log, you are respectfully requested to make such alterations and send the same to our secretary. Your agreement with the above will settle a long-standing grievance and allow of our working harmoniously together in the future.

'ADVANTAGES – To the Masters: Less expense for gas,

firing &c, work earlier in your hands, no disappointment to customers, no loss from bad work, or work left unfinished after payment; our society will pay all such from their funds.

'To the Men: It will lessen the number of votaries to the shrine of Saint Monday, make their homes more comfortable, their wives more pleasant and smiling through the regularity of their husbands, better satisfied with their work, through having no cause to quarrel with their employers, or employee having no excuse for losing time through being overworked.

'Signed by 54 members of the Luton Association of Journeymen Tailors.

Sir – You will signify your approval of the above by your signature or otherwise. Sending on or before the 30th of March, 1867, to the following address:–

Secretary, Tailors' Society,

Royal George, Stuart Street, Luton, Beds.

We remain, Gentlemen, your obedient servts.

THE WHOLE OF THE CLUB.

CLUB ROOM, 4th March, 1867.'

This was typical of the way in which branches all over the country seized the initiative when opportunity seemed to offer. The employers used similar guerilla tactics. Week after week notices appeared in *The Tailor* announcing a new trouble spot:

'The following important notice is requested to be kept before the Trade: According to present appearances a lock-out is inevitable, and journeymen are respectfully requested to avoid the town and not to enter into any engagements that may be offered by calls, or advertisements. Secretaries are also requested to be on the alert. All communications to be addressed to the Secretary, Jas. Hanly,

Oddfellows Arms, North Street,

Cheltenham.'

When the lock-out was in progress the announcements take on a terser note:

'LOCK-OUT

'The Tailors in Cowes and Ryde (Isle of Wight) are at present locked out on the Log question.

'Workmen are requested not to make engagements for the present.'

One of the larger lockouts occurred in Manchester, headquarters of the Amalgamated Society. After three weeks funds began to run short and an appeal was launched. Within a fortnight £467 13s 10d had been subscribed by branches all over the country, ranging from the £50 of Manchester No 2 and £30 from Liverpool down to 5s from Wisbech and the 4s from Gainsborough. The funds were augmented by a fifteen per cent levy on all tailors not locked out in Manchester, by donations from other unions and by collections from private individuals, bringing the total to £863 0s 9½d. Of this £779 14s 7d went on strike pay and £53 2s 6d to men leaving town.

In his report Peter Shorrocks speaks of the warm wishes that came with the subscriptions and proudly ends: 'We wish to record here, that of the whole number thrown out of employment, there was but one man who did not stand to his colours, though many overtures were made, and some very tempting offers to shake the men's fidelity; but they stood to their text, and performed their heavy duties cheerfully in order to benefit the condition of our trade.'

The Manchester lockout thus provided a shining example of solidarity. One of the most encouraging facts was that the Manchester No 2 branch, which had headed the subscription list, was almost entirely composed of outworkers. The dream of bringing all sections into one union was being expressed in terms of hard cash from these workers who were least able to afford it. The failure of the masters to entice more than one worker back was all the more remarkable in that the men had allowed themselves to be manoeuvred into an utterly untenable position.

Attempts to agree a new money log had been the cause of several minor strikes when the employers with bad grace for the most part accepted the men's demands. Some of them announced they would undermine the new agreement by installing machines and recruiting men on a weekly wage. There were frequent disputes about what work should be machined and how it should be priced. In exasperation the men passed a series of resolutions including one which said that nothing should be deducted from the normal time allowed when a machine was used to make plain garments.

The masters offered to meet the men, but at their next meeting the union members were so busy dealing with routine business and passing more resolutions that they failed to appoint a delegation. The masters rejected the resolutions, and some of them tried to reduce the prices paid for machine work. A strike in six shops where this happened was met with a lockout.

The Amalgamated Society was less than six months old when this dispute presented the executive council with the first real test of statesmanship. They considered a report on the extent to which machines were already in use all over the country, and studied the broad agreement which had already been made in Scotland on payment for machine work. They knew that in the United States machines were used wherever possible and that those journeymen who had emigrated there were the highest paid in the trade. They considered the history of other industries where machinery had been introduced. In the light of all this the executive decided the men had no case for their resolution 'that nothing be stopped for work done by the machine in the making of the garments'. They agreed to face the men and tell them the unpalatable truth.

The facts were argued out at an open meeting and so persuasive were the union leaders that there was a unanimous vote to withdraw the offending resolution and to leave the question to a joint committee of masters and men. After some delay the committee produced a machine log with a recommendation that any disputes about it should be referred back to a joint arbitration committee.

In the fifth week of the lockout the men were still completely united and were cementing their friendship with the outworkers. They had the evidence of the successful financial appeal to show they had the backing of tailors all over the country and of other organised workers as well. It was to men still very much in a fighting mood that the executive came to say they had been wrong to provoke the lockout in the way they had, and that they should return to work. This needed courage, and Messrs Green and Holly who spoke for the executive lacked neither courage nor eloquence.

This was the most important of the earlier occasions on which the executive had no hesitation in disagreeing with the action of branches. In its quarterly reports and in articles in *The Tailor* each case was temperately but cogently argued so that tailors all over the country could understand the issues involved and the reasons for the executive action. Even if they were wrong, the men grew to know they could be certain of the fullest support but they found, too, that they were subjected to the politest 'reasoning' about their attitude from headquarters.

The circulation of *The Tailor* increased rapidly, and soon every tailor in the country was kept completely in the picture week by week. No other union had a better service of information and education. To Williamson and his journal must go a great deal of the credit for the way in which the unions were built up on a sound basis.

The actual launching of *The Tailor* had its amusing side. Williamson planned the first sixteen-page issue for about the end of 1866.

Preoccupied as he was with the tedious but necessary preparatory work, he did not miss an interesting advertisement in *The Times*. This was inserted by J. D. Landon junior of Messrs Landon and Gledhill, Burlington Street, W. It invited master tailors from every town in the kingdom to a conference the following August at which 'the present and future prospects of the labour question can be thoroughly discussed, a more satisfactory arrangement among themselves may be arrived at, and a system adopted by which work may be efficiently carried on in case of strikes'.

The masters had watched the growth of the unions, and evaluated correctly the meaning of the help forthcoming from all over the country whenever men were in trouble through strike or lockout. The men were growing stronger at a time when the masters remained divided in their outlook and attitude. There were those like the partners in Andrew and Smethiorst, who celebrated the opening of new premises in Manchester with decent healthy workrooms by inviting the whole staff to a 'house-warming' dinner party. Replying to the toast of 'health and prosperity' to the firm, Mr Smethiorst said: 'We have met to drink a social glass in union, to give expression to our various sentiments and in order to cement and renew our friendship. I am quite sure that if employers and employed could be brought together more frequently to reciprocate their ideas there would be more of concord and good fellowship than at present exists between them, and unpleasant differences would be avoided.'

Such employers had as little in common with the sweaters

as had the sweated themselves. Between these two kinds of employer there were infinite variations of good and bad, well-meaning and frankly brutal, but all were guided by the profit motive in a period of fierce commercial competition. The employees were now beginning to conduct their affairs with rather more intelligence. They were realising that to take a job at any price meant an eventual lowering of the standards of all; it seemed possible they might eradicate competition for work between themselves and then hold the divided masters to ransom. Even the best employers viewed such a prospect with anxiety; the worst saw ruin ahead.

Just as the unions had thrown up leaders of the calibre of Shorrocks and Lawrence, so the masters found their spokesman in J. D. Landon. His organising ability had made him a natural choice as secretary of the masters' committee during a lockout in London early in 1866. This had brought him into correspondence with masters all over the country about their grievances and difficulties with labour. From this correspondence grew the idea of a national association of master tailors to defend themselves against the encroachments of the unions.

Landon prepared the ground carefully. He canvassed the London masters first, and obtained the signatures of the sixty-five leading firms before taking any further steps. He then advertised in *The Times* and elsewhere, following up with letters to key firms in all the provincial, Scottish and Irish towns. The response was sufficiently good for him to call a conference at St James's Hall, London, on 30th August.

John Williamson, who saw himself as the contemporary historian of the tailoring trade, was naturally keenly interested in this projected meeting, and bitterly disappointed to find that it was to be held in secret with admission limited to those who could produce a personal invitation backed by a firm's business card. All this seemed singularly undemocratic to a member of a union which threw its meetings open to the public and sought every means to gain publicity for its discussions. With the help of a friendly master tailor, Williamson was able to pass a triple barrier of flunkeys, the first of whom took his gaily coloured ticket, the second examined his trade card and the third wrote his supposed particulars on a sheet of foolscap. He tells us that at one stage he was almost drafted to serve on one of the sub-committees set up to deal with various problems.

F

His notebooks filled with a verbatim report of a vital meeting at which the masters had spoken uninhibitedly about their ideas and intentions, Williamson had as yet no vehicle in which to publish it. He pressed on with the preparations for *The Tailor* with even greater urgency and was able to bring out the first number on 6th October. This was a double-priced 'special' at 2d almost entirely devoted to reports and comments on the meeting of the masters. The delegate who had warned the conference that the unions 'were always on the alert and watch our actions very narrowly' was speaking more truly than he knew. The masters were dumbfounded when they saw their carefully edited handout to the press thus elaborated by a full report in the union journal together with many ribald comments.

Some two hundred delegates attended the meeting and many of them represented all the master tailors in their home town. Landon, 'a little man, with short cut hair, and a face reddened by excitement' was decorously cheered when he told them that the proposed association was not being formed to oppress the workmen, injure their interests or ignore their just claims. He was much more loudly cheered when he said: 'As long as the workmen have a well-organised and strong association putting forth its strength at its will, and the masters are weak, disunited and unable to cope with them, it requires no reasoning to show that unless we organise ourselves into an association, we must go to the wall. The men are well cemented together, and we should be the same. They can attack us whenever they like, and we are powerless to resist . . .

'The men having formed a union so strong that they can coerce and tyrannise over the masters, I think it high time we were also united . . . and further, gentlemen, I think one and all must admit that the coalition of the working classes at the present day is commercially, socially and politically dangerous. (Loud and continuing cheering.)'

In the debate which followed, speaker after speaker paid tribute to the way in which the men had organised themselves and pointed to the petty jealousies which had disrupted all previous attempts to bring the masters together. Mr Thompson of Conduit Street drew a sad picture of the way the London masters had been defeated that spring. The latest census showed there were over 32,000 men, women and children working at tailoring in London. Only 1,500 of them had been locked out, but the union had been able to get an increase in wages for all 32,000 as a condition of their resuming work. Could he urge a stronger reason for the masters to form a counter-association? With his hands thrust deep into the cross-pockets of his tight drab trousers, he called for the union of all masters great and small, whether in the east end, the west end or any other part of the kingdom. 'Then, with a long pull, a strong pull and a pull together, we shall be sure to attain the end in view.'

Mr M'Gee, a Pickwickian character with 'a glowing countenance and rotund figure wrapped in respectable broadcloth and with a vest of snowy white' represented two-thirds of the masters in Belfast. His was by far the most conciliatory speech, for he not only scouted the idea that the association should injure the men, but said its object should be to 'elevate them and put them in a proper position.' This was by no means the idea of most of the speakers. Self-made men like Mr Davis of Halifax – he would certainly have called himself a 'bluff Yorkshireman' – or Mr Mowat of Bromley, were at pains to explain what practical men they were. Everyone knew, said the first, that the journeymen as a body were the most degraded and demoralised. 'They are not only prepared to defend themselves, but are ready to tyrannise over the masters. Shall we, as masters who have risen from the ranks of the journeymen, suffer them to lower us in ratio of intelligence below themselves? I say not.' Mr Mowat ('We all know what a coat is when it is made, at any rate I do') ended with a plea for mutual understanding between masters and men. The body of his rambling speech contained spicy anecdotes such as the story of the branch official of the union who had been forced out of his trade and compelled to get a job as a lamplighter. He had, of course, some very estimable men working for him, men who would not sit in the same room with a union man!

There was a note of nostalgia from Mr Stuart of Newcastle who had helped to break a strike by going over to Hamburg to bring back 'a live cargo of journeymen tailors which completely knocked the wind out of the strike.'

Talking as they thought in private, those who supported the idea of the new association most strongly made it quite clear that if they had their way it would be an instrument of naked oppression. But even the most hot-headed realised that the masters were on the defensive. There was no talk of reintroducing the 'document'; they all knew that unionism had at last come to stay. They were now concerned to find means of rising from a position of inferiority to one of equality with their men.

An unseemly wrangle about the size of the subscription – a guinea a year was held to be far too much – and incompetent chairmanship which permitted several amendments and motions to be debated together threatened at times to allow the meeting to end in chaos. Nevertheless, the Master Tailors' Association of the United Kingdom was finally launched. Among its objects was free and friendly communication with the unions in order to avoid strikes, but at the same time 'prompt and united resistance of any attempt on the part of the men to enforce unreasonable demands or to limit the free action of any individual master'. The weakness of the association lay in the fact that individual employers were their own judges of what was a reasonable demand and what constituted freedom of action.

The great step forward was that there was general agreement that the masters must now negotiate with the men on their central demand – the establishment of a universal time log applicable all over the country. There were some who welcomed the idea because they thought it would mean reductions in existing time agreements, but the more sensible among them realised that there would have to be real negotiation with, perhaps, concessions on both sides.

Thanks to Williamson's ingenuity and persistence, journeymen all over the country were able to read a full report of this curious meeting. No better recruiting pamphlet could have been devised by the union leaders. Here was admission after admission from employers all over the country that they felt powerless before the strength of the unions, and hint after hint that they saw their only hope in sinking their own differences and exaggerating those between different sections of the workers.

Gleefully though Williamson and the union leaders joined in laughing at the discomfiture of the masters under this merciless exposure, they nevertheless joined in a chorus of welcome to the new association, as providing a platform on which the two sides might fairly and honestly discuss their differences. A warning accompanied the welcome:

'One thing that is indispensable to harmony is that masters and men *meet together* to consider what is right and just to both. But if the masters continue to hold their meetings within closed doors, and having concocted their schemes and plans, come forth with the idea of enforcing them, they will see the words of their leader verified, and find such a coalition to be "POLITICALLY, SOCIALLY AND COMMERCIALLY DANGEROUS".'

So wrote Williamson in *The Tailor*, with the full approval of the executives of the London, English and Scottish Amalgamations.

Chapter Eight/Towards a Showdown

LONDON-SCOTTISH NEGOTIATIONS ON UNIFORM TIME LOG BREAK DOWN; ACCESSION OF BELFAST AND DUBLIN TO THE AMALGAMATED; FORMATION OF MASTERS' ASSOCIATION; DEADLOCK ON MASTERS' LOG PROPOSAL; MATTHEW LAWRENCE'S ULTIMATUM; ALHAMBRA PALACE MEETING CARRIES STRIKE RESOLUTION

The Scottish tailors had been in the lead in the formation of the new unions and amalgamations. Their union had won considerable concessions at the outset of its existence. The fifty-seven hour week was nominally conceded, together with an immediate pay increase of fifteen per cent. This was to be replaced within twelve months by the adoption of the new London log paid at the rate of 5½d an hour. It was the representative of the masters who told the union executive that this new log was being prepared in London, but in fact the information was completely false. No London log existed, and none was being prepared. Most of the more prominent houses were paying roughly the same for whole garments, but there was no agreed standard for all the extras.

The Scottish leaders were anxious to co-operate with the masters and to develop friendly relations in which differences could be reasonably discussed and settled. They therefore felt bound to show their own good faith by carrying out the agreement on which a return to work had been negotiated. When they found they had been misinformed about the new London log, they willingly accepted a proposal for a compromise. A joint deputation of masters and men went to London and visited about two dozen representative shops, collecting information about the prices paid in each. An average of these was struck and a log made up on this basis. There was something to be said for this hasty and ill-considered way of dealing with an extremely complex subject. On the narrow view of purely Scottish interests, it was a means of consolidating the gains made as a result of the strike and lockout. By demonstrating their willingness to act in the spirit rather than the unworkable letter of an agreement the men might hope to induce a similar sensible approach in the masters.

Laudable though this attitude may have been, it ignored the changes which had taken place since the Scottish settlement. Soon after the so-called Scoto-London log had been drawn up, the masters of the United Kingdom met in London to form their own association. At that meeting the Scottish masters were well to the fore in suggesting a uniform time log for the whole country and spoke as if a basis for it already existed in the Scoto-London log.

The speeches at the masters' conference showed clearly that there was a large and powerful group of masters who hoped to profit from the lack of complete unity among the men. If an agreement on a log in Scotland could be concluded the whole weight of the masters' association could be used to force the same log on the rest of the country.

Peter Shorrocks was quick to see that the masters, who had thought themselves weak and divided in the face of the unions, were now likely to reverse the positions if their new nationwide association prospered. He therefore sent an urgent appeal to London and Scotland calling for a conference at which the three unions should discuss a closer alliance. The Scots refused to attend. They were hurt at the refusal of London to approve and endorse their log and were getting to the end of the twelve-month truce during which their temporary agreement with the Scottish masters was to run. They foresaw endless delays if they joined with the English and Irish in an attempt to make a new uniform log applicable to the whole country which would compel them to break the terms of the truce.

Matthew Lawrence and his colleagues in London were however as fully alive to the implications of the new situation as their comrades in the English Amalgamated. They accepted the invitation to go to Manchester where the agreement was reached in January 1867 which to all intents and purposes merged the two unions.

The London union had been surprised and dismayed to hear that the Scots were working out a log with their masters supposedly based on an agreed London log. The slapdash way in which it had been botched together bore as little relation to their own ideas of careful preparation and wide consultation as did a coat made in an East End slop shop to the workmanship of Conduit Street. They had replied to the Scottish union's request that they should endorse it with an emphatic rejection of the whole document as being utterly unacceptable to the London tailors. They begged the Scots not to go ahead with negotiations on this basis.

The administration of the Scottish union was poor enough for this correspondence to be lost or mislaid. Feelings in London were further exacerbated when the Scottish executive announced that 'because of the seeming indifference and silence' of the London men, they had been compelled to abandon the log and begin negotiating a new one with the Scottish masters.

Repeated efforts by the leaders in London and Manchester to persuade the Scots to call off their own separate negotiations and to join in presenting a united front to the masters proved vain. Cajolery and persuasion gave way to what the Scottish executive interpreted as a threat to appeal directly to their members to set them aside. This was sufficient to stiffen resistance and make any agreement virtually impossible. The breach between the Scottish union and the rest of the country was to last for many years.

The Scoto-London log was described by Matthew Lawrence later, when it had become impossible to keep the differences between the unions private, as 'one of the worst logs that ever existed.' It was a terrifying thought that the men's representatives might have to enter negotiations with masters who could say it had already been accepted by a large body of the workers and that they, representing the united voice of the whole kingdom, considered it reasonable to apply it everywhere.

There were already well over 150 different time logs in existence in England alone. The difficulty in reducing them to uniformity lay in their essential unreality. They were not arrived at as a result of any technique resembling the modern time and motion study. Their value lay in the fact that they established the *relative* times for which payment would be made.

Thus:

PAGE'S JACKET

	hours
Page's jacket with one pocket inside	18
Edges turned in and stitched	1½
Edges piped	3
Piped round bottom, extra	1
Button cuff, two holes	1
Button holes in breast, above fourteen, each	¼

This by no means meant it took a competent tailor eighteen hours to make a jacket for a page, or that he required fifteen minutes to make a buttonhole. But unless the minor variations required by customers were expressed in a minimum of quarter-hours, the log would have to be expressed in stopwatch terms of minutes, seconds and tenths of seconds. Once the ancient practice of one man one garment had been abandoned, time logs were bound to suffer from one or other defect. Either they would ignore small extras or log-time would be appreciably longer than actual work time. Since the definition of 'small' is capable of wide interpretation it was natural that the men should resist the first. With a change of fashion, one extra button on a cuff might become six. The journeyman who had done one buttonhole as an unconsidered extra would then find his employer expecting him to do six, which meant a real increase in the time spent on the garment. On the other hand the employer disliked a system under which work which he knew could easily be done in ten and a half hours was being rated at eighteen hours. It needed goodwill and a dispassionate appreciation of relativity on both sides to make the system work. They were not always present.

Some logs would approximate more nearly than others to the real time taken to do the listed work. This did not mean they were necessarily worse than those which grossly inflated the real work-time. On the contrary. A log which lists a page's jacket at twelve hours is infinitely preferable to one giving eighteen hours if the first is paid at a rate of 7d an hour and the second at 4d an hour. The earnings on the first will be 7s and on the second 6s.

Local customs and craft traditions had both played a part in producing these widely different logs. They were constantly being varied as the men won some new concession or the master imposed some new reduction. Changes in fashion would make a satisfactory time log unsatisfactory. It was therefore vital that if a new log applicable to the whole country was to be worked out, there must be careful and diligent inquiry.

Using the existing money log in Manchester as a basis, the Amalgamated converted it into a time log and sent the result to all branches for comment and amendment. The London association was similarly consulted, and a joint committee of the two unions then drew up an agreed log in the light of all the information and comment which had come from all over the country. It needed patience and much steady propaganda through the columns of *The Tailor* and by speeches to branch meetings before the objectives were clearly understood. There were the inevitable outcries from those working at low hourly rates on a log with greatly inflated times, who thought their earnings were to be cut because the draft log was more realistic. They had to be persuaded that a nationally agreed log which was reasonably realistic would provide a firmer basis for wage negotiations than the existing chaotic system.

There was further trouble for the leaders when the final draft of the log was published, and branches all over the country began to demand its implementation by their employers under threat of strike action. The union leaders knew that they themselves would not accept a log presented by the masters on a 'take it or leave it' basis. They did not expect the masters to do so either. What they envisaged was a negotiated settlement in which each side would have to make concessions. The hotheads had to be restrained.

There were reasonable grounds for qualified optimism about the future. The unions were steadily growing in strength and the accession of Belfast and Dublin to the Amalgamated early in 1867 brought the number of branches to more than 200, representing almost the whole of the country except Scotland. There were some small signs that the more well-disposed of the masters were in the ascendant in the masters' association. A dispute at Messrs Hill's in Bond Street was settled in a hitherto unheard-of way. A joint committee from the London union and the masters' association visited the shop and reported in favour of the men. After some delay, and further negotiation between the two associations, Mr Hill found himself compelled to accept the verdict.

In Stafford the masters not only welcomed the formation of a branch of the Amalgamated, but urged, in a notice printed with the local log, that all journeymen in the town ought to join it. There were many of these signs of goodwill.

The unions were able to demonstrate their ability to protect their members, as in the affair of the Marquis of Anglesey's dress livery coat. The firm of Jackson and Company decided to pay only 17s 9d for the making of this splendid garment, while the proper price was 21s. All thirty of Mr Jackson's men were withdrawn and he came into line with other first-class shops.

Conscious of their own growing strength and the many examples of a more conciliatory attitude among the masters, the unions were nevertheless well aware that the battle had not been won. The London masters in general acted in the spirit of their association's charter which spoke of 'free and friendly communication' with the men on any matter in dispute. In the provinces many masters relied on the phrase 'united resistance toward any attempt on the part of the men to enforce unreasonable demands or to limit the free action of any individual master' as giving them at once the right to declare any request unreasonable and the right to dictate their own terms in the name of individual freedom.

It was with this in mind that George Druitt, President of the London Association told a meeting of the Notting Hill branch, 'Let us meet them (the masters) with all the friendship and conciliation they profess; at the same time let us be fully prepared to take up the aggressive, or stand on our defence if necessary. Let the old and sterling motto, which has a thousand applications, be ours. Fear God, but keep your powder dry.'

The union leaders, said John Williamson in one of his editorials, considered it the noblest achievement they had yet attained, that their action should have led to the formation of a masters' association. It provided a platform on which free and equal men could meet together to discuss reasonably and amicably their mutual problems.

It was thus with supreme self-confidence, in a spirit of perfect goodwill, but with a watchful and wary eye that the joint committee of the unions invited the masters to meet them to take up the problem of the uniform time log in January 1867. The reply from John Goodwin, secretary of the masters' association, was couched in the same urbane and well-mannered terms as the invitation itself.

> 'Sir, – I am desired by the committee to thank you for your communication of the 10th inst, which was last evening handed in to them by our Hon Sec, Mr Landon.
>
> 'The spirit of the document was most fully appreciated by the committee; and I am authorised to acquaint you that it shall receive their best consideration, and that you shall hear further from them on the subject.
>
> > 'I am, Sir, your obedient servant,
> > > 'John Goodwin, Sec
>
> Mr M. Lawrence, Sec London Operative
> Tailors' Protective Association.
> 15th Jan 1867'

What could be more amiable, more prophetic of a new dawn in the relations between masters and men? The unions refused to be soured by what seemed to them unconscionable delays in fixing the meeting thus warmly welcomed by the masters. Holding their own impatient followers in check as best they could, the leaders waited while the masters went through the process of calling a full delegate meeting and then appointing a sub-committee with power to negotiate. It was not until 8th March that the first meeting to discuss procedure was held.

It was decided that the two sides should meet daily from four to eight o'clock in the evening to suit the convenience of the masters who had their businesses to attend to. Commented *The Tailor*, 'The proceedings were most harmonious, each heartily expressing an earnest desire that a speedy and amicable settlement might result from their united deliberations on this most important question. For our own part, as the representatives of the tailoring interests at large, we shall anxiously await the result of their labours, earnestly trusting meanwhile that the culmination of their praiseworthy efforts may be a practical realisation of the most sanguine anticipations of all who have even the most trifling interest in the matter.'

The obverse of this shining medal appeared in the same issue in a hastily written paragraph saying, 'We have just received intelligence as we are going to press, that, with the exception of Mr Kirkbridge's firm, the whole of the masters in Carlisle have locked out their men.' The representatives of the Master Tailors' Association of the United Kingdom were speaking fair, while some of its members at least were acting very differently.

The first business meeting was held on 20th March with seven representatives on either side. They decided to go through the log item by item and began with a dress or frock coat. This was rated at thirty-three hours in the Amalgamated's log, and at twenty-nine and three-quarter hours in the log prepared by the masters. The difference was argued out and an agreed figure of thirty-two and a half hours finally reached as being fair and reasonable by both sides.

The following day seven entirely different masters appeared at the conference. They refused to discuss the next item, except on the basis of their own log, or to go to arbitration. When deadlock was reached they asked for an adjournment of five days. At the adjourned meeting the masters' representatives announced they were not empowered to alter the log already agreed by the masters among themselves and could not therefore continue the procedure of discussing it item by item.

After two more days' fruitless discussion negotiations were broken off, the men refusing to accept the masters' log as it stood, and the masters saying they had no authority to negotiate any but minor alterations in it. George Druitt, leading the union delegation, obtained a promise that the general committee of the masters would consider the deadlock on 1st April and communicate with the union the same evening.

It had been agreed at the outset that the two sides to the negotiations should make no report even to their parent committees before their whole work was done. The masters broke faith. When their full committee saw how things were going after the first day, their representatives were promptly disowned and replaced by seven tougher characters with instructions to present the masters' log and to accept no modifications.

Though John Williamson was himself present throughout the meetings, not a word about them appeared in *The Tailor* until 6th April when the final rupture had taken place and the whole affair was the subject of common, and ill-informed, gossip throughout London.

A meeting of the London Association committee was called

to receive the considered statement from the masters promised for that evening. It was terse and very different from the polite exchanges of the previous January.

'Sir, – I am directed by the committee to inform you that in consequence of the failure of the negotiations of last week, they have resolved on allowing the "Time Log" question to remain in abeyance.

'I am, sir, your obedient servant,
John Goodwin, Secretary.'

The contents of this forbidding message were telegraphed at once to Manchester where the council of the Amalgamated was in session. The 'Dragon' public house where the London committee was meeting on the evening of a mild and sunny April day was filled with rank and file members who had heard whispers of what was afoot and had come to urge their leaders to militant action. The committee as a whole was incensed at the arbitrary way in which the masters had treated the union representatives and there were demands for an immediate mass meeting of the membership to declare a strike.

Matthew Lawrence, supported by George Druitt, urged that the masters should be asked how long they intended to let the log question remain 'in abeyance' and be told that the union considered it must be settled soon. This was agreed, but at the same time a deputation of the two leaders was sent post haste to Manchester to consult with the council of the Amalgamated before it broke up.

Matters were swiftly arranged in Manchester. The relevant articles of the agreement under which the unions had merged were reaffirmed; that each union would give full support to the other in the event of a strike or lockout and help to meet strike pay of 12s a week, and that they remained determined on a uniform time log based on the Amalgamated log. Implicit in this was that the London men should be the spearhead of the fight for the log and that the rest of the country would be behind them, trusting them to use their own judgment in what action they took.

A report of this satisfactory outcome of the journey to Manchester was made to a committee meeting on 3rd April which also considered this ambiguous reply from the masters' committee:

'Sir, – The Committee's letter was dictated by the feeling that they did not see their way to the settlement of a "Time Log" by the means hitherto employed; but that if any other course could be suggested which seemed to offer more probability of success, they would be happy to entertain it.'

The knowledge that they had outside backing which would be freely and loyally given increased the ardour of those demanding immediate strike action. In spite of this, and the evident unlikelihood of the masters remaining sincere in their former offer to negotiate, it was decided to make a final bid for a peaceful settlement. Those inveterate travellers Druitt and Lawrence were instructed to 'take a walk' down to Bond Street to the offices of the masters' association to seek means of reopening negotiations. At the same time preparations were put in hand to issue a circular to be issued to the public explaining the issues involved. The masters were to be asked to communicate with the committee which would meet on 9th April. The militants were promised that the committee would decide on action if nothing was settled within two weeks. Meanwhile all branches were urged not to take individual action.

While the national committee of the masters in London was becoming more intransigent, there came worse news from Leeds. A breakaway organisation calling itself the National United Master Tailors' Association took the offensive by issuing a circular calling for the formation of an 'active committee' of all local masters' associations in the Midlands and the North. With the circular was a list of nearly 200 journeymen. All employers were asked to blacklist them.

The committee of the London union met on 9th April to receive the masters' reply to their latest request for a resumption of negotiations. When it came this was a suggestion that the London union and the London masters should hold a conference to draw up a purely London log. There was an immediate motion that no answer should be given but a mass meeting of all members be called to decide on strike action.

Matthew Lawrence, who had hitherto been so strong an advocate of united action by the whole body of tailors, gave a curious display of wobbling uncertainty in this new situation. In an unusually rambling speech, he appeared to lay most of the blame for the failure of the negotiations on the presence of representatives of the Amalgamated on the joint committee, and said that if the London men did strike, sooner or later they would have to meet the London masters and reach a settlement. He thought it quite consistent with their obligations to the Amalgamated that they should enter separate negotiations, and was sure the masters would agree to no other course. Though he had some support, in the lengthy discussion that followed the tide was definitely against any separate talks without the full approval of the Amalgamated obtained beforehand.

Lawrence was convinced this consent would be readily forthcoming, and telegrams were sent asking for an immediate meeting of the council of the Amalgamated in Manchester. William Neal, chairman of the powerful City of London branch, was selected to accompany Lawrence to Manchester to discuss the situation. He was one of the many who had spoken strongly against the Lawrence line.

The following night the committee met again, but the deputation had not yet returned. Instead a series of telegrams from Manchester showed that Lawrence had completely abandoned his position. The important one was a copy of a wire already sent to the master tailors announcing that a general message on the subject of the uniform log was on the way and an answer would be required within three days. John Adamson and Alfred Bailey, president and vice-president of the Council of the Amalgamated, were on their way to London with Lawrence and Neal.

To the London committee Lawrence reported a day later in very different terms from his earlier speech. He now proposed that the masters be asked to reopen negotiations, failing which the unions should enforce the Amalgamated's log in its entirety. It had been agreed in Manchester that a levy of 2s per member should be raised on all men still at work. Labour would be withdrawn first from all members of the masters' association who refused to accept the log. Later other masters would be sent a circular with the log, and they too would be struck if they refused to pay it. Lawrence estimated that about 2,000 men would be withdrawn. The two Manchester delegates were co-opted to a small sub-committee which was empowered to run the strike.

In a letter to the master's association, the sub-committee

This elaborate dress of the 1860s is a product of the 'sweating dens'

Radio Times Hulton Picture Library

A tailor's sweating den at the turn of the century

reviewed the previous arrangement for joint discussion and then went on:

'We have, therefore, to request an answer by Tuesday morning the 16th April to the following:

'Whether you accept the enclosed log, or are prepared to carry out the original arrangement made by you for a fairly discussed log.

'We believe a satisfactory log can only be made by the united committee of employers and employed, and do not desire to press anything of our own as perfect, but we are in this position that a log must be had, and if you cannot fairly arrange the matter we have no other alternative but to immediately enforce our own, we being ready to fairly discuss and arrange with you.'

To this the masters replied that they could not meet a mixed delegation including members of the Amalgamated pledged to the Amalgamated's log which was unacceptable to the London masters.

'Nothing in your letter in any way alters our conviction upon this point, and though we regret that our refusal to attempt what we hold to be an impossibility is likely to lead to an antagonism we would gladly have avoided, we must leave you to judge for yourselves of the probable ultimate results of the forcible means by which you propose to convert us to your views.'

This was the expected answer, and masters outside the association were promptly circularised with the alternative of paying the log or having their men withdrawn. The full committee unanimously endorsed the action taken, and issued a call to a mass meeting at the Alhambra Palace for the afternoon of 16th April when the ultimatum would have expired. A few of the masters inside and outside the masters' association agreed to pay the log, or were already offering better terms. The vast majority ignored the circular or sent contemptuous replies.

The crowded meeting at the Alhambra Palace shouted down the lone voice raised in favour of separate London negotiations and the strike resolution was carried without dissent. Other resolutions declared the willingness of the journeymen to continue in work at all shops paying the Amalgamated log and to

G

call off the strike if the employers would agree to resume discussion of a new log. The meeting was followed the next day by one at which outworkers pledged their support to the strike.

The masters made their own efforts to rally support. The employers in Manchester were asked by telegram to lock their men out if necessary, and a delegation headed by J. D. Landon visited Birmingham, Sheffield and Liverpool seeking similar co-operation if it should become necessary.

Chapter Nine/The Great Strike of 1867

LONDON TAILORS CALLED OUT ON STRIKE; EMPLOYERS COUNTER-ATTACK; SUPPORT FROM OUTWORKERS AND WOMEN; STRIKE ORGANISATION; TROUBLE OVER PICKETING; PRESIDENT DRUITT OFFERS ARBITRATION; INFLUENCE OF *The Times*; STRIKE GAINS WIDESPREAD SUPPORT FROM WHOLE MOVEMENT; MASTERS REJECT COMPROMISE MOVES

The strike was called as the prolonged agitation for a new Reform Act was reaching its successful climax. In the session of 1867 Parliament gave the vote to a limited number of working-class householders and lodgers, new electors who would henceforth have an increasing influence on the composition of the House of Commons and therefore on the policy of the government.

This new step towards political democracy was not matched in the industrial field. On the contrary, while the campaign for Parliamentary reform was gathering strength, a violent anti-union agitation was being mounted with increasing ferocity. In the realm of business the capitalist felt he should be free to buy his materials in the cheapest market and sell his products for the highest price he could obtain. The doctrine was applied to human labour. Any interference by an outside body in negotiations between masters who wished to buy labour and those who were presumed willing sellers of it was regarded as an unwarrantable interference with the freedom of the market. The unions represented an outside body seeking to intrude into these negotiations between master and man.

The new larger unions of the builders, engineers and others

had proved strong enough to resist the 'document' and they were growing in size and wealth. They, like the tailors, were led by men who preferred negotiation to industrial strife and who looked on strikes as symptoms of the failure of society to organise itself intelligently rather than as an end in themselves.

The employers did not wish to see society organised – intelligently or otherwise; they wanted to be left alone to conduct their own business as they saw fit. They resorted with increasing frequency to the lockout as an alternative to the document. Even where a great majority of workers were willing to accept the employers' terms, all were locked out to break the resistance of small bands of militants in particular firms.

To meet the threat of the lockout the unions formed the United Kingdom Alliance of Organised Trades, a nationwide organisation based on Sheffield whose main objective was to give financial support to members who were locked out. Its rules precluded support for strikers. This purely defensive organisation was for a time the only truly national voice of trade unionism. It soon ran into difficulties for it was well-nigh impossible to draw a strict line between a strike and a lockout. Almost from its inception in 1866 the Alliance was in financial difficulties and was under attack from those who felt their right to support was being unreasonably withheld.

There remained innumerable small societies all over the country whose leaders shared none of the statesmanlike ideas of the larger unions. Among many of these smaller societies there was a tradition of violence and intimidation, and a series of outrages had been reported from the industrial north. The climax was reached in October 1866 when a keg of gunpowder was thrown down the kitchen chimney of a man who had offended against the Sheffield Saw Grinders' Union.

The act was brutal enough in itself to arouse widespread public indignation. It was eagerly seized upon by those who were running the anti-union campaign. In the jargon of modern times it helped temporarily to create an 'image' of trade unionists as anarchistic terrorists without respect for either life or property.

The Queen's speech at the opening of Parliament in February 1867 not only announced the forthcoming Reform Bill but also the appointment of a Royal Commission to investigate the Sheffield outrages and the activities of the unions. Responsible

union leaders welcomed the inquiry and began at once to prepare their evidence. Here was an opportunity to clear themselves from the irresponsible smear campaign being conducted
against the movement as a whole. The more searching the inquiry, the less they had to fear from the eventual report.

It was against this background that some 2,000 of the 36,000
tailors working in London were called out on strike against the
eighty-eight leading firms.

The masters held their own counterpart to the mass meeting
of the tailors in the Alhambra Palace when about 300 of them
gathered in the Hanover Square Rooms. The small voice of
reason and compromise was overwhelmed in a thunder of
denunciation and the meeting finally agreed to resist the
uniform time log and to support those masters whose shops
were being struck.

John Williamson was present at the meeting and reported
faithfully the more extravagant speeches. There was Mr Black-
more of Brook Street, who claimed to be no more than a
humble individual, but with the advantage of being a 'practical man.'

'This strike,' he said, 'is only kept up by paid agitators.
When once the men join them their freedom is lost; they must
follow and obey to their own ruin as well as that of their wives
and families. These are not idle words, they can be corrobor-
ated by the men in each of your shops. They have placed themselves in the hands of their Executives, and thus they are led.
This is a great oppression.

'By giving us your support on the present occasion you will
prove yourselves the friends of the working man; by crushing
this agitation and destroying what is ruining the men and their
families you will merit and receive the thanks of the community
at large.'

Here is a picture of the men and their leaders which bears
no relation to the events which led up to the strike, the speeches
of the leaders or the militancy of the members. Yet Mr Black-
more's was typical of nearly all the speeches made.

The *London Review* of 11th May reported on the meetings of
the men and of the masters, and found the latter decidedly
inferior to the former.

'The masters used scarcely any arguments; indeed they
made little attempt to parade more than one, which was that

the men wanted more money but did not deserve it. But if they were weak in argument they were strong in abuse, and they voted with enthusiasm against acceding to the demands of the men, whom they seemed to hold in hearty detestation. Some of them evidently bore an equal grudge against the letter "h" and displayed it with considerable determination.

'After hearing both sides, we profess ourselves utterly unable to decide whether thirty-two or thirty-four hours ought to be allowed for making a dress coat, but we have formed a strong opinion on the subject of the respective claims of the masters and men to have displayed good feeling and good temper in the discussion. And that opinion is certainly not in favour of the masters.'

There were few who were willing to listen as carefully to both sides and to make up their minds on the merits of the actual dispute. Most employers, led by *The Times*, were against the tailors because they were organised in a union and were making their demands through the union.

The masters entered the strike with a fund of no less than £5,587. This fund, which was rapidly augmented by donations, was used to subsidise those who were losing business through the strike. A combination of bribery and intimidation prevented those masters who were willing to come to terms with their men from making any concessions. A call was issued to masters outside London to lock out their men, and substantial bonus payments were offered to any competent non-union labour prepared to work for the strike-bound masters.

The employers got off to a slow start. The Manchester branch of their association promptly denied rumours that they were about to lock out their men. Emissaries from London were more successful in raising funds from their colleagues as they toured the Midlands than they were in persuading the provincial masters to join the lockout.

The union met with a much better reception from the outworkers. Unthinking customers of the West End shops might give a ready ear to the assertion of the masters that they were paying £3 and more a week to journeymen. A packed meeting of outworkers held in the Albion Hall, London Wall, scarcely needed to be told that such money could only be earned if four or five shared in the work.

For the first time the city branch threw open one of its business meetings to women as well as men and some 200 attended. Women were not yet eligible for membership, but they now played so important a part in the tailoring trade that their help was essential to the successful prosecution of the strike. The meeting unanimously agreed that none of the outworkers would accept work from any of the firms affected by the strike, and pledged support to the strikers in their fight for a uniform time log.

Similar meetings were held in other parts of London with an equally enthusiastic response. Money began to pour in from other unions. A levy of 2s a man was raised from those – the majority – still at work in London and of 1s throughout the Amalgamated Society. At the time of the merger between the London Association and the Amalgamated it had been agreed that strike pay would be 12s a week and that the two unions would support each other financially to meet this figure. In fact it was found possible to pay the London men a guinea a week. Women workers who agreed to refuse work were enrolled at their respective shops and were paid equally with the men strikers.

The strike was organised by a small sub-committee of five, two delegates from the Amalgamated and three from the London Association, who remained in constant session. A perpetual stream of callers came to the committee to give information or ask instructions. They were admitted one by one, their business dealt with and clear instructions given about such problems as finishing off work already begun before the strike, negotiations with masters who wanted work done and the picketing of the strike-bound shops.

A tight system of pickets was thrown around the shops being struck. They took their duties seriously but were always willing to extract what fun they could from the critical situation. Two pickets were approached by a footman employed by Mr Robert Lewis, the president of the masters' association. Acting dumb, they went along to Mr Lewis's shop in St James's where they were solemnly assured by the president that the strike would be over in a day or two and they would be able to earn big money by working for him. Meanwhile he arranged to send work to them at their homes which was to be returned by parcel post in order to escape the vigilance of their fellow pickets outside the shop.

This and similar incidents were all related to the strike committee and published with gleeful comments in *The Tailor*. There were other less amusing incidents. The pickets outside Mr Poole's shop in Saville Row asked an elderly woman to show them what was in a bundle she was carrying as she left the shop. She agreed to show them, but while they were examining the bundle Mr Poole who was watching had the three pickets arrested on a charge of intimidation.

The union engaged a solicitor for the hearing at the police court, and despite some hard lying on the part of Mr Poole's companion, who swore to seeing the elderly woman manhandled and reduced to tears, the charge of intimidation failed. The woman herself said she had been quite willing to open her bundle, had been treated courteously by the pickets and had no complaint to make against them. Nevertheless, the magistrate thought this was an affair that might lead to something worse and on these grounds bound over all three defendants to keep the peace for six months.

This was the first of many prosecutions launched by the masters against the pickets. The frequency with which these cases were brought before the courts was in itself a demonstration of the effectiveness of the picket system. Non-union labour from the provinces and outworkers in London were easily persuaded against helping to break the strike. The masters were compelled to smuggle work out of their shops and back again in garbage carts, milk floats and other vehicles.

The union leaders made every effort to keep their demands and those of their members restricted to a reasonable and sensible programme of reform. They consistently reminded the public that it was the masters themselves who had passed a resolution in favour of a uniform time log at the inaugural meeting of their association and that it was the masters who had broken off negotiations after this had been welcomed by the union and the first steps had been taken to implement it.

Mr Druitt in a letter to *The Times* offered to submit the whole dispute to arbitration. *The Times* printed the letter but followed it the next day with a two-column article telling the employers it was imperative that the 'presumption and tyranny' of the workmen be checked at once. While welcoming the offer to go to arbitration *The Times* assured the masters there was no need for them to entertain such a proposal from a trade union.

Heads of individual firms could refer any dispute with their own workpeople to arbitration without the intervention of a third party.

President Druitt at least had little doubt about the effect of the rodomontade from *The Times*. Speaking to the first annual meeting of the South Western branch, one of the largest and wealthiest in the union, he said: 'Even *The Times* has raised its mighty voice and devoted two columns of its valuable space to our cause. While many have lamented this, from the false statements, together with the ignoring and perverting of facts it contains, I myself consider that it has done us more good than anything else could, since it is universally known that so soon as *The Times* begins to misrepresent and oppose any movement, that is the surest evidence that the cause is both good and on the threshold of victory.

'Its object has always been to malign and keep down labour; by every effort they can call forth they strive to abuse and put down trades unions. But in doing so they are rendering us more essential service than all the speeches that are being made on platforms in their behalf.'

In spite of the virulent anti-union propaganda a majority of the full committee of the masters' association which was called together in the third week of the strike were in favour of entering negotiations. They were dissuaded from pressing their view by an influential minority who held that the strike would collapse within a fortnight.

The union promptly increased the levy on men still working in London to 3s a week while the council of the Amalgamated meeting in Manchester appointed delegates to tour every district and town in the country on a fund-raising expedition. These efforts within the tailoring trade itself were supplemented by a heartening response from other unions. The small Alliance of File Smiths in Sheffield sent an immediate donation of £20 and promised £10 a week so long as the strike should last. A long list of subscriptions published each week included such items as the shilling from 'a barman'. A mass meeting of 5,000 unionists in Trafalgar Square launched weekly collections in all factories, workshops and yards and called on their unions to cut red tape and make immediate donations to the strike fund.

Money flowed in. The decision of 500 men and women

employed in West End shops making military uniforms to join the strike helped to raise the numbers of the strikers to 2,800, but even this additional burden on the strike funds was easily met.

With between 200 and 300 women on strike it was no longer possible for any but the most ardent anti-feminists to resist their admission to full membership of the union. In the fourth week of the strike a women's branch was formed for the first time, with fifty members.

Meetings of outworkers conducted in German, Polish or Russian were held in the East End and needed little persuasion to see that their own future lay not in reaping temporary advantage by accepting extra work but in supporting the strikers in their demand for a uniform time log on which they themselves would be able to bargain.

The strike had begun at the opening of the busy spring season and there were many among the masters who saw themselves faced with ruin if some accommodation could not be made with the men. It is fair to say that there were others who were filled with genuine liberal sentiments towards their workers and who still subscribed to the original ideas on which the masters' association had been formed – the negotiation of a uniform time log and free and friendly communication with the men.

Mr Augustus Bohte, who had been the first secretary to the masters' association, was speaking for this section of the masters when he wrote to Matthew Lawrence suggesting that some public figure of acknowledged weight and reputation should be called upon to act as peacemaker. He suggested as examples the Earl of Shaftesbury, John Stuart Mill or Thomas Hughes, M P.

The offer was taken up with enthusiasm by the union leaders. George Druitt and Matthew Lawrence replied that their committee would willingly submit to arbitration, adding significantly, 'We believe that anything settled by force on either side cannot be lasting, a just arrangement being only obtained when both interests are represented at the council board . . . We only want a fair discussion on the whole matter and if the employers were to agree to have a fair discussion their workshops could be filled tomorrow.'

Several members of Parliament, including Mr James Beal

and Mr Thomas Hughes, interested themselves in the problem and got in touch with the union leaders who assured them they would accept the masters' own choice of arbitrator and would abide by his award.

Mr Beal's offer to bring the two sides together was flatly rejected by Mr R. Lewis on behalf of the MTA. The men at that time in their employ, he said, seemed perfectly satisfied with their wages and the masters were equally satisfied with their men. There was therefore no dispute and no need for arbitration.

Mr Lewis claimed that the indulgence of the customers and the exertions of the master tailors themselves had reduced the loss and inconvenience due to the strike to nominal proportions and that after eight weeks of strike the busy season was now coming to an end.

Commenting on this exchange of correspondence *The Tailor* was able to produce evidence which appeared to show that Mr Lewis was talking nonsense. Instead of the normal 500 Mr Poole had only 24 men working in his two shops. Mr Smallpage had 16 instead of 50 and Mr Pulsford had 4 instead of between 90 and 120.

On the face of it the masters seemed to be whistling in the dark to keep up their courage. In fact, a slight drift back to work had begun on the part of the strikers. Those defecting included vice-president Cameron of the city branch who accepted an offer of three and a half guineas a week and a commission of four per cent on the trade done in the shop where he was employed. He failed to lead a mass return to work by the city branch, but some members were persuaded to join him.

Though it was true that only a handful of men and women crossed the picket line to work in the struck shops, the masters were improving their methods of smuggling work to the east end and to outworkers at their homes. The season was proving shorter than usual, for this was a year of general trade depression. The masters had less need of men.

It was at this point, when the strike was in its twelfth week, that William Broadhead, treasurer of the United Kingdom Alliance of Organised Trades, confessed to having played a leading part in instigating the Sheffield outrages.

In later months the affair was to be seen in perspective. The outrages would be shown to be the result of the degraded conditions of work in the Sheffield trades and to be an argument in favour of giving the trade unions a proper place in industrial society with reasonable protection for their funds and disciplinary powers over their officials and members.

In June 1867 the revelation that an official of the Alliance had been involved in a gunpowder plot was hailed as sufficient evidence by the anti-unionists of all they had ever said about the evils of the unions. Broadhead – the Alliance of which he was an official – the unions composing the Alliance – the tailors who belonged to one of those unions – the tailors on strike in London: in the wave of hysterical denunciation which swept the country, here was a clear connection between the pickets in the west end of London and a secret society of dynamiters.

The effect was to stiffen the attitude of those master tailors who had been willing to consider a compromise. Their more extreme colleagues now saw it to be not merely their right but their national duty to act as the spearhead of a move to smash the whole union movement.

After one or two unsuccessful attempts the masters succeeded in opening a call-house in Air Street to recruit non-union labour. The pickets prevented this from being as useful as it might have been, and renewed efforts were made to obtain convictions in the police courts. After one such hearing Matthew Lawrence defiantly asked the masters as they left the court together why they did not proceed against the union leaders rather than these poor fellows?

Mr Sleigh, the solicitor to the masters' association, advised that this was a challenge which might well be taken up.

Chapter Ten/Trial By Jury

EMPLOYERS SUMMON UNION LEADERS FOR CONSPIRACY; WIDE ISSUES FOR
WHOLE MOVEMENT; TAILORS' COUNTER-CHARGE AGAINST MASTERS; HEARING
AT THE OLD BAILEY; REFUSAL TO WITHDRAW PICKETS; BARON BRAMWELL'S
JUDGMENT; DRAIN ON FUNDS; STRIKE PETERS OUT

The acts of Parliament granting the right to combine for purposes of regulating wages and conditions and the right to strike
had already been shown to be full of loopholes. These acts were
read by the courts in relation to previous acts and the common
law and it had been held that even the posting of a strike notice
could be a criminal conspiracy because it was in restraint of
trade.

The Molestation of Workmen Act of 1859 had laid down
that no workman, by reason of his endeavouring peaceably and
in a reasonable manner to persuade others from working or
ceasing to work, should be guilty of an offence under previous
acts of Parliament. It was on this act that trade unionists had
relied in their organisation of pickets during strikes.

The picketing system was vital to the carrying out of any
strike by the tailors. The vast improvement in communications
brought about by the railway and the electric telegraph was
still in its infancy. *The Tailor* and other working-class journals
did not reach all members of the union in all parts of the
country, much less the larger numbers of non-union men and
women.

Tailors came to London from the provinces and from the
Continent in good faith, drawn by glowing advertisements of

work waiting to be done at good prices. The vast majority, when they were told by the pickets they were being asked to act as strike-breakers, refused the offers. The employers realised that an essential step towards winning the contest was to find some way of getting the pickets withdrawn.

Action against individuals and groups of pickets had failed. The decision to take up the challenge of Matthew Lawrence was on the advice of counsel that the whole system of picketing might be illegal in spite of the Molestation of Workmen Act.

Summonses were issued against George Druitt and Matthew Lawrence, the president and secretary of the London union, together with John Adamson, president of the Amalgamated Society who was acting as treasurer of the strike committee, and a number of other members of the union executive.

Taken out by Mr Thomas Bowater on behalf of the Master Tailors' Association, the summonses alleged conspiracy on the part of the defendants to impoverish a number of master tailors in their trade and business.

Serjeant Ballantine, leading counsel for the masters' association, rested his case on two propositions, first that picketing was illegal in itself, being a form of intimidation, and secondly that by combining together to obstruct employers in obtaining the services of people willing to work for them the leaders were guilty of conspiracy.

The points of law thus raised were far too important to be settled in a police court. They affected the whole trade union movement and would need to be decided by a higher court. Mr Edward Lewis, solicitor for the defendants, made no attempt to rebut the evidence of the prosecution, but agreed that the case should go for trial before a judge and jury. Druitt and Lawrence as the alleged ringleaders were compelled to find bail and the remainder were released on their own recognisances. All were sent for trial.

There had been no single act of violence reported throughout three months of strike. The leaders were on record as having made frequent appeals for a peaceful settlement of the strike by negotiation and as having urged all members time and again not to give way to provocation from whatever source it might come.

The tailors were quite sure they had acted well within the

existing law. They were by no means so certain that they would receive justice. Wrote John Williamson after the police court hearing, 'Few would be surprised if the wicked determination of the employers and the highest talent at the English bar, so materially assisted by the prejudices of presiding magistrates and judges, should be successful in removing for a short time those who have been the chief ornaments in that cabinet (the strike committee).'

Such language nowadays would ensure the immediate committal of the commentator for contempt of court when used about a forthcoming trial before judge and jury. In the atmosphere created by the Broadhead confession there was little hope of a balanced view being taken by any judge or magistrate, much less by a jury composed of middle-class traders.

Assuming that the leaders would probably be sent to prison, the strike committee promptly appointed substitutes to carry on their work. Picketing continued, and an appeal was launched for a defence fund in addition to the strike fund. Druitt and Lawrence set out on a tour of the country to rouse trade unionists to the dangers all were facing if the coming prosecutions were successful and to raise money for both funds.

An attempt was made to have the trial removed from the Old Bailey, where the jury would be composed of city merchants, to the Queen's Bench where it was hoped a special jury might take a more objective view. The masters offered not to oppose the application if the pickets were withdrawn pending the hearing. Since this would have meant conceding the point at issue, and meanwhile crippling the strike, this offer was refused. With the masters opposing, a judge in chambers rejected the plea for a transfer of the trial.

As much to demonstrate the essential unfairness of the law as with any hope of success, the tailors launched their own prosecution for conspiracy against the masters. Their solicitor argued that if it was an offence to molest or obstruct a workman seeking to hire himself, the masters were guilty of it by issuing a circular urging members of their association not to employ men unless they were registered at the employers' own call-house in Air Street.

Summonses were granted against Mr Robert Lewis and four other members of the masters' association but they were dismissed when they came up for hearing in the police court. The union was given leave to take the question to a higher court but decided against doing so for it was clear, wrote John Williamson, 'that the law is made to protect and favour the masters and not the men; this being so, to carry it to a higher court would be risking an amount of expense which could not be justified by the probability of success.'

The question of expense had now become the major preoccupation of the strike committee. Depression was spreading throughout all trade and industry, and unemployment was mounting. However willing other unions were to support the tailors, they themselves were suffering from lack of funds. With the coming of the end of the season those master tailors who had not been struck were now beginning to turn off their workers.

With the prospect of heavy legal charges before them, the strike committee took steps to remove as many as possible from the strike fund. Strikers were offered 10s and a clean card to leave London in search of work elsewhere on the understanding that they would not return for at least three months.

One suggestion made early in the strike was that support should be given to those wishing to emigrate. The emigration scheme gained considerable impetus, and increasing numbers of the most proficient tailors sought their fortunes overseas. The ending of the Civil War in the United States had brought new opportunities in that country. Glowing accounts of the high wages and good conditions enjoyed by the best craftsmen on the eastern seaboard and in the south came back from those who had already emigrated.

These efforts to reduce the strain on the strike fund were successful as far as they went, but income was falling faster than expenses were being reduced. The question of reducing strike pay was now becoming urgent, but it was postponed to await the outcome of the trial.

The hearing was fixed for Friday 5th July at the Old Bailey, before Baron Bramwell. The day before the trial was due to open the prosecution put in thirty-six pages of proof of evidence from thirty new witnesses who had not been called at the police court. Defence solicitors were unable to brief counsel with this new material until midnight on 4th July.

The chief defence counsel, Mr Coleridge QC, protested to the court that the prosecution had made it impossible for him

The Mansell Collection

*A sweated outworker returns
a bundle of finished coats to the factory*

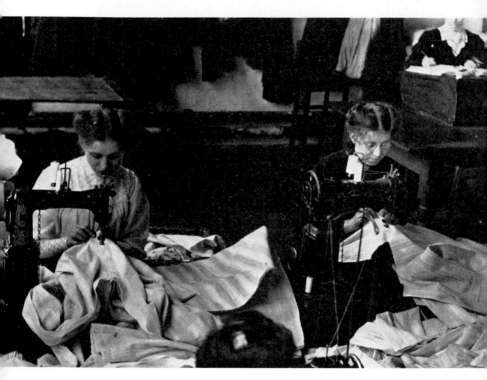

Machining shirts in a Manchester factory, 1909

to prepare his case and asked for a twenty-four-hour adjournment to consider this new evidence. The judge was unsympathetic and refused the adjournment on the grounds that it was no concern of the court if the prisoners had not properly briefed their counsel.

Prosecuting counsel said they were prepared to agree to an adjournment until the August session provided the pickets were withdrawn pending the hearing. Once more the defence argued that this was precisely what the case was all about and that they would prejudge their case if they agreed to stop what they claimed was a perfectly legal activity. The judge brushed this aside and said it would have no effect on the outcome of the trial if the pickets were temporarily withdrawn. He ruled that he would grant no adjournment at all unless the defence gave an undertaking to stop picketing.

Mr Coleridge said he would withdraw from the case if the court tried to compel him to proceed without proper preparation. He was given time to consult with Druitt and Lawrence who were thus faced with the alternative of agreeing to withdraw the pickets or of not having the defence properly conducted. From a legal point of view Mr Coleridge advised that the proper course was to accept the ruling of the judge that withdrawal of the pickets would not affect the outcome of the trial.

The problem was not only that with the judge already clearly against them the prisoners might well face a heavy sentence of imprisonment if they were found guilty. The trial was also of immense importance to the whole trade union movement. The prisoners therefore reluctantly accepted the conditions for an adjournment in order that the defence could be properly prepared.

Seeing that the judge was on his side, Serjeant Ballantine pressed home his advantage and demanded the fullest assurances that the pickets would in fact be withdrawn and added that if in the interval before the postponed trial the union tried to take advantage of the situation, he would bring it to bear against the defence to the utmost. The trial was thereupon adjourned until Wednesday 21st August.

The masters thus appeared to have gained the whole of their objective, which was freedom from the annoyance of the pickets, without the trial having begun. They were quickly disillu-

H

sioned. The tailors were in no mood to accept what they regarded as a piece of blatant trickery even if it had been backed
by the full authority of the court.

Having studied the reasons for the action of defending
counsel, the union executive decided they were in no way
bound by promises given in court on behalf of the prisoners.
Since the police court hearing, deputies had been acting for the
three union officers who were waiting trial. In order to protect
them the three were now formally deposed from office, and
new men were elected in their places.

This left the executive free to pass a defiant resolution that
in no circumstances would pickets be withdrawn until they
had been declared illegal by a competent court. The three
ex-officers, now debarred from taking part in the running of
the strike, set off on a new propaganda and fund-raising tour
of the country.

On the eve of the original summonses the strike committee
had announced that a new policy statement was about to be
issued. This had been held over during the preliminary legal
hearings, but was now published. It was another appeal from
the union leaders for joint discussions on the troubles of the
trade to be held on a national basis.

The masters had rejected the idea of compromise when they
provoked the strike. They were certainly in no mood for it now
that their hopes of ending the picketing had been so rudely
disappointed. They met briefly to consider the appeal but made
no direct reply. No record of their deliberations can be traced
but their decisions were soon translated into action. A
further twenty-five summonses for conspiracy were issued
against leading members of the two unions and individual
pickets. These were apart from the summonses for intimidation
and breaches of the peace by pickets which were being brought
almost daily in the police courts.

The summonses for conspiracy against Messrs Partridge,
Bailey and Shorrocks (vice-president of the London union and
president and vice-president of the Amalgamated Society respectively), together with twelve pickets, were heard on Friday
16th August, five days before the trial of Druitt, Lawrence and
their companions was due to begin. One was discharged for lack
of evidence but the remainder were sent for trial. The five
leading defendants were released on bail of £100 each, and the

remainder on bail of £20 each. Outside sympathisers stood surety.

Under the criminal law as it then stood the prisoners were not allowed to give evidence on their own behalf. Both in the police court and at the Old Bailey evidence was given by ex-policemen employed by the masters' association, by foremen who had remained at work during the strike and by a selection of the masters themselves. These witnesses had to face cross-examination but no other evidence was before the court. This one-sided procedure naturally told against the trade unionists.

At the trial of Druitt, Lawrence, Adamson and their six companions, evidence was given that the three leaders had all been involved in organising the picketing system. This was not denied, but cross-examination elicited the fact that Druitt and Lawrence had always behaved in a 'gentlemanly manner' to the masters, that they had insisted all along that they wanted negotiation, and that they had repeatedly set themselves against any form of coercion or intimidation. Though they were not allowed to speak for themselves in court, a transcript of the speeches made at the Alhambra Palace meeting which decided on strike action was, with the consent of the prosecution, put before the court.

The worst evidence that could be adduced, and this by ex-policemen admittedly in the pay of the masters, was that there had been mass picketing, that workers and masters had been followed, and that some workers on leaving their shops had been greeted with such cries as 'Curs, cowards and dungs'. This last epithet had of course a special meaning to tailors.

For the rest, the pickets were said to have stood about or sat on the pavement smoking 'vegetable substances' with a disagreeable smell, in short pipes. While there were general allegations of interference with workers and customers of the tailors no single witness came forward to complain of such treatment.

The masters themselves in evidence admitted they had used the lockout as a weapon and that the previous year sixty-six firms had locked out their men to break a strike in three shops. They admitted too that they had advertised during the strike for workers with notices saying 'Good hands wanted; no unionists need apply.'

In his summing up the learned judge dismissed as irrelevant

the plea that the anti-union activities of the masters were far more heinous than anything done by the prisoners. The jury were told to dismiss this, and most of the rest of the case for the defence, from their minds.

He went on to say that intimidation need not involve physical violence or the threat of it, but could result from an attempt to control the liberty of mind and thought by compulsion and restraint. The Molestation of Workmen Act of 1859 laid down that no workman merely by reason of his endeavouring peaceably and in a reasonable manner and without threat or intimidation, direct or indirect, to persuade others from working or ceasing to work should be guilty of an offence under previous acts of Parliament. If picketing were carried out in a way which excited no reasonable alarm or did not coerce or annoy those subjected to it, he thought it was not an offence in law.

But the judge went on to say that picketing would not only be illegal if abusive language and gestures were used, but also if the acts of the pickets were 'calculated to have a deterring effect on the minds of ordinary persons by exposing them to have their motions watched and to encounter black looks.' It was 'probable' he said, that since Druitt, Lawrence and Adamson had authorised the system of picketing they knew what the pickets were doing. If the jury were satisfied that the system, though not carried beyond watching and observation, was still so serious a molestation and obstruction as to have an effect upon the minds of the workpeople, then they ought to find these three men guilty. If the jury believed the evidence of one of the ex-policemen witnesses who had said he had seen the other prisoners on picket duty, they too should be found guilty.

The jury came to the conclusion that the three leaders were guilty and that those who had actually been on picket duty were not guilty. Extra bail was demanded by the prosecution before the three were released to come up for sentence later.

The following day Messrs Partridge, Bailey and Shorrocks and twelve others were brought before the same court on similar charges. Similar evidence was given with the addition that this time a woman, a man and his son all gave evidence that one of the prisoners named Knox had ill-treated them.

In his summing up Baron Bramwell elaborated on his ruling of the day before. It was true, he said, that picketing might be carried on without being illegal, but he added 'it is only legal if it is practised in such a way that it will be no greater inconvenience to anyone than if it did not exist.'

He doubted if there was enough evidence to convict Shorrocks and another prisoner named Stokes, and these were found not guilty by the jury. The remainder were found guilty. They and Druitt, Lawrence and Adamson came up for sentence the following day. All were bound over and released with the exception of Knox who was sentenced to three months. Neither counsel for the defence nor the other accused had attempted to excuse the conduct of Knox.

Baron Bramwell's judgment was severely criticised by many eminent lawyers as giving a completely false interpretation, but nevertheless, it now stood as the law of the land until such time as Parliament should decide to pass a new act. The judgment was a profound shock to the whole trade union movement. Its effect on the tailors' strike was disastrous. In accordance with their claim that they would never act illegally the union leaders were compelled to withdraw the pickets. In their absence a new drift back to work began on any terms that could be obtained.

The legal costs, amounting to more than £1,000, imposed a new and intolerable burden on the dwindling resources of the unions. The strike had already cost £30,000, of which some £23,000 or more had been contributed by the London and provincial tailors themselves. The delay in imposing cuts on strike pay had made them all the more drastic when they were eventually made.

A meeting of strikers was called at the Cambridge Hall and the bald facts were placed before them. Matthew Lawrence made no attempt to hide the fact that without the pickets they were beaten. The question was whether they should seek a general resumption of work on the best terms obtainable by the union or continue to watch the 'constant skedaddle' from the union ranks by those who were already returning to work.

The meeting voted unanimously for a return to work, and a conciliatory letter was sent to the masters' association on 28th August saying that the union accepted the legal decision which had gone in favour of the masters. Announcing the withdrawal of the Amalgamated's log, they asked on what terms the masters would be prepared to end the dispute.

By 5th September no acknowledgment or reply had been received and a new meeting of strikers decided to continue the struggle and to renew the appeal to trade unions throughout the country for support.

Mr Thomas Landon, secretary of the masters' association, later claimed he had been out of town when the letter was received in his office and that it had not been forwarded. His reply, when it did come, was dated 12th September, and showed that the masters considered their victory was complete:

'I beg to state that as the Master Tailors Association have no dispute with their men, but are perfectly satisfied with them, and that they have abundance of labour at hand; and that independently of this yourself and Mr Druitt are acting on behalf of a society which avowedly declares its objects to be to prevent masters of their free right to employ men whom they please and on what terms they please, and to prevent the operative tailors working for whom they please and on such terms and with such fellow workmen as they please. The Master Tailors' Association must decline to have any communication either personal or by letter with the representatives of such a society.'

The leaders of the union had scattered all over the country to address meetings of trade unions and to seek support for the men still on strike. Though they met with an enthusiastic welcome the nation-wide depression in trade and industry meant that the enthusiasm could not be matched with money. The Amalgamated Society had thrown in sickness and burial funds to aid the strikers, and many of its branches had gone out of existence, bankrupted by their efforts to support the London tailors.

Meetings of the branches of the masters' association all over the country were passing resolutions declaring their right to engage whom they wished at what wages they wished. In Scotland the Glasgow tailors had succeeded in negotiating a log with the masters and this had been reluctantly and under protest accepted by the masters of Edinburgh. Now the Scottish masters decided to present their own new log drawn up without consultation with the men and locked them out when they refused to accept it. It was a delegate from Chester who moved the resolution at a meeting of Belfast masters that a time log should be drawn up and imposed on the men.

Here was an open conspiracy on the part of the masters to destroy the legally constituted union of the men. The law, as laid down by Parliament and interpreted by magistrates and judges, had no cognisance of this type of conspiracy.

After five months the strike was virtually at an end. Of the 2,800 who had been receiving strike pay at the height of the struggle, only 800 remained on the roll. More than 200 of the best and most adventurous had emigrated while another 200 had crept back to work. The remainder had left London to seek work elsewhere.

The policy of subsidising men to leave London so as to relieve the strike fund was in line with tradition. It was afterwards seen to have been something of a blunder. Many of the strikers had moved to the outer suburbs and had found work in the second and third class shops there. Having come from the best West End firms they were naturally welcomed by the masters and they themselves had no compunction about displacing non-union labour from these shops. This non-union labour tended to become anti-union in consequence and all the more willing to work for London masters who were offering good money while the strike lasted.

The sewing machine would have led to a revolution in tailoring as inevitably as the electric telegraph revolutionised communication and the steam engine travel. The strike accelerated the process. In the early days the masters were at their wits' end and for all their boasts they lost some £33,000 of business. But as trade slackened off they found they could in fact get their work done not too badly by the second class operatives from the country and by accepting a greater proportion of machine working in garments. It was true, as the union claimed, that the workshops of the leading masters had very few men working. The masters found they could get along with far fewer than they had hitherto thought necessary.

Once the admission had been made at the Cambridge Hall meeting that the union had been beaten, the masters had nothing more to fear. They promptly began to reduce the prices they had offered to induce men to work for them. In one shop where a workman protested, he was summarily dismissed and threatened with a prosecution for intimidation. The masters now knew the law was on their side.

Though the strike continued, those who remained out were

simply men the masters refused to employ on any terms. The London Association collapsed and was reformed the following year with George Druitt as secretary. But the men had lost heart and the new society slowly withered. The remains of the city branch joined directly with the Amalgamated Society which also recruited a new West End branch. The skeleton of the London Association which remained met at the 'Dragon', famous as the headquarters of the strike, and decided to dissolve and become a new 'Dragon' branch of the Amalgamated.

Chapter Eleven/Factory Workers Unite

LESSONS OF THE STRIKE; EMERGENCE OF NEW TYPE OF MASTER; FOUNDATION
OF TRADES UNION CONGRESS; SHORROCKS' ROLE; GROWTH OF LEEDS AS
FACTORY CENTRE; CONFLICT BETWEEN CRAFT AND FACTORY INTERESTS;
AST MEMBERSHIP; UNIONS IN LEEDS; FORMATION OF AMALGAMATED UNION
OF CLOTHIERS' OPERATIVES

The great strike, as it came to be called in the annals of the
tailors, was defeated by a ruling which in its widest interpretation meant that no two workers could discuss the pros and cons
of taking a particular job without one of them being guilty of
intimidation and therefore liable to imprisonment. The judgment was in tune with the wave of anti-union hysteria sweeping
the country as an aftermath to the Sheffield outrages.

The national campaign against the unions was not in itself
sufficient to explain the change of front on the part of the
masters when they suddenly broke off hitherto amicable discussions and precipitated the strike. Sensible men on both sides
had recognised that constant strikes and lockouts could do no
more than settle how much workers or employers could afford
to sacrifice at any particular time. A rational discussion of the
problems of the trade conducted in a spirit of good will seemed
a more attractive alternative to unprofitable strife. These
ideas had been in the ascendant in the masters' association
when negotiations were opened, but they were quickly abandoned.

The problem facing the masters came into the open when
they held their meeting at the Hanover Square rooms soon

after the great strike began. Mr A. W. Miles, from the East End, attended the meeting, although he was not a member of the masters' association. He made two contributions. One was to offer the advice that the union should be broken by the extensive use of sewing machines, and the other was an offer of £1,000 to the fighting fund.

A docket from the premises of Mr Miles fell into the hands of a picket and was printed later in *The Tailor*. It showed he was paying 11s for a coat and the elaborate instructions for its making ended with the reminder that the customer had brought his previous one from Mr Poole. On the making of this coat would depend future orders for the firm! *The Tailor* found it amusing that the West End masters should accept a donation from one whose main interest was to keep the strike going while he stole their business by underselling them.

Mr Miles recognised neither the union nor the masters' association. He was quite prepared to support the latter in a struggle with the former and was frank enough to say why. If the union were to win 'it will be my turn next.'

In spite of the unanimous agreement that a uniform time log was desirable, the inaugural meeting of the masters' association had clearly shown the ambivalent attitude of an organisation which some were joining in order to resist 'unreasonable demands' from their workpeople, while others were looking to 'free and friendly discussion' with them. If it meant anything, an agreement on a uniform time log would have been binding on any member of the masters' association who respected his own reputation for integrity and fair dealing. Yet the association had no power to enforce such an agreement on its own members, much less on those like Mr Miles who remained outside its ranks.

Mr Miles was the personification of the new type of businessman who had been emerging since the beginning of the Industrial Revolution. In 1867 relations between employers and employed were still governed by the Master and Servant Act. The implications of the title of this act were already a dead letter and a new relationship was soon to be recognised by the passing of an Employers and Workmen Act.

Under the old law it was possible to imprison a workman for leaving his workplace before he had completed the work assigned to him. Master tailors had often taken advantage of the law by starting a man on a new piece of work before he had completed a previous job. He could by this means be kept in bondage to the same master.

The Employers and Workmen Act was a progressive measure in that workpeople and their employers were made equal partners to a civil contract and imprisonment for breach of engagement was abolished. It was also an unspoken admission that the employer no longer had any responsibility at all for the well-being of his workpeople. Household slaves, serfs and the inmates of the establishments of the medieval guild masters had all been to some degree members of the family group. Self-interest alone demanded that the masters should treat them with some degree of consideration. However widely it was dis-honoured in the breach, a tradition had remained that the master had responsibilities towards his servant.

Men like Mr Miles had long since abandoned their right to imprison their servants when the new act was passed in 1875. They hired and fired men, women and children in the same spirit as they bought or scrapped a sewing machine. A con-sumptive operative had no more call on their sympathy and interest than a worn-out machine; they bought labour in the cheapest possible market, and scrapped it when it was worn out or broken down.

Liberal-minded employers in the limited field of the very highest class of workmanship might still treat their most skilled craftsmen as human beings, but for the majority the challenge of Mr Miles to their business seemed best met by adopting both his methods and his outlook. It was Mr Miles and those who shared his philosophy who were the real victors of the great strike, and their victory brought with it a further lowering of standards in an ancient craft together with a new and even more bitter degradation for those working in the trade.

The union had hoped it would be possible to negotiate a reasonable time log with the most enlightened and prosperous employers and that this would form a basis for a gradual eleva-tion of the status and economic position of workpeople through-out the trade. Mr Miles was quite right in supposing that it would be his turn next if they had succeeded in their first objective.

Starting with no more than £300 in cash the union was able to collect and disburse well over £30,000 in the course of the strike, three-quarters of which came from levies on the tailors themselves. Though the struggle could be represented as being in aid of the élite of the workers employed in the best West End shops, there was heartening evidence that many of the lowest paid outworkers, including some of the most recent immigrants who had not yet learned to speak English, saw that this was their own struggle and were willing to support it by making sacrifices which could come from nowhere but their own inadequate supplies of bare necessities.

Compared with anything in the past, these were gigantic efforts and unheard-of demonstrations of solidarity. The fact that the union could claim a membership of only one fifth of the tailors then working in London was not so great a weakness as it might appear. There were vast numbers of tailors who, though not union members, would have felt it a betrayal of their craft to do the work of a man on strike. The attitude of the women, who were not even eligible for membership at the outset of the strike, was typical. They won their right to union membership by going on strike first.

The struggle for a national agreement had been lost before the strike began. The disappearance of the representatives of the masters' association who had negotiated the price of a frock coat marked the triumph of the Miles philosophy. Those who took their place were not prepared to negotiate; as the mood hardened, they sought the destruction of the union.

If it failed in its supreme objective, the strike was not without its valuable results. It provided one more example of mutual support among workers in many trades and the lesson was not lost on the working-class movement as a whole. The steady stream of militant unionists emigrating overseas brought fresh vigour to the trade unions in the newer countries. The garment workers' unions in the United States owe much of their present strength to the infusion of this new blood during and after the London strike.

As in the past, the tailors provided outstanding individuals whose personal experience in their own struggle fitted them to become leaders in the wider movement. Ever since the miserable failure of the Owenite Grand National Consolidated the trade unions had been groping unsuccessfully towards some form of national association. The United Kingdom Alliance, torn by internal dissensions and shattered by the Broadhead confession, was the latest to claim national status and was already staggering towards its inevitable end.

From 1861 onwards an unofficial group consisting of the leaders of the newer national unions had been attempting to guide the movement along conservative and respectable lines. The 'Junta' as the Webbs called it, was self-appointed, exclusive and suspicious of other unions. Though it did valuable work in bringing pressure to bear on Parliament on a number of issues and helped to create a new image of trade unionism, it was unrepresentative of the movement as a whole and was unwilling to adapt itself to the changing times.

It was Peter Shorrocks, in his capacity as secretary of the Manchester and Salford Trades Council, who called together a conference of trades councils from all over the country in 1868. He was elected secretary of the conference which was to become an annual one. It proved to be the first annual Trades Union Congress.

The first TUC was in danger of becoming yet another idealistic debating society. Delegates from all over the country who had gathered together precisely because they were convinced of the need for strengthening the trade union movement were compelled to sit through long dissertations on such topics as 'Trade unions, an absolute necessity.' Peter Shorrocks was among those who sought to give the congress more practical and immediate objectives. His own paper on 'the present inequalities of the law in regard to conspiracy, picketing, coercion etc' was an admirable exposition of the lessons learned by the tailors in their strike and provided a clear plan for a campaign designed to remove some of the worst disabilities imposed by the law on trade union activity.

Having thus firmly put the question of Baron Bramwell's dubious judgment on the agenda of the very first meeting of the TUC, Shorrocks was in the forefront of the struggle for the amendment of the law. We find him at the next annual conference leading a debate on restrictions of union activity, and a little later as a member of the powerful Parliamentary Committee (precursor of the present day General Council). By 1875 this committee was able to report that collective bargaining and peaceful picketing had been legalised and henceforth no act by a group of workers would be illegal unless the same act would be punishable when done by an individual. The

tailors who had suffered from the obscurity of the law of conspiracy were thus instrumental in getting it clarified for the
benefit of all trade unions.

The congress to which this report was made contained two
women delegates, the first ever to be admitted in their own
right as representatives of women's organisations. Of the two,
one represented the Society of Shirt and Collar Makers. Both
tailors and garment workers, men and women, were thus in the
vanguard from the very earliest days of the T U C. As individuals
they played their notable parts in building the modern trade
union movement.

Within their own trade the tailors were less successful. The
industrial revolution was now catching up with them, bringing
with it profound changes in both the conditions and methods
of work. The tailoring trade was to remain, but only as a small
part of a new clothing industry.

As early as 1860 the London firm of E. Moses and Sons was
advertising its claim to have invented the new system of ready-
made clothing. 'The public,' they said, 'were amazed to find
that we could give ready-made suits that a Beau Brummel
would have been proud to wear at prices that a mechanic
could afford to pay.'

If their claim to have been first in the field was justified, this
firm was by no means alone in exploiting the revolution. John
Barran, who had opened the first ready-made clothing establishment in Leeds in 1856, had installed the first cutting
machine two years later. This was an adaptation of a bandsaw
for cutting furniture veneers. By substituting a knife for the saw, it
was possible to cut through two dozen double thicknesses of cloth
all to the same pattern in one operation. By dividing up the rest
of the work, semi-skilled sewing machine operatives could be
used to complete all but the most difficult parts of the garment.

Two other devices were installed by the same firm. A series
of goose irons, all working from the same gas supply, were
fitted with a small flame inside. By pressing a pedal under the
table each ironer could vary the heat of her own iron. Two
hundred sewing machines were driven by a single engine.
The speed of each could be controlled by a similar device
operated by foot. Other inventions were to follow, but these
three were alone sufficient to make factory organisation possible as an alternative to the old workshop system.

The ready-made clothing industry opened up a new market among the growing number of small tradesmen, office workers and others of the *petite bourgeoisie*. It provided a cheaper alternative to those who had hitherto bought their clothes from the less expensive made-to-measure establishments. It thus set a limit to the expansion of the traditional trade and began to encroach on its markets. This gave fresh impetus to the cheapening of made-to-measure clothing by fresh attempts to reduce the cost of labour.

The new industry developed most rapidly in Leeds, though there was a steady expansion in Colchester, Norwich, Bristol and the east end of London. Conditions in Leeds were particularly suitable for the new development. The declining linen industry provided factory space and a pool of female labour in an area where engineering firms were alert to the possibilities of adapting machinery to the new ideas.

The steady flow of Jewish refugees from eastern and central Europe which had been maintained during the early part of the second half of the nineteenth century increased rapidly with the pogroms of 1881 onwards. The ports of London and Hull were the point of entry for many of these unfortunate victims of persecution; those who arrived at Hull tended to gravitate towards Leeds where relatives and friends had already settled and where there was work to be found.

The Jewish people had been the traditional tailors in Europe for centuries, and this new influx brought with it a combination of highly skilled workers and a body of poverty-stricken men and women who had no alternative but to accept economic exploitation as an alternative to the inhuman persecution from which they had fled. There were, too, acute business minds who were not slow to see the possibilities of an industry needing no specialised type of factory building and in which the means of production were available for hire.

Though the census reports give only a rough guide, they provide telling evidence of the changes brought about by industrialisation. In 1851 there were only 935 men and 29 women tailors in Leeds. By 1871 when John Barran was beginning to instal his machinery, there were 1,523 men and 483 women. Ten years later the number of men had risen to 2,148 but women had jumped into the lead with 2,740. By the turn of the century there were less than 6,000 men and over 14,000 women. By this time there were more women then men engaged in the industry in the country as a whole, while in the ready-made clothing centres this predominance had been achieved between twenty and thirty years previously.

These bare figures of the increase in the number of women at work in the clothing industry reflect not only the expansion of the factory system in which large numbers were employed, but an enormous increase in outworking. The simpler operations such as button sewing and plain machining did not always require factory space or special equipment. They were within the compass of the elderly, the sick and the young mother tied to her home by growing children.

It was the exploitation of workers such as these and of new immigrants seeking work as an alternative to starvation which set new low standards of earnings in the industry. By 1891 a woman investigator was describing the East End of London as 'a sink for the deposit of unskilled and good-for-nothing husbands and inefficient women compelled to support themselves and their families.'

The division of interest between trained craftsmen and many other sections of the tailoring trade had been steadily growing and had become increasingly difficult to bridge. That between those who claimed to be tailors, with all that this implied by way of traditional skills, and the new groups of semi-casual machinists grew wider and deeper. It is against a sombre background of declining wages and worsening conditions in an industry adjusting itself to entirely new methods that the failure of trade unionism in the last quarter of the nineteenth century must be judged.

The reconstituted Amalgamated Society of Tailors confined itself more and more to sectional interests in the years following the great strike. Even with the absorption of the remnants of the London Association, it could claim no more than 4,000 members by 1870. Thereafter its membership rose gradually until it had quadrupled in 1890. This was during a period when the numbers engaged in the industry rose from about 150,000 to more than 200,000.

The counterpart of the Amalgamated Society in Scotland continued its separate existence. It was under the auspices of this Scottish National Operative Tailors' Society that an unsuccessful strike was launched in Aberdeen in 1875. It created a record, for it lasted for fifty-seven weeks. The unfriendly feelings between the two societies which had arisen out of the dispute over the Scoto-London log persisted and there were frequent disputes in the border country over allegations of poaching members in each others' territory.

Neither of these two feuding organisations could claim to speak for all the workers in the industry. They soon lost any desire to do so. They represented the skilled tailors in the bespoke trade and the élite of the newer clothing factories. In the early days they remained militant. Strikes were organised on a strictly local basis in single towns and by this method piecemeal gains in wages and conditions were won for their members. Many of the strikes were defeated, but over the years a general advance for a very small minority of workers was obtained. As time went on, the membership of these unions became more and more conservative in outlook and less inclined to resort to the strike weapon either in their own interests or in those of their fellow workers in the industry.

The Amalgamated Society had its greatest concentration of membership in London, which remained the largest centre of the bespoke tailoring trade. It was in London that at last agreement was reached between it and the Master Tailors' Association for a uniform time log at a conference in 1891. The aspirations of the union leaders of twenty-four years earlier were achieved in form only. The agreement was merely an acceptance of the rates already being paid to almost all the workers in the leading establishments of west and central London. It was far more valuable to the employers who were agreeing not to undercut each other than to the employees.

The London log was accepted by employers with similar interests in the provincial centres. In London the log rate was 6d an hour, in Leeds 5d, in Norwich 4½d. Attempts to widen the application of the log were defeated. In 1893 twenty-eight skilled workers in Leeds who struck to obtain the log were all dismissed and replaced or re-engaged on the employer's terms. So far from fulfilling the vision of a universal time log forming a basis from which the whole trade could be elevated, the 1891 agreement was a cosy arrangement between a small minority of workers and employers for their mutual benefit which was broken by those employers who found it burdensome, and ignored by those who were strong enough to defy it.

The increasing numbers of those engaged in the clothing industry in the rapidly expanding provincial centres found little attraction in the aims and policy of the Amalgamated Society. They attempted to fight their own battles, often without any organisation at all. The workers in a particular factory or workshop would refuse to work by mutual consent when they found conditions or the suggested rate for some particular order intolerable. This type of protest frequently led to the formation of small societies which dissolved as soon as the issue giving rise to them had been settled – more often than not by the defeat of the strikers. The picture of this period is of a plethora of small societies ranging from the club with purely friendly society aims to militant but purely sectional trade unions.

They were helped by the activities of a twenty-six-year old newly married woman, Mrs Emma Ann Paterson, a pioneer of modern women's trade unions, who began her work in this field in 1874. In the remaining twelve years of her brief life she was responsible for organising a number of unions among garment workers and tailoresses and for founding the National Union of Working Women in Bristol. Many of the small societies formed under these and other auspices had brief lives, but all kept alive the idea of trade union organisation among the employees.

It was in the 1880s that the Jewish tailors in Leeds made their first attempt to organise themselves into a single all-embracing union to include all the main branches of the trade. It coincided with a trade depression and in 1888, under the leadership of Morris Kenter, there was a general strike to press the claim for a reduction in hours from sixty-two to fifty-eight and a closed shop. Some 3,000 workers responded to the strike call, but union funds were insufficient to continue the fight, and when the strike failed the union collapsed. It was not until 1893 that a new Jewish union was formed, the Amalgamated Jewish Tailors', Machinists' and Pressers' Trade Union. It started with a membership of only one hundred, but grew rapidly and before the turn of the century could claim over 1,200 members in Leeds.

The Amalgamated Society of Tailors itself had some 270 members in Leeds, but took no organised part in the strike of 1888.

In the meantime, a number of small societies with limited

membership and sectional aims grew up. The most important was the Leeds Wholesale Clothiers' Operative Union, formed by cutters and pressers in November 1889. Similar organisations were formed at about the same time in London, Bristol, Manchester and elsewhere.

In 1894 the Leeds and Bristol branches amalgamated and subsequently joined forces with a number of local organisations in other garment-making centres, notably Manchester, Wigan, Liverpool, Nantwich, Glasgow, Leicester and Hebden Bridge. The banner under which they united was the Amalgamated Union of Clothing Operatives.

The union started on slender foundations of men and money, but it was to develop into a national organisation embracing all workers in the industry, whatever their skill or their job.

Within six months membership had risen to 268 full members and 239 probationers, but the union was facing serious difficulties. Three strikes had been organised in Leeds, two of which were successful and which cost the union no more than £2 18s 6d in all. The third strike absorbed all but a few pounds of the branch reserve fund and ended in total failure, broken by blackleg labour. 'We have had an uphill battle from the beginning of this, our new society,' wrote William Pitts the general secretary in his first half-yearly report. They had been compelled to fight 'not only against the capitalists, but against so-called working men who in our opinion are not worthy of such a name.'

In the second half of the year both branches lost more members than they recruited. Leeds gained forty-nine and lost ninety-five. Commenting on this 'deplorable state of affairs', William Pitts added: 'The majority of the ninety-five were the men who came out on strike, and after receiving all the benefits they could, and greatly reducing the funds of the union, thanked us by leaving the Society.'

These disheartening results were only slightly bettered in the following year, which ended with a net increase of three members in spite of new branches being opened in Wigan and Glasgow. Both new branches lost members during the year. This proved, however, to be the turning point in the affairs of the union. A year later there were 827 members, an increase during the twelve months of 329. Progress was slow and unspectacular for the next ten years, but unlike so many other organisations the AUCO remained in being with an ever-increasing number of branches, a steadily improving financial position and a growing list of small but important successes to its credit. In 1900 a Leeds Tailoresses' Union was formed, but collapsed after a few months. AUCO then opened its ranks to female clothing workers.

Chapter Twelve/*The Nation is the Sweater*

EFFECTS OF MECHANISATION AND FACTORY PRODUCTION; JEWISH WORKSHOPS
IN LONDON AND LEEDS; JEWS NOT RESPONSIBLE FOR GROWTH OF SWEATING;
CONDITIONS OF OUTWORKERS; JOHN GALSWORTHY VISITS THE EAST END;
CONDITIONS OF LEARNERS; JACOB FINE

By the turn of the century clothing factories were well established and new inventions such as buttonholing machines and
blind-stitching machines made it possible to improve the
efficiency and quality of factory production. At first sight it
seems surprising that this new system did not rapidly displace
the workshop and the outworker. In fact all three methods
continued side by side with the high-class made-to-measure
trade of tailoring.

The ideal aimed at by the factory owner is to keep his
premises and machinery continuously employed. As early as
1864 John Barran of Leeds was making the claim: 'Our
business does not depend much on orders; we make our goods
in anticipation and send out our travellers to sell our work.'
Here was the beginning of a planned production which would
make the fullest use of the factory and labour, but the total
clothing demand nevertheless did remain seasonal. It was
cheaper to off-load the peak demand rather than extend the
factory and have the new premises and machinery idle during
the slacker seasons.

In Leeds and London the Jewish workshops provided one
means of solving this economic problem. The Jewish immigrants with their common religion and language brought with

them alien customs from foreign lands. It was natural that they should tend to live and work together, but in Leeds there was never any absolute segregation of Jewish and gentile workers.

The largest Jewish workshops grew up in Leeds. Their success depended on the fact that they supplemented the work of the factory. In one field they excelled – the organisation of the work. The master tailor worked alongside his employees and was able to exercise the closest supervision and set the pace of the whole shop. Sub-division of labour was brought to a higher pitch in these Leeds workshops than anywhere else in the country.

The Jewish workshops in London were neither so large nor so well organised as those in Leeds. They competed with gentile sub-contractors for the thriving export trade to South Africa, producing clothing of a shoddiness and cheapness almost unknown to the home market.

In London, Leeds and elsewhere, small Jewish workshops gave impetus to a new development, the wholesale bespoke trade. The retailer of ready-mades saw profit in offering a service of made-to-measure clothing to those of his customers who wanted something a little above average. Some retailers took measurements and sent them to a factory which returned the goods for finishing; others cut out the order on their own premises and passed it to a Jewish shop to be made up. With their divisional methods of making these shops encroached on the trade of the older tailoring establishments still working on traditional lines.

The last quarter of the nineteenth century saw an expanding clothing industry within which new methods and machinery were being tried out with varying success. While firms competed fiercely for the market, the real struggle was that of flesh and blood against machinery. The bankrupts who were forced out of business by their rivals or by their own lack of organising skill were symptoms of the struggle; the real victims were the increasing number of sweated workers whose earnings fell steadily while the cost of living rose.

The tailors and garment workers were not alone in suffering the effects of industrialisation. The public conscience had been aroused about the conditions of factory workers long before this system was introduced into the making of clothes, and

Factory Acts seeking to limit the hours of work and to impose minimum conditions of employment had been passed by Parliament. In spite of a loud outcry against the invasion of the privacy of the home, these were extended by the Factory and Workshop Act of 1895 to workshops as well as factories. This social legislation was well-intentioned, but the lack of factory inspectors made it less effective than its authors intended and evasions were widespread and notorious. Nor was it wholly beneficial, particularly in the clothing industry. The individual working at home could not be controlled by its provisions either as to hours of work or the state of the workplace. The pressure of the Factory and Workshop Act, when it was felt at all, was an extra inducement to the employment of outworkers. Work went to those who were prepared to do it most cheaply and who in consequence lived in the most squalid surroundings.

The larger and better equipped factories should have been able to compete with all comers and at the same time pay reasonable wages. These were the factories which most readily attracted the attention of the factory inspectors; attempts by the in-workers to win higher wages could, when pressed too hard, be met with a diversion of work to unorganised and ill-equipped workers in their separate homes.

All these developments could not but affect even the high-class tailoring houses providing expensive clothing for the wealthiest and most fashionable clientèle. The centre of this trade remained in the west end of London, but the lessons learned by the masters in the course of the great strike of 1867 were not forgotten. The tailors and tailoresses working for these establishments found their own meagre wages being depressed by the development of factory-made garments. Though turnover increased, fewer and fewer skilled workers were employed direct by the fashion houses on their own premises.

The increase in the use of sweated labour and the lowering of real wages among the sweated had coincided with the rapid rise in the number of refugee Jews fleeing the pogroms since the 1880s. Dislike and distrust of foreigners has always been one of the more irrational English characteristics. It helped to obscure the fact that the evils of the clothing industry were due to underlying economic causes affecting all who worked in it, irrespective of their social background, country of origin or religious beliefs. The inference was drawn that the arrival of the Jews was responsible for, instead of being coincidental with, the worsening of sweating. The Jews were made the scapegoat and subjected to outrageous attacks, even in union journals and by union officials.

James Macdonald, secretary of the London West End Tailors and from 1896 to 1907 secretary of the London Trades Council, summed up a widely-held view when he said that even if the Jews had not introduced sweating 'they certainly are responsible for its rapid development. Their fellow Gentiles have not been slow to follow the lead, but the Jew can always beat them.'

Yet sweating had been known in the tailoring trade long before the Jews formed any significant proportion either of workers or masters. It was a characteristic of other 'needle' trades such as button or hook-and-eye carding, umbrella covering, sackmaking, lacework and embroidery, boot and shoe stitching and others, whether Jews played a part or not. It spread beyond the needle trades to the making of chains and nails, boxes and clay pipes and even to Bible folding.

Professor R. H. Tawney, the eminent socialist economist, attributed the success of the Jews to their efficiency and high degree of specialisation. 'The popular association of the Jews with sweating is an error,' he wrote.

A great deal of energy and thought were dissipated in attacking various symptoms rather than in diagnosing and attempting to eradicate the disease. The enemies of a 'better life' were not the small minority of Jews nor the host of poverty-stricken people who worked for less than a subsistence wage, but an economic system based on a philosophy of anarchic freedom from all restraint.

Beatrice Webb summed up the position succinctly with her phrase: 'The nation is the sweater.'

Typical of the sweated outworkers in the East End of London at the turn of the century was the widow Turnhouse. For her story, we are indebted to the late J. J. Mallon, who visited her home in Hackney with the novelist John Galsworthy. Anxious to see things for himself, Galsworthy found there material for a saga of a very different nature from the world of the Forsytes.

Mrs Turnhouse was one of many women in a slum street, who worked at home on her own treadle sewing machine, making trousers. The machine had been bought on hire purchase – a system introduced by the Singer sewing machine company – many years before.

She was fifty-eight years old and did not complain of her failing eyesight. There was no one to listen to her, and she had little time for talk. She collected, in her own time, work from a gentile factory some half an hour's walk from her home. It consisted of cut-out cloth which she machined up into trousers. This work took more than an hour a pair, though as night came on and she worked by candle light she found herself slowing down.

She bought her own thread and used about 4½d worth for each dozen pair of trousers. When they were finished she carried them in bundles to the factory and walked back with a fresh supply of work. She was punctual and reliable and always willing to work a little harder and longer if the factory had a rush order. She was thus kept in fairly regular employment though there were slack seasons when there was little or even no work at all for several weeks on end. At these times she trudged back and forth between her home and the factory so as to be on the spot if anything should turn up.

Mrs Turnhouse was self-respecting and wished to be respected by others. She could have got some relief from 'the parish', but by her code this was to be reduced to begging, and to beg she was ashamed. She preferred, when the work was there, to sit far into the night at her treadle and to start again as a matter of course when dawn broke. It was less costly both in candles and eye-strain to work continuously while daylight lasted.

When Galsworthy asked how much she was paid for her work she replied 'Twopence a pair'.

'How much do you earn in a week then?'

'Oh, four shillings, perhaps even five or sometimes six.'

'And what do you pay for your room?'

'Two shillings a week.'

'Are you really telling me you *live* on between two and four shillings a week?'

'Oh yes, my dear.'

'But what do you live on?'

'Well, I haven't got a very good appetite and sometimes I go without.'

Galsworthy turned to the landlady. 'She doesn't really go without food for a whole day, does she?'

'Yes, she does. Sometimes I take her a cup of tea but she gets nothing to eat.'

Galsworthy broke down and was led away in tears. From then on he was a vigorous and active supporter of the campaign to abolish sweating.

Another social pioneer who went to see for herself was Mary Macarthur, the great leader of working women. Having seen some curious advertisements for baby outfits in the newspapers, she sent for one and traced the clothes to their source. In one of the worst slums of London she found a young girl, with incipient diphtheria, making little lace-trimmed garments by the dozen, at 1d each. She was so poor she could not afford bedclothes, and so covered herself at night with the baby linen she was stitching. Through handling the garments, Mary Macarthur herself contracted diphtheria and had to spend six weeks in hospital. Later she said it was worth it, in order to bring home to the public the evils of sweating.[1]

Hundreds of similar cases were brought to light by the patient social investigators, and later used in evidence before government or Parliamentary commissions of enquiry. A great many examples were collected and published in the catalogue which formed the backbone of the *Daily News* anti-sweating exhibition of 1906 (see Chapter Thirteen). They showed that the grinding poverty and misery which John Williamson found in the East End of London in 1866 had, if anything, become even more desperate.

It was no wonder that Margaret Irwin concluded from her investigations into the conditions of shirt-makers that Hood's *Song of the Shirt*[2] might still be accepted as a thoroughly up-to-date report.

The high-class men's trade produced much the same sort of picture. One social investigator went down to Bethnal Green where he found a small living room 'so filled with piles of waistcoats that there was only just room for the sewing machine and

---

[1] *The story is told by Mary Agnes Hamilton in her book on Mary Macarthur (1925).*

[2] *It is somewhat surprising to learn that the* Song of the Shirt *first appeared in a Christmas number of* Punch – *in* 1843.

the three occupants, the mother, the married daughter, who comes in to help her and the son who had come in for a meal.

'The mother, Mrs G, is a waistcoat maker, i.e. she does all the machining in the ready-made waistcoat and makes the button-holes. Each one takes her from two to three hours. She is paid from 8s to 10s a dozen, but as she has the cotton to provide herself, and the silk for the buttonholes, 1s for materials must be deducted from every 8s she earns. Her rate of pay therefore works out at rather less than 3d an hour. If she and her daughter are both on full work for a week they can between them earn £1. But weeks of full work come irregularly and from August to Christmas, work is always very slack.'

Sitting eleven hours a day at a machine was described, with deliberate understatement, as 'very trying,' while Mrs G admitted that she 'suffered much with her eyes.'

In the majority of homes visited, the members of the family appeared to regard their lot with a dumb, almost brutish acceptance of their conditions as part of the natural order of things. Not so in this Bethnal Green house. The son of the house burst out in a savage denunciation of the system as 'slavery' and declared that the only possible answer was political action. 'Everything will soon be altered now that the Independent Labour party are having it all their own way,' he told his mother.

Political action and trade union organisation – these were the ultimate solutions preached by the pioneers of the late nineteenth and early twentieth centuries, as distinct from the charitable, Sunday-school, 'do-good' approach of the many well-meaning social workers whose horizon was limited by the concept that 'the poor are always with us.' (Indeed, it would not be an exaggeration to say they regarded the poor as a necessary outlet for their conscience and charity.)

Frances Hicks, secretary of the London Tailoresses, said as long ago as 1894 that while more inspectors were needed to eliminate the evil and unhealthy workshops that abounded in the centres of the tailoring trade, the real answer lay in forming trade unions.

She was glad to note that men, who had found it impossible to stem the tide, were beginning to assist, instead of obstructing, the organisation of women into trade unions. We find the union journal denouncing the men who still look upon unions for women with 'something akin to suspicion' or who 'still cling to the old idea that the proper sphere of women is in the home.' 'It behoves every union workman to encourage the women to organise until they can secure the same wages as are paid to women for similar work performed.' (The struggle for equal pay for equal work, which is still not resolved, has very early origins.)

Miss Hicks had herself been an apprentice in the trade, so she knew what she was talking about when she described the forerunners of the 'Madame' shops. 'In every suburb and working class district there are to be found a number of women who having worked for a few years in some fashionable dressmaking establishment, have set up for themselves in business and give West End style to neighbouring tradespeople, upperclass servants and perhaps a few wealthier patrons.'

These women who thus pandered to the 'keeping up with the Joneses' instincts in the suburbia of the nineties, needed very little capital, since customers provided their own materials and a sewing machine could be hired for 1s 6d a week. 'The chief requirements are a tidy room with fashion plates and magazines, a mirror and long white curtains which admit a good light, yet screen the customer while garments are being tried on.' Other requirements were 'perseverance and a pleasant manner', not to mention a stream of willing, unpaid or underpaid young helpers whose only ambition was to launch themselves similarly into the business. It was quite common to pay a premium of £20 and over to 'Madame' to become apprenticed.

'At the place where I was apprenticed,' Miss Hicks recalled, 'the workroom was shop and kitchen combined. The family consisted of the dressmaker, her two sons at school, a lazy husband and a gentleman lodger. The dressmaker, one assistant and I sat all day at a table near the window. Our hours were from eight in the morning to eight at night, with one hour off at midday for dinner. Tea was given us at the worktable and we did not cease working for that meal.

'It was my duty as apprentice to fold up and put away all material carefully and to pick up the pins from the floor before leaving at night. This was especially annoying, as it made me always later getting away.'

Apprentices usually worked for from six to twelve months

or nothing, and after that, for another year as an improver, at
2s or 2s 6d a week. Her apprenticeship finished, a girl was
generally glad to leave and try her hand in the West End. At
the right season, the end of March or the beginning of April,
she could almost certainly get taken on as a season hand at one
one of the large dressmaking firms round Oxford Street, starting
with about 8s a week. The majority worked from March till
August. 'What they do until the season begins again cannot be
said.'

Concern for the moral welfare of the young girls was a
recurrent theme. Miss Hicks commented on the dangers of a
life in which a girl becomes dazzled by beautiful materials and
hears gossip about the private affairs of the grand customers.
'It is here that the girl's eyes are opened to the ways of the
world. This is a time that tests a girl's character very severely.'

Another social investigator Mary Neal expressed fears for
the effect on character, as well as health.

'I think the display and luxury with which young girls, just
at the age when they love finery and pleasure are brought into
contact is very bad for them. The contrast between their lives
of drudgery and the lives of the girls for whom they make pretty
frocks, for parties of all sorts, for open air pleasures and indoor
revels, cannot fail to implant a bitterness which no after
experience can obliterate.'

She drew the conclusion that there was 'much to be done
before either men or women can wear good and expensive
clothing with a clear conscience.'

This attitude may seem utterly 'square' in these days when
mass production and multiple shops enable a factory worker
to be as well turned out as a debutante and fashion is no longer
the prerogative of the wealthy. But to women like Frances
Hicks and the other pioneers of the women's trade union movement must go much of the credit for the changes in social
structure during the past sixty years.

Attention has been focussed on the condition of the women
outworkers, but things were often just as bad for the men. The
exploiters and the sweaters did not discriminate between the
sexes when they imposed intolerable hours and miserable
wages on their workers.

The story of Jacob Fine illustrates the plight of the early
Jewish immigrants who flooded into Britain at the turn of the

century. About the time when the widow Turnhouse was
finding her eyes increasingly troublesome and Frances Hicks
was seeking to protect the young apprentices in the 'Madame'
shops, a slightly-built lad of seventeen stepped ashore at the
London docks from a cattle boat plying between Britain and
the Baltic ports. There could have been no lonelier person in
the world than this shrimp of a youth who walked from the
dock gates towards the yellow flare of gaslight reflected from
the shops and public-houses on the rain-soaked pavements.

His first human contact in London was the policeman who
found him wandering along clutching his bundle of possessions,
unable to understand or make himself understood in the
strange tongue of this foreign city. He was taken to the police
station and given a hunk of bread and a cup of hot cocoa. The
scrap of paper with a name and address in the Jewish quarter
of the East End was deciphered and he was guided by signs and
a scrawled sketch map to his destination.

Jacob Lewis Fine had arrived in the land of his dreams and
had found in the first hour of his stay that one at least of the
stories he had been told of this fabulous country was true. He
had met the 'London bobby' and found him even more kind,
generous and helpful than he had been led to believe.

He was on the whole fortunate in finding an immediate
refuge. This was at a workshop on the fourth floor of a house in
Bethnal Green where the Jewish proprietor and the eight
members of his family worked with twenty or so other tailors
and tailoresses. He was taken on as shop-boy with the promise
that he might be taught to become a machinist if he stayed until
the new year. As odd-job man and errand boy he was first in the
shop in the morning lighting fires and last out at night sweeping
and clearing up. From a wage of 3s 6d a week he paid 2s for
sleeping quarters in a cellar (using rolls of cloth as blankets)
and by living on black bread and salted herring could save as
much as 3d a week.

Observance of the law in the pious home meant that all work
stopped on Friday afternoon. To prepare for this keeping of
the sabbath, it was usually necessary to work through most of
Thursday night with perhaps an hour or two of sleep snatched
lying on the shop floor or the work tables.

It was a harsh and unhealthy life, but those like Jacob who
had fled from Europe had known worse. Looking back some

sixty years later he could remember not only the bitterness and squalor but many simple pleasures. There were the trips to the British Museum with a ½d buttered roll as the day's food. There was the pawnbroker who refused to advance 6d on his gun-metal watch but gave him 1s and refused to take it back when it was offered after several weeks' saving up.

Jacob Fine was destined to play an important part in building up trade unionism among the Jewish workers – we shall meet him again later in this story.

Chapter Thirteen/The Anti-Sweating Campaign

PUBLIC OPINION AWAKENED TO EVILS OF SWEATING; EARLY MOVES TO WIN
STATUTORY PROTECTION; SIR CHARLES DILKE'S BILL; J. J. MALLON AND THE
NATIONAL MINIMUM WAGE LEAGUE; *Daily News* EXHIBITION 1906; BERNARD
SHAW'S LECTURE; EAST END TAILORS' STRIKE; DEPUTATION TO ASQUITH
GOVERNMENT; WINSTON CHURCHILL TAKES A HAND; TRADE BOARDS BILL

Looking back on this period in the light of subsequent history
it is easy enough to pick out the threads which were later to be
woven into a pattern of strong and virile trade unionism
Lacking the gift of prophecy, those living and working in the
industry at that time can be forgiven for looking on the struggle
to build the unions as hopelessly visionary. The Amalgamated
Society had fewer members in 1900 than in 1875, and member
ship fell further in the following decade. AUCO had 1,400
members in 1900 and the figure remained static for the next
five years. These were the largest and most stable unions in
an industry with more than two hundred thousand workers

All attempts to keep alive the idea of a broadly based union
speaking for the whole industry failed in the face of the growing
conflict of interest between different sections in the industry
No common purpose existed among the workers; new method
and new machines intensified the competition for work at any
price; it was as fierce as that between the employers seeking
customers.

The evils of the outworking system had been apparent to the
leaders of the great strike. They had sought to solve them by
bringing these workers into the union and to achieve universal

betterment of wages and conditions for all engaged in the industry. Instead of the hoped-for improvement, the state of the outworkers had grown steadily worse, until it was no longer possible to consider organising them with any hope of success. Nor could the numerous agitations for the prohibition of outworking offer any better prospect. Such a ban could never have been enforced in the conditions of the age.

Even if the will had been there, workers and employers alike were faced with such revolutionary changes in their industry that they could not have solved their problems without outside help. Since the will was lacking, such outside help was imperative. Parliament was to provide it.

The Reform Act of 1867 had laid Parliamentary candidates open to the increasing pressure of a new working class electorate. The failure of the Liberal party to meet the demands for social reform voiced by the TUC encouraged the formation of the Labour Representation Committee in 1901. This alone was sufficient to impose a more radical platform on the Liberal party as it sought to defend itself against encroachments from the left.

Systematic scientific inquiry had resulted in many of the new inventions which revolutionised industry. The same method applied in other fields led to such developments as the formulation of Darwin's theory of evolution. The fundamentals of religion and morality which had been thought to be immutable were seriously questioned, openly challenged and to many minds proved false. Charles Booth, a wealthy Liverpool shipowner, applied the method in the field of social inquiry. His monumental *Life and Labour of the People in London* provided a vast mass of facts and figures about the actual conditions of the working population in the capital.

The work of pioneers like Pasteur, Lister and Koch demonstrated the connection between dirt and disease and pointed to the means of prevention. The discovery that insects and airborne microbes could carry contagion showed that personal cleanliness was not enough; self-interest demanded that no one could tolerate filthiness in his neighbour.

There were thus practical reasons why the condition of the poor should be of increasing concern to thinking people. To say this is not to detract from the devoted work of all those who for a variety of reasons found it ethically intolerable that a large part of their fellow countrymen were living in a state of squalid misery and abasement while they themselves enjoyed increasing comfort. The pioneers of social justice were given new arguments with which to combat the philosophy of Mr Miles[1] and his like.

It was not an easy argument, for it rested on theories which had not yet been put to the test. Charles Booth had painstakingly brought to light the stark facts of working-class life in London, but to diagnose an ill is not to provide a simple means of cure.

The fact remained that under the system of competitive free enterprise the total wealth of the country was rapidly increasing. Might not interference with this system so far from curing the evils of poverty merely result in sapping the very qualities of self-reliance and initiative which were held to be the mainspring of the wealth-producing mechanism? This was a real dilemma to many men of goodwill. It was certainly more comfortable to hope that a system which had already made Britain the richest and most powerful nation in the world would, if left alone, achieve further triumphs, including the conquest of poverty.

The process of conversion to the view that the community as a whole had a responsibility for, and a duty towards, all its members was therefore painfully slow; nor was this snail's pace wholly due to vicious selfishness or uncharitable disregard for suffering. Fears that concessions to progressive ideas might lead to excessive demands were none the less real for being both absurd and shortsighted. This was the thought-barrier which had to be overcome before even the most modest schemes of amelioration could find sufficient acceptance to make them practical politics.

Though the emphasis had been towards complete *laissez-faire* during the nineteenth century, Parliament had never completely accepted the doctrine of non-interference. Attempts to revive any form of legal control over the level of wages were however resisted not only by employers, but also by those of the growing trade union movement who knew enough history to believe that Parliamentary interference with the freedom of collective bargaining had in the past been in the direction of imposing maximum rather than minimum wages.

[1] *See chapter eleven. Mr Miles was the personification of the businessman of the* 1860s.

In the face of this general hostility those who were trying to obtain legal protection for the sweated workers had to move slowly and on a narrow front. Sir Charles Dilke introduced a modest bill into the House of Commons as early as 1898. This Wages Board bill would have given bodies formed from both sides in a limited number of trades power to fix minimum wages. It made no progress either that year or when Dilke re-introduced it at the beginning of each subsequent session.

Involved in an unsavoury divorce suit, Sir Charles Dilke could no longer hope to become leader of the Liberal party. He and his wife remained influential and spent the rest of their lives working for the 'underdog'. They joined forces with such pioneers of women's rights as Mary Macarthur, Susan Lawrence, Gertrude Tuckwell and the many others making ceaseless propaganda in the cause of social reform.

The campaign against sweating was given drive and impetus by a National League to Establish a Minimum Wage. James Joseph Mallon, who became secretary of this league in 1906, had many of the qualities and none of the defects of Francis Place. A master of detail, he could out-argue any opponent with irrefutable facts. His acute and penetrating thoughts were communicated with Irish urbanity and wit. He had the supreme gift of self-effacement and could bring a committee of men and women with widely divergent views and beliefs to a common purpose without any of them suspecting they were acting under his guidance.

An ardent socialist, Mallon was convinced that the best hope of the future lay in stronger trade union organisation to assist the growth of the infant Labour party in the political field. At the end of an anti-sweating meeting in Bristol which he and Mary Macarthur had addressed, a young man tackled him and he outlined his ideas. The young man was Ernest Bevin, who years later admitted that this conversation had turned his thoughts towards becoming a trade union organiser.

Among the many friendships Mallon made at this time was one with A. G. Gardiner, the radical editor of the *Daily News*. It was through this friendship that Mallon met his future wife, Stella Katherine, Gardiner's eldest daughter, whom he married in 1921. With the full support and cooperation of Mr George Cadbury and his family, owners of the *Daily News*, Gardiner and Mallon began to organise a giant exhibition 'to acquaint the public with the evils of sweating and to cultivate an opinion which shall compel legislation that will mitigate, if not entirely remove, those evils.'

A small exhibition lasting two days had been held in Bethnal Green in 1903, and a larger one had made a big impression in Germany the following year. It was now decided to make an all-out effort to shock public opinion into demanding action. The sympathy of the future Queen Mary was enlisted and the interest and approval of the Royal Family were demonstrated when Princess Henry of Battenberg agreed to open the exhibition at the Queen's Hall on 2nd May 1906.

With A. G. Gardiner as chairman of the executive committee and George and Edward Cadbury prominent among its patrons and active supporters, the exhibition was assured of a blaze of publicity in the foremost radical newspaper of the time.[1] Nor could the rest of the press ignore a six-week long exhibition supported by such a wide range of public personalities as to include royalty and the cloth-capped Keir Hardie.

The exhibition covered all the sweated industries, 'from trouser making to bible folding, from jumping jacks and mousetraps to babies' bibs and coffin tassels,' commented the *Daily News*, and called it 'a bazaar belonging to Dante's Inferno.'

Soberly, and without exaggeration, the exhibition catalogue set out case histories giving the stark facts which were illustrated by demonstrations at the various stalls. A first edition of 5,000 copies of the catalogue was sold out soon after the opening. Daily lectures by prominent and controversial figures underlined the story. George Bernard Shaw gave a characteristically brutal talk to some 1,600 fashionably dressed men and women who had paid to hear him halfway through the exhibition.

'I see,' he said scathingly, 'you are not interested in sweating but you are interested in me. That may be very flattering to me, but it is characteristic of the present day.

'If you all felt very strongly on the subject of sweating, you wouldn't be listening to me today. You would be out in the streets, burning people, burning houses and generally upsetting

---

[1] *The* Daily News *at that time boasted a circulation of two hundred thousand copies a day, a very substantial figure for those days. It advertised itself as 'the biggest morning halfpenny paper in the world. It contains no betting and horse racing news or alcoholic drink advertisements.'*

the whole social system. I have been trying for a long time to make you do that. It would result in immediate and thorough attention being given to the question of sweating, but of course you haven't the slightest intention of doing anything of that sort.

'I notice some of you are standing. It serves you right. You have been suffering for about half an hour from a mild form of fatigue. Many thousands of women are compelled to suffer fatigue of that kind while working for fifteen and sixteen hours a day.'

Apart from the verbal fireworks and taunting insults inseparable from a Shaw speech on politics, he forced his audience by cogent argument to face the need for a minimum wage for all industry and if possible the complete abolition of all outworking.

The exhibition exceeded the most extravagant hopes of its organisers. It had been visited by nearly 30,000 people and some 20,000 copies of the catalogue had been sold when it closed on 13th June. A new League for the Abolition of Sweating was formed to carry on the struggle.

The fashionable world which had attended a gala performance of *Tristan and Isolde* at Covent Garden on the day the exhibition opened, or had applauded the acting of Irene Vanbrugh in Pinero's new play *His House in Order* at the St James's Theatre, could no longer plead ignorance of the way the other half of their countrymen were living.

This airing of their grievances encouraged the workers in the East End sweat shops to take action on their own behalf. On the day the exhibition closed, the East End branch of the Amalgamated Society of Tailors and Tailoresses called an unofficial strike. Non-unionists joined with the branch members and some 10,000 strikers marched behind two brass bands to form a mile-long procession through the streets.

The strike was directed against the middlemen who were receiving as much as 10s a garment from the master tailors and paying their workers only 3s 6d. The strikers demanded a twelve-hour day from 8 am to 8 pm with an hour off for dinner and half an hour for tea. The six-day week should include a 'short day' of eight hours from 8 am to 4 pm. A joint committee of the union and the employers should be set up to decide on fair prices according to the proficiency of the workers concerned.

The strike brought the holiday suit trade to a complete standstill, and the master tailors joined with the strikers in bringing pressure on the middlemen. The executive council of the union decided to declare the strike official and to give 15s a week strike pay to members of six months' standing and between 10s and 12s to others. This solved the problem of rent-day which otherwise might have proved disastrous to the strike.

With public opinion already strongly against them as a result of the exhibition, the sweaters could not withstand the pressure. They capitulated on the question of hours. A protest meeting planned for Trafalgar Square on 25th June 1906 was turned into a victory march from Whitechapel to Whitehall with votes of thanks to the public and the press for their support. The police had turned out in force, but their services were not needed as, reported the *Daily News*, 'the demonstrators were in far too good a humour to cause any trouble.' The report went on:

'The strikers' demands have been conceded. They will work from eight to eight, with one hour for dinner and half an hour for tea and no piece-work . . . Thus has this struggle peacefully and satisfactorily ended and the men claim the result as the biggest victory ever achieved by a trade union in such a short period.'

The twelve-hour day with two meal breaks was hardly a revolutionary innovation. The illegal unions had established it in London, Sheffield, Aberdeen and other centres as far back as 1710. Two centuries of ceaseless struggle had led to a grudging acceptance of hours that had been thought appropriate in the reign of Queen Anne. But past experience showed that the employers would dishonour the agreement as soon as they felt able to do so.

Bernard Shaw had pointed out that neither agreements nor laws could be enforced so long as the doctrine that 'an Englishman's home is his castle' remained. 'You can sweat people in their homes to an extent that you cannot in factories. You can make as many laws as you like enabling factory inspectors to enter these private homes, but they can't get there. All the evil deeds done there are hidden away.'

To attempt to abolish sweating or homeworking by law would have meant an invasion of privacy by an army of inspectors on a scale which few would have had the temerity to suggest, and none of those concerned would have tolerated. It was J. J. Mallon who persuaded increasing numbers of those interested in the subject of sweating to concentrate all effort on a single small but positive objective, the passing into law of a Wages Board Act under which the two sides would be compelled to agree on minimum wages with penalties for any employer paying less.

In spite of the enormous impact of the *Daily News* sweating exhibition in 1906 and the return of a Liberal government with an overwhelming majority in the same year, another three years of ceaseless propaganda were needed before action on these modest lines was eventually taken.

By 1909 the campaign had been brought to the pitch where it was possible to demand an interview with the Prime Minister. Headed by the Archbishop of Canterbury, a representative delegation including Sir Charles Dilke waited on Mr Asquith in his room behind the Speaker's chair in the House of Commons.

The chosen spokesman was that master of detail and ardent Fabian, Sidney Webb. It proved an unfortunate choice. The urbane and scholarly Asquith had little enough in common with this dry statistically-minded expert. Webb soon forgot that his business was to state a case, and started arguing. Asquith's temper was ruffled and something like a quarrel developed before the deputation was abruptly dismissed from the august presence.

Dilke, who considered himself to have at least as great a grasp of detail as Webb, and who had in the past certainly shown himself a master at negotiation, was pleased neither with the choice of spokesman nor with this sorry outcome of all their labours.

He stalked angrily from the room, so far forgetting the rules of precedence as to push past the Archbishop. He addressed the deputation with a majestic 'We have done no good at all today,' and swept into the corridor. This magnificent exit was spoiled by the discovery that he had lost his hat and he returned even more angrily to the anteroom to search for it.

Greatly though his irreverent and impish sense of humour prompted Mallon to burst out laughing at the somewhat ridiculous tableau, his long years of dealing with temperamental committee members helped him to keep a straight face in the interests of the cause he had made his own. Realising that the missing hat was in the Prime Minister's room, he slipped through the door and snatched it from a chair across the room. In those few moments he overheard a brief but pregnant exchange.

Asquith, Herbert Gladstone, C. G. F. Masterman, John Burns and Winston Churchill were sitting round the large table discussing the deputation. Churchill was saying, 'Mr Prime Minister, I am interested in this. You give that question to me and let me play with it and I will make something of it.' To which Asquith answered, as Mallon was creeping from the room, 'Very well, if you feel like that, take it.'

Mollified by the recovery of his silk hat, Dilke was disarmed by the news Mallon brought with it. 'Oh, if Winston gets it, something will happen,' he commented and the rest of his ill-humour dissolved at the prospect. Sir Charles was right. Three days later Mallon was bidden to the President's room at the Board of Trade and asked to bring one or two experts. He took Mary Macarthur and Clementina Black. They were met by Winston Churchill, William Beveridge, Lord Askwith the industrial arbitrator and Clara Collett, whose work as a Board of Trade investigator had done much to bring the facts about the employment of women to public notice.

Churchill welcomed the delegation and disarmingly confessed himself to be a mere amateur among experts. He had, however, instructed his officials to prepare him a graph which was pinned on the wall. This showed average wages plotted against all industries for which facts or estimates were available. The peaks on the graph showed the 'good wages' which were as much as 45s or more. The troughs sank as low as £1 or less.

Throughout his turbulent political career no one has accused Winston Churchill of lack of enthusiasm. He had the Prime Minister's permission to 'play with' the problem and he now outlined to the startled experts the results of two days of this process. He wanted advice on what was a 'reasonable wage'. He proposed to draw a line across his graph at this level and to ask Parliament to give him power to deal with all industries in which wages were 'below the line.' This would have involved at least one-third of the working population.

Mallon and his friends represented those who had fought for years to interest the government in the evils of the sweated industries. They had come in the hope of prodding the minister into a small experiment of a new kind. Expecting to have to push hard at a door which was merely ajar, they found themselves sucked into a powerful wind-tunnel. They were overwhelmed by this sweeping plan which, if it had been put into effect, would have abolished want at a single stroke.

They knew that the Liberal party, which had won so great a victory in 1906 was, as a later commentator was to describe it, 'one of the most incoherent groupings that have ever formed a British administration.' The 377 Liberal MPs at Westminster had little in common but their title. They ranged from extreme radicals to hard-bitten industrialists willing to assail every privilege but that of their own rights over the workers in their factories. It was these last who had provided most of the party funds. This curious agglomeration could hardly be expected to cohere if any large sectional interest were at stake.

To the objections from the deputation that, much as they would welcome so glorious a crown to all their efforts, it would be impossible to get this revolutionary plan through Parliament, Churchill replied with an impatient gesture towards the lower half of his graph, 'I would call all these sweated trades. If you give me a word like "sweated" to use I will guarantee to ride down any opposition.'

It is interesting to speculate on what might have happened if Churchill's enthusiasm had carried the day. The agricultural workers would have been included in any reform of this scope and grandeur, and this alone would have ensured the opposition of the House of Lords. Nor is it conceivable that the industrialists backing the Liberal party with their money would have countenanced so wide and gross an interference with their liberty. Either the ultimate struggle with the House of Lords would have come on an issue on which public opinion had been insufficiently prepared, or the Liberal party might have split and foundered earlier than it did. But had these and other very considerable obstacles been surmounted, the four years before the first world war would not have earned the title of the Great Unrest.

Those like Mallon who had spent years in pushing, prodding, intriguing, cajoling and proselytising, were convinced that they were in danger of losing a prospective small, but real, victory if an attempt were made to leap at a bound toward these larger and more distant horizons. They sought allies in their efforts to curb Churchill's overmastering enthusiasm. It was Arthur Henderson who finally persuaded the impetuous President of the Board of Trade to adopt the principles of the Dilke Bill which, like its author, had by now become almost respectable.

That this bill, moderate and experimental though it was intended to be, was perhaps as far as one could hope to go was demonstrated in its passage through the Commons. Churchill made it clear that his intentions went far beyond the limited provisions of the bill. 'Where you have sweated labour you have no organisation, no parity of bargaining. The good employer is undercut by the bad and the bad employer is undercut by the worst. The worker is undersold by the worker who only takes the trade up as a second string. His feebleness and ignorance generally render the worker an easy prey to the tyranny of the masters and middlemen only a step higher up the ladder than the worker, and help in the same relentless grip of forces. Where those conditions prevail you have not a condition of progress but a condition of progressive degeneration.

'In these sweated industries it is a particular class which has been constituted of the widow, the womenfolk of the poorer class labourer, the broken, the weak and the struggling . . . I ask the House to regard these industries as sick and diseased industries. In passing this Bill the House will not only be dealing manfully with a grave social evil, but will also take another step upon that path of social organisation on which we have boldly entered, and along which the Parliaments of this generation, of whatever complexion, willingly or unwillingly, will have to march.'

The Bill was fought tenaciously by those like Sir Frederick Banbury, the Conservative member for Leicester, who interpreted Churchill's speech as an admission that this was the thin end of the wedge and would lead to state regulation of wages in every trade and industry. It would spell the final ruin of all our economy. The inevitable crocodile tears were shed over the plight of the poor widow; with these higher wages her work would go to the factory and she would be left to starve . . . (The widows of Britain have always attracted some curious champions.)

During the committee stage there were exhibitions of delaying tactics which were to be repeated on a grander scale in modern times when Brendan Bracken and John Foster spoke with lengthy passion on the vital issue of whether nationalisation should be spelt with an 's' or a 'z'. On the last day the committee had been compelled to sit throughout the luncheon hour and at three o'clock in the afternoon Mr E. H. Carlisle was protesting vigorously to the chair that it was preposterous that they should be faced at this late hour with such cryptic words as 'hammered, dollied and tommied chain-making' without a word of explanation from the minister.

Churchill, robbed of his own luncheon and his customary nap after it, remained unruffled. He blandly told the committee that because he assumed such processes were so well known he had not wished to waste time with unnecessary speech. A hammer was, of course, a hammer. The other two words, dolly and tommy were also in fact hammers, but hammers worked by hand or by foot. The schedule of which these words were the last line was agreed and the bill ordered to be reported to the House.

Churchill was asked afterwards how he had known what dollies and tommies were. He confessed he had seen neither in action, but had thought it prudent to get drawings of them put before him when he first presented the bill to the Commons.

The bill passed through its later stages in the face of the same determined opposition. It is noteworthy that some 200 of the Liberal MPs were not present to vote for the third reading. The party had an enormous majority and the absentees were not needed to ensure the passage of the measure, but these figures do not indicate wild enthusiasm; it seems probable that Mallon and his friends were correct in thinking that anything more radical would have met opposition rather than acquiescence.

Chapter Fourteen/Revolution in the Clothing Trad

SLOW PROGRESS OF TRADE BOARDS ACT; COMPOSITION OF TAILORING BOARD
WAGE RATES AND THEIR EFFECTS; DEVELOPMENT OF TRADE BOARD SYSTEM
FIRST WORLD WAR — EFFECTS ON PRODUCTION OF CLOTHING; POSTWA
CHANGES — MULTIPLE SHOP METHODS; MONTAGUE BURTON'S ; WOMEN'S TRADE
NEW PATTERN ESTABLISHED

Any hopes that the passing of the first Trade Board Act, whic
received the Royal Assent on 20th October 1909, would be c
any real and immediate benefit to the sweated workers of th
tailoring industry were bitterly disappointed. For fourtee
months nothing happened at all.

The act empowered the Board of Trade to set up a board t
regulate wages in any branch of a trade where they wer
exceptionally low. Bad though conditions were in tailoring
they were even more appalling among the women employe
in making chains and nails, cardboard boxes and machine
lace. These worst trades were dealt with first and it was no
until mid-December 1910 that the first meeting of the Tailorin
Trade Board was held.

This was a cumbersome body of forty-nine, made up of fiv
independent members and twenty-two from each side in th
industry. It set up seven district committees and so brought i
a further 161 representatives. These district committees wer
largely time-wasting.

The board's authority was confined to the wholesale bespok
and ready-made sections of the industry, but even within thes
limits there was a wide diversity of interest which led to long

rawn-out and tedious discussions. Those of the employers who
ere already paying higher wages were not averse to trying to
mpose what they themselves knew might be burdensome rates
n other employers producing lower quality goods in quite
ifferent circumstances.

The bargaining and cross-voting are well illustrated in the
xing of an hourly minimum for women workers. The master
tailors who had a smaller proportion of women workers sug-
ested 4d an hour, and the workers' side was defeated when it
ried to increase this to $4\frac{1}{2}$d. These master tailors then combined
vith the workers' side to support a compromise figure of $4\frac{1}{16}$d
ut this was rejected by the factory owners, the vast majority
f whose workers were women. The independent members
acked the factory owners in their resistance.

The independent chairman then suggested $3\frac{1}{2}$d, but the
factory owners would not rise above 3d and the workers would
ot accept less than $3\frac{3}{4}$d. The deadlock was broken by a final
agreement on $3\frac{1}{2}$d with the factory owners insisting on their
dissent being recorded in the minutes.

In the subsequent outcry from workers who thought the
figure too low and employers who thought it too high, the
employers were more successful in building up pressure by
odging 'objections' with the board. Ultimately they succeeded
n chipping $\frac{1}{4}$d off the rate which was fixed at $3\frac{1}{4}$d.

By much the same process the workers' demand for 9d an
hour for men was countered by an offer of 7d from the better-
off masters and of 5d from the factory employers and a final
figure of 6d was agreed. Rates for learners and apprentices were
fixed for a fifty-hour week. Girls under fourteen would get a
minimum of 3s a week rise to 12s 6d at the age of twenty-one,
while boys under fifteen were to have 4s 2d rising to 21s 11d at
the age of twenty-two.

The board decided against fixing minimum piece rates, the
employers being left to base them on the time rates. A general
guidance was issued providing that eighty per cent of female
piece workers should be able to earn at the minimum rate of
$3\frac{1}{4}$d with the workers' side registering their protest in the
minutes. No provision was made for overtime, and the board
had no power to limit the length of the working week.

The protracted negotiations did not reach finality until the
latter half of August 1912, and the Act provided for a further

six months' delay before the decisions of the board becam
legally binding on employers in February 1913.

These results of years of agitation and long months o
bargaining seemed to many to be worthless. The new rate
meant a minimum weekly wage of 25s for men and 13s 6d fo
women.

Only a small proportion of men and women in Mancheste
and the still rapidly expanding industry in Leeds were gettin
less than the new rates, though some juveniles in these centre
benefited. In Leeds union action soon resulted in agreed mini
mum rates of 4d for women and 8¼d for men compared witl
the 3¼d and 6d laid down by the Trade Board.

In London the men's rates were already generally higher
but in other southern centres increases had to be granted. The
biggest benefits came to the women workers in London and th
southern counties. In the country as a whole it was calculatec
that something over one-third of women workers receivec
increases.

Hebden Bridge in Yorkshire had been notorious for its lov
rates of wages, for there was little alternative employment
From one of the employers came the cry, 'This sort of legisla
tion only tends to create unrest. The workers have beer
pandered to, and now they are asking more.' A survey carriec
out by AUCO showed that in this centre nearly sixty per cen
of the workers gained increases.

While many workers complained that the Trade Board rate
were giving legal sanction to a 'sweated wage', employers whe
had been paying women 2d an hour in the factories and fai
less for homework were loud in their protestations that they
would be thrown out of business if they were compelled to fac
such enormous increases in their wage bills. The passage o
time proved how false were these lamentations; the clothing
industry did not fall into ruin but on the contrary prospered
even though the women's rate was raised by the board to 3½c
in 1915.

Though the original orders did not cover hours of work they
did abolish the system under which workers had been com
pelled to wait for work in the factory, but were paid only fo
the work actually done. When idle labour had to be paid for
factory managers were compelled to plan production more
carefully to avoid this addition to their overheads.

Homeworkers benefited least of all. Employers were supposed to keep a register of all outworkers and in theory there was a piece rate based on the hourly wage for them as for others, but as all the authorities agree, evasion was easy and enforcement extraordinarily difficult. It was almost as hard to control activity in the smaller workshops. By 1915 there were only twelve inspectors working under six different trade boards responsible for regulating the wages of half a million workers. They could hardly be expected to clean out every pocket of evasion.

As late in the day as 1924, The *Daily Herald* found it necessary to run an anti-sweating campaign, though the evil had by then been much reduced. The report of the chief inspector of factories and workshops for that year claimed that illegal employment had become exceptional. Nevertheless it quoted one workshop making coats and dresses where the women had been working from 9 am to midnight for six consecutive days and had been given work to do at home on Sunday. After about a fortnight sufficient stocks had been accumulated for the employer to dismiss all his workers. Even so, the chief inspector reported that the women were reluctant to give evidence and added that, but for the dismissals, the offence might never have come to light.

In spite of all evasions, however, the worst evils of sweating and outwork in the clothing industry faded gradually in the years following the Trade Boards Act.

J. J. Mallon, a member of all the original boards, commented, 'About the substantial success of the boards in their first application there is no longer any question. Everywhere they have succeeded in considerably raising the lowest levels of wages, in forwarding organisation among both employers and workers and in diverse and subtle ways releasing and stimulating forces that make for the efficient and humane development of their trades.' In 1913 the National Anti-Sweating League urged that the act should be extended to six other trades – the Board of Trade agreed to five: sugar confectionery; shirtmaking; hollow-ware making; linen and cotton embroidery and certain processes in laundries. To the quarter of a million workers already protected by the act were thus added another 140,000, nearly all being women.

Earnings in the shirtmaking trade, according to a Board of

Trade report in 1906, ranged from 9s 9d a week in Londonderry, to 13s 7d in Yorkshire and Lancashire, to 15s 10d in
London, where rates were raised by the West End trade. Over
a fifth of the women received less than 10s a week and the
figures would be further depressed if the report had taken into
account the earnings of home-workers. Dr Mallon quoted a
case of home-workers making shirts at 1s 3d a dozen against
the factory price of 1s 6d, and said that factory workers could
earn 15s or 16s a week without difficulty, compared with the
7s a week which 'only strenuous women' could earn.

The 1914-18 war gave a tremendous impetus to the trade
board movement. At the beginning, some employers wanted
to suspend the operation of the machinery for the duration, but
public opinion had come to accept the principle and the experience of the war years served to strengthen the idea of
statutory control. In 1919, 15 new boards were set up; and
another 37 in 1920/21, bringing the total to 63 boards covering 39 trades and regulating the wages of about 3 million
workers.

This burst of new boards followed the passing of a new
Trade Boards Act in 1918, which was a considerable improvement on the old Act. The boards were given a wider authority
and the early stigma of 'sweating' was removed; instead of
confining action to trades where wages were excessively low,
the factor 'lack of organisation' among both employers and
workpeople was brought in. The boards were also empowered
to fix weekly or daily normal hours and overtime rates. Most
declared that the forty-eight hour week was 'normal' and so it
remained for another twenty-eight years.

The wider definition brought in *all* clothing workers who
had not been covered by earlier-established boards. The nine
broad divisions catered for were: shirtmaking; ready-made and
bespoke wholesale tailoring; retail bespoke tailoring; corset;
fur; wholesale mantle and costume; dressmaking and women's
light clothing, with separate machinery for Scotland. Hat, cap
and millinery, ostrich and fancy feather and artificial flower-
making were borderline activities of the trade similarly covered.

Despite all the statutory paraphernalia for protecting
workers and the large number of representatives of the industries and outside independent people associated with the
activities of the boards, the problem of enforcement remained.

'*The sweater's victim*': *a postcard produced by the National Anti-Sweating League*

Andrew Conley

It was not only the old problem posed by Bernard Shaw in 1906 of forcing people in their own homes to observe the rules. There were difficulties in applying the regulations to factories and workshops. In 1915 there were only twelve inspectors for six trade boards; by 1922, the number of boards had increased sevenfold, but there were only three times as many inspectors. The fears expressed by Conservative back-benchers in the debates in Parliament that the 1909 act would lead to an 'enormous army of inspectors' invading the privacy of homes and interfering with the liberty of the employer were groundless indeed.

Other factors, unconnected with the trade boards, were changing the character of the clothing trade, and reducing the importance of the home-work element during the second decade of the century. Changes in social custom and in taste played their part.

The change in fashion from Edwardian tailor-made coats and skirts to dresses transferred a great deal of the women's clothing trade from the home-worker and sweat-shop to the factory where dresses and coats were made in the same way as the cheaper ready-made men's clothes. The dressmakers who had protested against the Trade Board rates as vigorously as any, had been attempting to sell at a price which would prevent the customer making her own dress. They were now themselves undersold by the factories. The greater demand created by changing fashion coupled with the growing disinclination of women to 'do it yourself' led to a sharp increase in the turnover of factory-made dresses with consequent economies in costs. Competition from the factories led to the gradual decline of the type of exploitation described by Frances Hicks, when young girls were employed as learners by private dressmakers.

The Aliens' Immigration Restriction Act of 1911 cut off the inflow of skilled and unskilled labour from the Continent. In the years that followed, a shortage of skilled labour developed and there were no penniless immigrants who had to work or starve. There was a tendency towards greater regularity of employment and better wages in consequence. The workshop which had been able to compete with the factory by the use of sweated labour became less competitive.

Small though they were, judged by the still inadequate standards of today, the earlier social service payments helped to

L

alleviate the direst poverty and so remove another incentive
to accept sweated conditions in homework.

But far and away the most decisive factor in eliminating
homework and changing the character of the clothing trade
was the first world war. Although mobilisation was never so
complete, or the control over the economy as rigid as in the
second world war, the whole of industrial production became
geared towards meeting the needs of the armed forces. Large-
scale production of uniforms kept both private firms and War
Office factories working at full stretch, and with the drain on
manpower, more and more women took up war work. Married
women were no longer compelled to accept any kind of work,
or to work long hours in their homes, in order to keep the
family together. They worked long hours, but they worked in
munition factories and clothing factories, where they acquired
a new sense of independence and wider interests.

The war had profound and lasting effects on production
techniques. The need for steady long runs and the building up
of stock to meet the continuous demand for uniforms and
military equipment had lessons for those managements which
cared to learn them. The scarcity of workers encouraged the
introduction of labour-saving machinery. The immediate
post-war years brought a continued boom and for a time the
clothing trade could claim a 'never had it so good' period. Not
only was there an inrush of orders for ordinary consumer goods,
but the millions of returning soldiers required demobilisation
suits.

At the same time, it was a period of startling change and
clearly any firm which thought in terms of going back to pre-
war methods could not hope to survive. The trend for simpler
fashions swept the country. No longer were small boys to be
dressed in knickerbockers and velveteen suits, or their sisters
in voluminous petticoats. Knitted jerseys, short trousers and
skirts for children took their place. Women celebrated their
newly-won emancipation by cutting not only their hair but
their skirt-lengths, and emerged in short, skimpy and shapeless
dresses and coats. Men's clothes did not change to the same
extent, though they too tended to become more simple and
casual in character.

It is against this background that the developments of the
clothing industry during the inter-war years must be seen. The

most spectacular feature of this period was undoubtedly the rapid growth of the multiple firms and the made-to-measure tailors.

Originally, the clothing manufacturers sold their products through a multiplicity of small shops. But they found these inadequate and unable to carry sufficient stock and during the latter part of the nineteenth century, several clothing firms began to develop their own outlets. At this time J. Lyons and Liptons were beginning to be household names and, some of the more forward-looking manufacturers argued, why should direct trading be confined to tea? Two Leeds businesses which early on started their own shops, to cut out the middleman and sell direct to customers, were Hepworths and Blackburns. From the opposite end, the Cooperative Society reached back from its retail end to establish clothing factories. The so-called 'special order departments' flourished. These were precursors of the wholesale bespoke business, where customers were measured and fitted for coats and suits. Prophetically, the journal *Men's Wear* had remarked in 1902, 'Some very shrewd men in the clothing trade express the opinion that in the near future the whole industry will be run on the lines of the Special Department . . . All garments will be made to measure . . . the trend of things is certainly in this direction.' Yet wholesale bespoke tailoring then accounted for only a tiny proportion of men's clothing.

Thus, even before Montague Burton came on the scene, 'made-to-measure' was getting established, if only on a small scale. Burton's name, however, is associated in the public mind with the wholesale bespoke business.

One of the outstanding figures in the history of the industry, Burton set up a retail shop in Sheffield in 1900 on £100 he borrowed from a relative. His make-up was a mixture of business acumen and philanthropic idealism. He was deeply shocked by the prevailing state of squalor in the trade, and wished to raise the general standard of those he clothed and those who clothed them. He judged that men were not only individuals but were sufficiently conscious of their own individuality to dislike the uniformity of the ready-made, and aimed to offer individually tailored clothes which would compete with the quality of existing bespoke tailoring and with the prices of ready-to-wear.

Burton spent six years managing his shop in Sheffield and learning everything there was to learn about the trade.

In 1906 he opened up the first shop at which measurements were taken for clothes to be made up in his own factory in Sheffield; and soon established shops in the north. The demand strained the resources of the Sheffield factory to such an extent that he moved his headquarters to Leeds, with a factory in Concord Street. The firm was still small and his ideas came under fire from both the traditional bespoke tailoring and the cheaper ready-made trade.

The demobilisation of millions of men who were anxious to escape from uniformity, and wished above all to put the horrors of khakidom behind them, led to a boom in all sections of tailoring. The Burton system, with its integration of shops and factory, retail and production, was able to reap the benefit and expanded with almost incredible rapidity. By 1921, at the age of thirty-six, Montague Burton headed the largest clothing firm in Europe and was planning to establish the largest clothing factory in the world at the Hudson Road Estate in Leeds. By 1938 his firm employed 10,000 workers in Leeds and a further 1,500 in Lancashire.

Burton's was the biggest but by no means the only firm of its kind. The market for cheap or moderately priced made-to-measure garments appeared to be unlimited and many other multiple firms entered the field.

The other main firm in the multiple business was also a Leeds concern, Prices Tailors Limited, which traded under the title of Fifty-Shilling Tailors. Before long there were few towns in Britain without a branch of a multiple tailor, where a man could walk in and be measured, and walk out again with the knowledge that in a matter of days, he would be wearing a suit tailored to his individual requirements in a Leeds factory. Multiple tailors selling direct through their own retail outlets had by 1938, captured a substantial part of the men's suit trade.

The methods of making and selling women's clothes followed a somewhat different pattern. Between the two wars, the drive came from the retailer, rather than the manufacturer, and there was little direct selling to consumers. The Co-operative Wholesale Society, with its numerous factories for large-scale production of women's coats and dresses, was a notable exception. Few retailers went in for their own factory production and the big department stores preferred to place their orders through manufacturers – or, in the case of underwear or children's clothes, through wholesalers. During the 1920s there were many amalgamations of stores, though this was mainly a financial operation and they kept their own names and individualities.

The most significant feature of the inter-war period was the growth of the so-called variety chain store, like Marks and Spencers, which first became a public company in 1926, and operated on a system of placing individual contracts and bulk orders with a number of different manufacturers. In the north of England the thirties saw the growth of the chain stores of Lewis's.

Yet despite these developments, the multiples still took a relatively small share of the total women's trade, compared with that of the men. More than half the total supply of women's outer clothing was distributed by small, single-shop retailers – the draper in the market towns and suburbs who offered personal service, or the specialist 'Madame' shop whose origins we saw in an earlier chapter. Certainly this period brought a big improvement in the quality and range of ready-mades; British retailers looked to the example of the United States where 'off the peg' clothes were firmly established. The American large-scale retail stores carried big stocks and offered so wide a choice of fittings that only the most fastidious buyer felt he or she could do better by having individually tailored clothes.

The pattern of the modern clothing industry was definitively established during the war and inter-war years.

The age-old craft of tailoring which had been confined to men and served the needs of a minority of the population had seen many changes in the course of centuries. It is still possible to buy handwoven cloth and take it to be made up by an individual tailor, working by himself on the old principle of one man, one garment; but the vast majority of the clothes we wear, whether specially tailored suits, or ready-made underwear, raincoats, shirts, skirts and the rest, are factory-produced in an industry serving almost the whole population.

The swing towards the factory had two profound effects. It tended to break down the old divisions between those working as individual tailors, as employees of tailoring shops, as employees in workshops and as factory workers. It also brought about a situation in which women workers far outnumbered the men in the industry.

This presented the unions with an even bigger challenge of recruitment and organisation.

Chapter Fifteen/Inter-Union Divisions

While an expanding clothing industry was evolving towards factory-dominated production in the early years of the present century, the unions were struggling to solve their own organisational problems. These problems were themselves a reflection of the changing character of the industry, and the struggle was not made easier by the legacies of prejudice and mistrust which lingered long after they had become irrelevant to the conditions of the day.

The Amalgamated Society, with its ancient lineage and long history of active leadership, had pretensions to speak for the whole industry which were as strong in theory as they were becoming hollow in fact. The policy adopted for the great strike in which all the tailors in the kingdom had been called on to support the two thousand on strike in London was continued in miniature during the latter part of the nineteenth century. All the resources of the society were concentrated on one special locality and by these means small gains were registered over the years. These tactics were sufficiently effective for the employers to found their own organisation, the National Federation of Merchant Tailors, in order to counter selective strikes with equally selective lockouts.

The gradual decline in the relative importance of bespoke tailoring in the industry had the effect of bringing the leaders of the society and its membership closer to the employers. The strike weapon was virtually abandoned and when it was used the results were disastrous. The rules of the society may have appeared realistic but they were essentially defeatist since they stated the objects as being to maintain uniform rates 'as far as possible'. The emphasis was on Friendly Society benefits for the members and 'friendly representations' to the employers about wages and conditions.

The executive council in Manchester was the supreme arbiter, but it lacked any apparatus of real control over the branches spread throughout the kingdom which were for the most part run by honorary officials. While administrative costs were low this simply meant there was little administration and branches were frequently closed when they went bankrupt through inefficiency or worse.

One of the last strikes backed by the executive was in Dublin in 1900 and was designed to end outworking in the Irish capital. It had no possible chance of succeeding, for the branch would not have welcomed the outworkers as members of the society even if they had been able to afford the union dues out of their beggarly earnings. The net result was to impoverish the branch and to encourage the employers to give even more of their work to the poorer and therefore more docile out workers.

This experience made the executive still less willing to sanction strike action for any reason. The cautious and conservative elements were in the ascendant at a time when the society was in decline. The permanent fund, under the control of the executive, had reached a peak of more than £20,000 in 1884 but had fallen almost every year until it reached £5,618 in 1900 Membership had dropped from its highest level of 17,573 in 1891 to 13,439 in 1900. To meet this situation the executive sought to build up the funds and to come to terms with the employers wherever possible.

The tailors in the West End branch of the society considered themselves the élite of the country's craftsmen. They were producing the finest quality clothing for the wealthiest customers but though their earnings were higher than most, they were still well below those of many craftsmen in other trades. The were not prepared to accept this position of inferiority. From Manchester it seemed more desirable to try to bring others up to the London standard than to risk the society's dwindling funds in efforts to improve the Londoners' standards.

The West End branch felt that its members were being called upon to subscribe to a society which was doing nothing to further their interests. They refused to raise the levy in support of the Dublin tailors and had to be coerced into doing so. The executive, in trying to build up the permanent fund, was not slow to claim that the West End branch's affairs were being badly managed and that it was not pulling its weight. Manchester could rightly claim that it had bled the rest of the country white to support the London tailors in the great strike; the West End branch retorted with vigour that the London tailors had sacrificed their livelihood in that great battle on behalf of the tailors of the whole nation.

The quarrel came to a head in 1905 when the West End branch seceded from the society and formed the London Society of Tailors and Tailoresses. The breakaway organisation seems to have taken most of the old members with it, for six months later it could claim 999 members compared with the 1,051 in the West End branch of the AST & T a year before.

Terence Flynn, the secretary of the Amalgamated Society, was a son-in-law of Peter Shorrocks and was steeped in the history and traditions of the tailors. In resisting the breakaway move he pointed out that London had a record of continuous failure. 'Every kind of local society was tried and found wanting when any position of real danger had to be faced. It makes the most disastrous and humiliating reading not only because of the constant defeat of the local societies but because the issues fought were of paramount importance to all tailors throughout the kingdom. Yet we are told that a return to this futile, ineffective and fossilised system of organisation is better than the Amalgamation.'

An ardent admirer has left this pen-picture of Flynn: 'He is undoubtedly a man of constructive and administrative ability, far above the average, of a quiet and unobtrusive disposition, and one who has thought deeply upon the political, social and economic questions of the day. He has none of that swagger and ignorant self-assertiveness which unhappily characterises too many of those prominent in the Labour movement; a strong and convinced believer in arbitration and conciliation in industrial disputes, believing as he does that such disputes should be submitted to the arbitrament of reason rather than the arbitrament of force.

'He is a man of considerable literary ability. His report (to the Dublin Conference of the Society in 1904) was an admirable report, containing much sound philosophy and passages of real eloquence, altogether a brief but solid contribution to the literature of trade unionism.'

This thumbnail sketch from the Society's journal certainly does Flynn no injustice; it shows he could evoke respect and devotion among those working closely with him. The late Edith Maycock, who worked as a union official in the field, had perhaps a more objective view. While paying tribute to Flynn's urbane good manners and well-informed mind, she considered 'Agnes was the better man of the two.' Agnes Shorrocks had been born into the Amalgamated Society and as Terence Flynn's wife was its assistant secretary. Her own ideas, imbibed from her father, were more militantly radical than those of her husband and she was regarded by many as the driving force in the working as well as the domestic partnership.

In spite of Terence Flynn's denunciation of the breakaway West End tailors, they were not simply union-splitting wreckers. While still paying lip-service to the wider visions of forty years earlier, the society had in fact narrowed its outlook. It stood for the protection of the interests of a small section of the clothing industry and had no positive policy for broadening its basis. The West End tailors were carrying this attitude to its logical conclusion. They themselves represented a minority within a minority, but if it was good that the craftsmen tailors should act in isolation from other clothing workers, was it not equally good that the fairly well-defined section of craftsmen working for the leading London houses should also manage their own affairs?

What they proposed was that groups of clothing workers who, like themselves, had common interests should organise themselves in branches to run their own affairs without interference from others with different sectional interests. All these branches would pay into a central federal fund which would be used to further the more general interests of workers in the industry as a whole.

They were correct in their diagnosis that the Amalgamated Society was not facing the realities of a changing industry. Terence Flynn was equally correct in castigating their proposed solution as a return to a system which had been proved hopelessly ineffectual in the past. He lacked the inspired insight which would have led him to offer the alternative solution – the building of a single all-embracing union which would be run on democratic lines but with a strong central control.

The defection of the West End branch came when the anti-sweating campaign was already stimulating increased union activity throughout the industry. The quarrel itself with its attendant publicity and a protracted law-suit over possession of the union premises and funds provided an example of the public relations doctrine that any publicity is better than none at all. In spite of the loss of the West End members, within six months the Amalgamated Society recorded an increase in total membership of 1,091 and a permanent fund which was once more approaching the £10,000 mark. The London membership was only 169 less, so that new recruits had almost exactly balanced the losses.

Most of these newcomers appear to have been Jewish workers. The spread of Jewish workshops from the East End of London to the west had been frowned on by the Amalgamated Society since this meant a transfer of work from the tailoring shops to the sub-contracting workshops. As part of the general attempt to isolate the West End branch and later the London Society of Tailors and Tailoresses, the Amalgamated Society had been changing from an attitude of veiled anti-semitism to one of welcoming Jewish men and women into its ranks. The quarrel with the West End branch thus had the beneficial result of accelerating the entry of Jewish workers into an organisation which had hitherto been largely anti-Jewish. So long as the Jews continued to live in closed communities, mostly unable to communicate or receive ideas except in Yiddish, they were liable to fall under the sway of any orator who could speak their own language. Anarchists and other revolutionaries were responsible for some of the mushroom unions which sprang up and had a brief but startling growth before collapsing after a futile strike. It was this kind of organisation which gave the Jewish trade unionists the reputation among other clothing workers of being 'strike-happy'.

Two main Jewish unions did survive and grow. In Leeds the Amalgamated Jewish Tailors' Machinists and Pressers Trade Union, which had been formed in 1893 with about 100 members, had more than 1,200 members by the turn of the century. In London the London Jewish Tailors' was the longer lived. Both survived until they were absorbed in the first big amalgamation of clothing unions in 1915.

The position of the Jewish trade unionist in the industry was discussed by Emmanuel Shinwell in a letter from the Glasgow branch of the Amalgamated Union of Clothiers' Operatives to the union journal published in September 1909. Mr Shinwell's comments are all the more valuable in that he was writing as a Jew, and that his own turbulent early life showed he was not lacking in pugnacity, while his subsequent career demonstrated the high quality of his intellect. 'Organisations of Jewish workers have sprung into existence in as little time as it takes to tell, and have as quickly died away. Now, right here, let me say that independent organisations composed exclusively of Jewish workers, whether as a means of improving conditions of trade, raising wages, or even maintaining the *status quo* are absolutely futile. Their methods of fighting, their ignorance of trade union law, the social relationship between master and man, and the independent position of the small Jewish employer, all serve to render the efforts of Jewish trade unionists to improve their position of no avail.

'Perhaps the most insuperable obstacle in the way of effective organisation among them is their lack of discipline and trade union principle. They are for ever wanting to strike against some employer about the most trifling details and if, as often happens, the executive are opposed to such a course, then the organisation is as good as dead.

'Now, the question arises, what is to be the future of Jewish organisation in this country? Is the outlook favourable or gloomy? Does there appear to be any possibility of effective organisation among them? My personal opinion is that the immediate future of Jewish organisation is extremely unfavourable. The Jewish worker is passing through a process of trade union education and experience which will eventually teach him that his emancipation will come not through organisations based on racial sentiment, but from combinations of working men, whether they be Gentile or Jew, based on fellowship and human understanding in which the barriers of racial and religious intolerance have been transcended. But that time is not yet.

'The time will come when through the exigencies of the industrial system and bitter experience they will gladly seek our help. When it does, I trust that the hand of fellowship will be extended so that Jew and Gentile may be able to work together for the emancipation of the human race.'

Looking back more than fifty years later, Mr Shinwell's strictures on his own race seem indeed harsh; indeed it seems incredible that the Jewish issue should have aroused such bitterness. But the comments must be seen against the background of the early decades of the century, with their conditions of degradation and exploitation, when charity and tolerance were hardly the characteristic features of the age.

The Jews had been washed up like castaways on our shores by a wave of intolerance and oppression which has only been exceeded by the brutalities of Nazi Germany. They sought first a foothold on an alien land and secondly a living. Only thereafter could they be expected to throw off, and that gradually, their exaggerated exclusiveness bred by years of ostracism. They had to learn English before they could begin to learn English ways.

It will be noticed that while Mr Shinwell was opposed to the incorporation of purely Jewish unions as branches of his own Amalgamated Union of Clothiers' Operatives he was strongly in favour of accepting individual Jewish members working in the factories. This was in accord with the general policy pursued by AUCO of accepting all clothing workers into its ranks. The union benefited, like all others, from the nationwide anti-sweating campaign and also by the increase in factory production taking place at the same time. Its membership, which had been around 1,400 or 1,500 in the first five years of the century, leaped in two years to 2,500 (including 600 women) by 1907. From then on it was by far the fastest growing organisation in the industry and by 1915 had 12,000 members of whom two-thirds were women.

The passing of the Trade Board Act in 1909 gave fresh encouragement to workers to join their unions, so that their representatives on the employees' side of the board could speak with stronger voices. Union organisation was particularly poor in the south and west of England and it was necessary for the Board of Trade to select workers' representatives for the district committees. The south and west countries had long been the despair of trade union organisers, and, in passing, we may refer to some of the trials and tribulations which beset union officials in the early part of the century.

Some of the reports that appeared in the *Journal* show that the problems of apathy, poor attendance at branch meetings and turnover in membership are by no means a product of the post-second world war period.

In 1904 we find a letter in the *Journal* asking 'what could be done to arouse the members generally from their slumber or stupor? That very little interest is taken in the society's affairs may be seen at our quarterly meetings – the poor attendance of the members. Something is needed to rally the members and to create, or rather revive, the old enthusiasm . . . '

The reports from the south of England were the most discouraging. Messrs Rowlerson and Roland reported that 'for many years the south has been one of the worst organised parts of the country . . . Repeated attempts have been made to put new life into the movement, but with no lasting effect.' 'The tailors in the city of Bath,' according to one report in 1907, 'are as much outside the labour movement as if they were anchored where the east and west meet in the Pacific Ocean.' There were no branches in Chatham, Rochester or Gillingham, and Maidstone had only nineteen members. 'Kent may be the garden of England . . . it may be called a barren wilderness so far as we are concerned,' ran one lament.

Portsmouth was described as 'always a very difficult town to deal with,' despite 'a sympathetic press and an active trades council.' Against this, encouraging results were recorded from membership drives in Oxford, where the numbers increased from fifty to 145 in six months, Winchester and Basingstoke. Windsor was said to be 'a good town for the journeyman tailor,' but 'the sweater has got the thin end of the wedge in, and we had the opportunity of watching the fat-bellied individuals with their wives, combining business with pleasure.'

The time-honoured lament, 'Somehow the trade union movement does not appeal to young men as it used to do in the old days,' frequently appeared in the pages of the *Journal*, which was full of good advice. One letter suggesting that branch meetings should be made 'more than formal gatherings where balance sheets are passed and offices left to the few who are willing to take them' has a particularly familiar ring.

Some branches sought to enliven their proceedings with entertainment. Smoking concerts proved a successful and popular means of attracting members. The Norwich branch secretary reported that forty to fifty new members were recruited as a result of a smoker.

For good measure he included the programme of this 'very enjoyable evening' in his report. Mr H. Green sang *The anchor's weighed,* and Mr G. Dixon *Black-eyed Susan.* Mr H. Plunket rendered *Granny only left me the old armchair,* while Mr W. Lemon drew an encore with his *Star of my soul.*

By contrast with the somewhat gloomy news from the south of England, it is good to read that a large audience of women decided in November 1907 to form a female branch of the AST & T in Glasgow. 'The more revolutionary points of the speeches were met with spontaneous applause, and the eager attention of the women indicated a strength of character that will make their union a success.'

By 1910 the society claimed to have some 12,000 members organised in 280 branches. Bath, we note, still had only nine members, but Manchester, Liverpool, London, Newcastle, Belfast and Dublin Emerald showed strengths of 350 and more. Its peak had been reached in 1891, when it had 16,629 members. The society's income in 1910 was put at just under £17,500, raised mainly from contributions; main items of expenditure were sick, unemployment and funeral pay, with nearly £2,000 on strikes and lockouts, the largest amount since 1906. The general secretary, it may be noted, was paid at the rate of £39 per quarter.

While the AST & T was thus declining in membership and directing all its efforts to holding on to those it had, the young, rival AUCO was forging ahead in Leeds. The benefit of organisation was vividly demonstrated, when the Leeds branch negotiated its own considerably higher minimum rates with the Leeds employers, soon after the trade board rates came into force. This Leeds agreement, reached in April 1913, was a major landmark in the history of the clothing workers. It provided for rates as high as $9\frac{1}{2}$d an hour for men (formerly $8\frac{1}{4}$d an hour) and limited the working week to forty-nine and a half hours. It set a pattern of wage rates which was copied wherever the unions were strong enough to negotiate it, and it is significant that during that year 17,433 clothing workers won wage increases totalling £2,350 a week, six times as much as had been conceded in 1912.

The trade board could ensure minimum standards around the subsistence level. Only trade union action could achieve a living wage. The lesson was learned in Leeds at any rate. Men and women flocked to join the union and two years later, AUCO claimed 4,000 men and 8,000 women in its ranks.

At this time the national pattern of trade unionism among the clothing workers was somewhat confused.

Though the unions fell into three recognisable groups, the craftsmen, the factory workers and the Jewish workers, there was never any clear demarcation between them. A life-long member of the AST & T leaving a tailoring shop to take a better job as a skilled worker in a factory would retain his membership and if he were an active unionist would recruit new members among those working with him. Jewish women working in the east end of London, finding themselves excluded from the all-male Jewish unions, formed a branch of the AST & T. Having established itself in the east end factories, AUCO followed the westward movement of the workshops and, true to its policy of universality, began to organise cutters in the West End tailoring shops. The breach between the Amalgamated Society and its Scottish counterpart, the Scottish Operative Tailors' and Tailoresses', had never been healed, and the Amalgamated Society had its own branches north of the Tweed. In the border country there was already a long history of 'body-snatching' between the two unions when AUCO too began to organise in Scotland.

The relations between the Amalgamated Society and the breakaway London Society of Tailors and Tailoresses were understandably bad. The two bodies jointly negotiated with the London employers but, as conditions favourable to union growth developed, the newer society sought opportunities to expand at the expense of the older.

The London Society led a move for a revision of the London log and an increase of 2d an hour in advance of any award from the Tailoring Board to other sections of the industry. Without attempting serious negotiation, it called out its members at the first rejection of its proposals by the employers in

Dame Anne Loughlin

John Newton succeeds Dame Anne Loughlin as general secretary, 1953

1912, without prior consultation with the AST & T. The executive of the Amalgamated Society sent instructions from Manchester that its members should not join the strike and the branch committees in London endorsed this instruction. Nevertheless AST & T members joined unofficially in the strike which was not called off until the London Society's funds were exhausted six weeks later.

The London Society had thus unhappily proved Terence Flynn's prophecy that it could not hope to fight its own battles successfully, even though it had had the unofficial support of many of its fellow unionists. Rather than accept the loss of face which would have followed the logical next step – re-union with the Amalgamated Society – the impoverished London Society opened negotiations with AUCO for a merger.

The idea of an amalgamation of all the unions in the industry was already in the air. The General Federation of Trade Unions suggested such an amalgamation in 1911 and as a result of a conference at Nottingham in March 1912 agreement in principle on a nationwide merger was reached. The protracted negotiations which then began were suspended on the outbreak of war, but were resumed later.

The years from 1905 onwards, when conditions were favourable to the growth of unionism, coincided with fundamental changes in the pattern of the clothing industry which jumbled members of all the different unions together in the same factories, workshops and tailoring shops. Incensed by the recruitment of craftsmen into AUCO, the AST & T retorted by recruiting factory workers and had some success in towns like Huddersfield, Kettering and Plymouth.

Meanwhile general unions were busy recruiting members. J. J. Mallon recalled to us an incident when he wrote on behalf of AUCO to Ernest Bevin complaining that he was recruiting clothing workers along with dockers and transport workers into his Bristol union, and received the short reply, 'Who the hell do you think you are?'

The keen competition for new members thus transcended the artificial boundaries between the different unions which events were making yearly more artificial. This led to bitter recrimination, to slanderous personal attacks between local leaders and to deliberate refusals to co-operate when it was felt that united action might be of benefit to an 'enemy' organisation.

Chapter Sixteen/Enter Andrew Conley

CONLEY SUCCEEDS JOSEPH YOUNG AS AUCO SECRETARY; HIS BACKGROUND
AND CHARACTER; MOVES TO RECRUIT WOMEN; REFUSAL OF AMALGAMATED
SOCIETY TO CONSIDER MERGER; FORMATION OF UNITED GARMENT WORKERS
TRADE UNION 1915; FAILURE OF DUBLIN STRIKE AND DECLINE OF AST & T
UGW MERGER WITH SCOTLAND TO FORM TAILORS' AND GARMENT WORKERS
TRADE UNION 1920; ITS AIMS AND STRENGTH

The angry quarrels and widespread mutual poaching of mem
bers mentioned in the last chapter are unedifying to read in
detail and might well be omitted altogether from the story of
the clothing workers' unions since they occupied little more
than a decade in a history covering centuries. Nevertheless, to
gloss over this unhappy interlude would not only leave the story
incomplete but would detract something from the glowing
triumph of all those who worked for and achieved unity. It
would be to tell the story of an arduous ascent to the summit
of a storm-wracked Everest in terms of a summer's afternoon
stroll up a hillside.

From the outside J. J. Mallon watched these struggles with
patience and understanding but with a firm determination to
do all in his power to end them. He could claim a large share in
the credit for the establishment of the trade boards and was a
member of all the first thirteen boards set up under the act.

Joseph Young had taken over the general secretaryship of
AUCO in 1895 and from this commanding position had nursed
the infant union through its early troubles until it was firmly
established with some 4,000 members at the time of the first

Tailoring Trade Board. By then he was in failing health and slowly going blind. Though he bore his afflictions with fortitude and had earned his not inconsiderable niche in the history of his union, he was no longer capable of tackling the vast new problems and responsibilities of his job. He proved no match either for Terence Flynn and Gurney Rowlerson of the Amalgamated Society nor for the huge-framed, heavily bearded David Little and others on the employers' side of the trade board.

Noticing a letter in the press which seemed to reflect on his own capacity and good intentions, Mallon sought out the author intending to demand an explanation and withdrawal. The author proved to be Andrew Conley, one of AUCO's organisers, who was like himself born in England of Irish parents. What had promised to be a stiff encounter dissolved into warm friendliness and from this meeting there developed a fruitful partnership which was to be of inestimable benefit to the clothing workers.

Mallon found in Andrew Conley a man already imbued with the same ideas and vision as his own, and with an enormous capacity for putting them into practical effect. With Conley in charge of the union's affairs Mallon was able to follow his own natural bent, that of 'back-room boy' to the union. His high intelligence, broad vision and capacity for public affairs were always at the disposal of the organisation; respected and consulted by cabinet ministers, civil servants and others of the Establishment, he wielded an immense influence behind the scenes while Conley devoted himself to the task of organisation in the field.

Andrew Conley was one of those rich, full characters about whom legends are told even while they are living. Stories abound of the rollicking pugnacity with which he sometimes conducted his meetings. There was the stormy meeting in Whitechapel when he stopped short and slowly peeled off his jacket before saying to the hecklers 'I'll take on any half dozen of you, and if you haven't the spirit to come up here, I'll come down and wipe the floor with you.' There was the time when he was arrested while talking to a factory gate meeting in Belfast and so charmed the sergeant in charge of the police station that he led Conley back to the meeting and re-opened it himself by telling the men to join the union 'and not keep the gintleman here tellin' ye what ye ought to have the sinse to do without

being told.' There was the rough encounter with the proprietor of a Bristol factory who entered his work-room to find
Conley addressing his idle workers. To his astonished demand
'What the hell is going on here?' he got the swift and uncom-
promising reply, 'This is a meeting of the union and you bloody-
well hop it.'

Born in 1882 of Irish parents who had settled in Leeds,
Conley spent his early years in Yorkshire before being sent to
Ireland to study for the Roman Catholic priesthood. His studies
were interrupted when his father died and he returned to Leeds
to help support his mother and seven younger brothers and sisters. He found himself out of work at the age of seventeen when
the Boer war broke out, and although under age he enlisted in
the 17th Lancers. He was soon under embarkation orders for
South Africa. A typical Conley story is told of the ceremonial
embarkation parade. The Lancers' own bay horses had been
decimated by illness and they were compelled to borrow
mounts from the Scots Greys. Rather than present a piebald
appearance in the ranks, Conley's troop dyed their borrowed
greys with Condy's fluid so as to show a less uneven appearance
on the parade.

In South Africa his troop was ambushed and captured in a
defile by a Boer commando. The first thing the ragged tatter-
demalion guerillas did after disarming their prisoners was to
demand their trousers as replacements for their own worn
out clothing. This was in accordance with the rough and ready
rules of war operating in the campaign and it was not considered undignified to submit to superior force in this particular.
But when a fully armed Boer commando began to rummage in
Conley's knapsack in search of further spoil Conley went for
him bare-fisted. He might well have been shot out of hand but
for the appearance of an officer on the scene who ordered the
contestants apart and demanded an explanation.

Said Conley, pointing to his adversary, 'That son-of-a-gun
has already pinched my trousers and now he's pawing over my
love-letters.' The officer returned the knapsack with a rebuke
to his own soldier and apologised on behalf of the Boers for the
discourtesy. He introduced himself as Jan Smuts and sealed the
apology with a handshake. Many years later Andrew Conley
was to meet General Smuts in London and recall the incident.

By nature physically strong, Conley was toughened by his

wartime experiences in the veldt. On demobilisation he returned to Leeds where he had begun as a clothing worker
before enlisting and took up his old trade.

Recognising that under the factory system women would
play a predominant part in the industry, he saw that unless
they were organised equally with men they would form a
reserve of exploitable labour which could always be used to
keep standards down. In his first shop he therefore set out from
the beginning to bring all the women into the union. Where he
differed strikingly from many other trade unionists was in believing that women were quite capable of organising themselves
and throwing up their own leaders.

Women were as yet only on the threshold of emancipation.
The Victorian myth still persisted of the frail vaporous 'miss'
unable to understand the intricacies of a man's world and too
weak to undertake burdens beside which childbearing and the
management of a household were in reality comparatively light.
With notable exceptions, too many women accepted this
estimate of their own capacities.

To Andrew Conley must be given the credit of creating
self-confidence in a host of young women who by themselves
would never have dreamed of becoming unionists, much less
union organisers. By a mixture of bullying, Irish blarney,
charm and sheer inspiration he persuaded them they could not
only do the job but do it far better than most men.

He lacked the polished urbanity and controlled lucidity in
debate of Terence Flynn of whom it was said 'to see him bow
and get a chair for a lady was to enjoy a lesson in deport-
ment from a master of elegant good manners.' Instead, with his
warm deep voice lilting in Irish cadences, he could rouse and
inspire a mass audience to a pitch surpassed by few in an age
of huge public meetings and superlative oratory.

The impact made by Andrew Conley on those around him can
be judged by the address made by Herbert Tracey, an official
of the TUC at the memorial service after Conley had died.
Tracey was himself warm-hearted and affectionate, but after a
lifetime spent in devoted service to the trade union movement,
he had few illusions and small reverence for some of the leaders
of the movement. His tribute is for that reason all the more
moving in its sincerity.

'He gave to me, for more than thirty years, a full measure of his confidence, his kindness and affection; and the man of whom I speak is one who loved me and for whom I had a brother's love. What we shall remember most often, we who knew him in close personal association, was the strength and depth of his affectionate nature. He was generous and kindly almost to a fault.

'He gave himself freely in his friendships; perhaps too freely at times, some may say – but those who say this do not know, as we who loved him knew, how much of it was the outflow of his good will and his happiness in good companionship.

'He was a man of many moods, but there was a transfusion of gay and happy laughter in them, and he was rarely downcast and then not for long.

'Loyalty in his friendships and in personal associations was a manifestation of the deeper loyalty he held towards the ideals of the movement he served throughout his working life. The strongest fibres of his complex character were woven into his trade union faith.

'Without professing any formal religious attachments he was essentially a man of faith. He had a missionary zeal for the cause to which he devoted his considerable intellectual qualities and powers of organisation and leadership. He was by nature a leader, and early in his life he found the cause which gave him both a faith in which he could believe and a service he was eminently qualified to give.'

If Conley had been gifted with second sight enabling him to foresee the war and its consequences, he could not have chosen better means of strengthening his union, than the emphasis he had given on recruiting women and on encouraging them to play their full part in union organisation.

From its small beginnings AUCO's membership rose rapidly in the early days of the war and was soon in sight of equality with the old-established AST & T. The wage fixing authority of the trade boards was supplemented in 1916 by the Committee of Production which had power to make awards binding on both sides. The stronger the unions were, the more powerfully could their case be made out to these authorities and the better the opportunities for direct negotiation with the employers. Circumstances thus reinforced the cogent arguments for a merging of interests and his own dynamic personality marked Andrew Conley out as the obvious leader of a new amalgamation.

These moves were, however, unacceptable to the Amalgamated Society which refused to join the negotiations when they were resumed early in 1915. The society itself was prospering as a result of the war. Though not making the same headway in the factories as AUCO, it was nevertheless having considerable success in founding new factory branches all over the country. Its leaders were well versed in the history and traditions of the craft. They mistook the significance of AUCO and saw it as one more of those mushroom growths which had flowered in the past only to wither and die. Their own society seemed to be embarked on a new stage of steady development which would ultimately make it all-embracing. They therefore stood out against the merger proposals while continuing the policy of 'reprisals' by recruiting non-craftsmen.

Cautious and conservative in its attitude to industrial action, the Amalgamated Society was becoming more conservative in its political outlook. Where it had once stood in the forefront of the movement for political reform and had welcomed the birth of the Labour party, it gradually developed a lukewarm attitude towards left-wing policies. The officials of the rival AUCO stood for militant trade union and political action to achieve a fundamental change in the whole structure of society. Political differences helped to widen the rift between the two organisations.

These major differences between the two largest unions in the industry served a useful purpose in educating masses of workers throughout the country. In a situation in which unity was imperative, the rank and file trade unionist had little doubt as to the correct course to follow. There was a decisive swing towards AUCO. The merger negotiations once reopened were quickly brought to a successful conclusion in 1915 with the amalgamation of several smaller unions under the banner of the newly named United Garment Workers' Trade Union.

This amalgamation was, of course, far less than the most ardent visionaries could have wished. It was nevertheless a gigantic leap forward. For the first time elements of all the diverse sections of the industry were gathered in a single organisation. To the factory workers already enrolled in AUCO were added the former members of the Amalgamated Society's West End Branch which had become the London Society of Tailors and Tailoresses. Jewish workers in factory, workshop and tailoring shops were brought in through the Leeds Amalgamated Jewish Tailors, Machinists and Pressers and the London Jewish Tailors. Other smaller societies like the London and Provincial Cutters and the Waterproof Garment Workers (which later defected) lent support to the new union's claim to universality, embracing Jew and Gentile, craftsman, factory worker and homeworker without distinction of age or sex.

The United Garment Workers' Trade Union began with a membership of 8,000 men and 13,000 women – almost twice the total membership of AUCO – and in wartime conditions of full employment and rising wages it found little difficulty in enrolling new members. By 1919 it had absorbed a number of other unions, the largest of which was the National Amalgamated Shirt, Collar and Jacket Workers' Society with 6,000 members, and had reached a record membership of 79,000 women and 23,000 men. Though the old Amalgamated Society also expanded it never had more than 30,000 members.

The Amalgamated Society of Tailors and Tailoresses had a long-established hold on the handicraft tailors in Ireland and during the war had considerable success in recruiting hitherto unorganised factory workers and even homeworkers. It was spectacularly successful in the north, particularly among the shirt and collar workers. Its membership in Ireland rose to about 12,000, of whom the vast majority were factory workers. In Derry alone it had 5,000 factory members.

The newly formed United Garment Workers' began to recruit in the same field. Its small branch of 200 in Derry was called out on strike in support of a wage increase of 15s a week. The Amalgamated Society executive considered the claim unreasonable and refused to sanction strike action by its own 5,000 members in support, though many of them took unofficial action. The employers retorted with a lockout and switched their urgent work to branch factories in England and Scotland. Troops were called in to deal with the rioting which followed the lockout and the strike was defeated.

The Amalgamated Society spent no less than £4,000 from its permanent fund in supporting those of its members who were locked out. The failure to take any positive attitude towards the wage claim and the refusal to give grants to those who had joined unofficially in the strike destroyed confidence in the Society in spite of this heavy expenditure. The Amalga-

mated Society in Ireland disintegrated and left the United
Garment Workers as the only union organising factory workers.
Its strength reduced to one tenth, the AST & T could in future
claim no more than 1,200 handicraft tailors spread throughout
Ireland in small branches.

In Scotland the Amalgamated Society had never been able
to come to terms with the Scottish Operative Tailors and
Tailoresses, and the two unions were in open competition for
precisely the same membership. The Scottish Society grew at
the expense of the Manchester-based Amalgamated until its
membership reached 8,000. At this point, in 1920, the Scottish
tailors decided to merge with the United Garment Workers.

The new body was called the Tailors' and Garment Workers'
Trade Union, and became by far the strongest organisation ever
known in the clothing industry. It was firmly established as the
senior partner and its creation settled once and for all the question of whether or not all clothing workers should be organised
on an industrial rather than a craft basis. There could be no
looking back.

The Amalgamated Society, which had inherited the aspirations of those rowdy young men in their hostel in Garlykhythe
and had played so important a part in the subsequent history
and struggles not only of the tailors but of the trade union
movement as a whole had now outlived its usefulness. It was
no longer in the van of progress but was a stumbling block in
the path of unity and strength. It was only a question of time
before it too would be swallowed by the young and virile union.

The aims of the Tailors' and Garment Workers' Trade
Union were all-embracing. Its rules provided for the regulation
of apprentices and the establishment of a fair wage and uniform
hours and conditions of work. In addition to Friendly Society
benefits there was a fund for the education of members based
on 'independent working class principles' and a political fund.
Though it could not claim direct linear descent from the earlier
pioneers of trade unionism in the tailoring trade, it thus took
over their work of education and propaganda which the
Amalgamated Society was no longer either able or willing to
perform.

Its chief strongholds were in Leeds, where it had 7,000
members at the time of its formation, London with about 5,000,
Manchester with over 4,000, Londonderry and Glasgow with

3,000 each, Bristol with about 2,000 and substantial membership in Wigan, Hebden Bridge and Edinburgh. Industrially,
its strength lay in the heavy clothing and shirt and collar
sections; its organisation among workers in the women's clothing trade was still pathetically weak.

Chapter Seventeen/Inter-war Readjustment

JEWISH WORKERS REMAIN ALOOF; JACOB FINE AND THE UNITED LADIES'
TAILORS' AND MANTLEMAKERS' UNION; EFFECT OF SLUMP AND WAGE CUTS;
DIVISIONS BETWEEN LONDON AND LEEDS; THE GENERAL STRIKE OF 1926;
ANNE LOUGHLIN ORGANISES 'LIMITED STRIKES'

Apart from the Amalgamated Society and the small Water-proof Garment Workers' Union which first joined and then defected from the new merger, one other group of workers remained outside. These were Jewish workers employed in making women's coats and costumes in London.

Although the Tailors' and Garment Workers' union had embraced the two largest Jewish unions, one in Leeds and the other in London, there was still considerable opposition among Jewish workers. The TUC had supported the moves to restrict the entry of aliens into Britain on the grounds that this would protect the jobs of native-born workers. To most of the Jewish refugee community this seemed a gross betrayal of all the ideals of international brotherhood for which the British trade union movement was supposed to stand.

A Jewish Workers' Defence Committee, formed to resist the campaign for the restriction of immigrants, helped to reinforce at once the sense of isolation and the solidarity among Jewish workers in the tailoring and other trades. Among the immigrants were political refugees linked with the various revolutionary parties of eastern Europe who did not accept the 'reformist' policies of the TUC and the Labour party.

The influx of refugees which had been reduced to a trickle

by the Aliens Act was cut off completely on the outbreak of the first world war. Many of the sons and daughters of the earlier refugees did not take up tailoring. Instead of providing a constant supply of new skilled labour and of new trainees, the Jewish community thus became a dwindling instead of a constantly increasing source of skilled manpower.

The growth of the factory system for making men's clothing at the expense of workshop production in the larger centres such as London and Leeds threw the workers together in a way which compelled them to recognise their common interests irrespective of their religious or other differences. The defence campaign launched by the Jews had brought about the amalgamation of many small Jewish societies into the two large groups in London and Leeds with branches elsewhere in the country. The system under which these men and women were working made it possible for the London and Leeds Jewish unions to join the United Garment Workers' Union.

There was less reason for those engaged in making women's clothing to follow the same line. The more rapid changes in women's fashions made it impossible to supply this market by means of the long runs of identical garments which were typical of factory production for men's wear. The smaller workshop with an efficient system of sub-dividing work between the operatives was ideally suited to short run production and quite sudden switches to a new line at the dictates of fashion.

These were Jewish workshops at first confined largely to the East End of London but later spreading westwards. The workers in them were slowest to become assimilated to the ideas of the country of their adoption and remained for many years the last strongholds of isolationism among the Jewish workers. They retained their close cultural, linguistic and religious relationships with the members of their community who had joined the Garment Workers' Union. Both inside and outside the Garment Workers' Union there were Jewish trade unionists who were open to the influence of Jewish isolationist ideas and of the revolutionary propaganda which permeated the Jewish Workers' defence committee.

Among the considerable figures in the refugee movement was Rudolph Rocker, a German who had been brought up as a Roman Catholic and who had come to Britain as a political refugee. A powerful orator and notable propagandist, he exercised a great influence over the refugee population as editor of the *Workers' Friend*. Throwing himself wholeheartedly into the cause of the Jewish immigrants, he linked with various anarchist and other groups in a campaign for social revolution.

Among those attracted by the teaching of Rudolph Rocker was Jacob Fine, the youngster we first met making friends with his legendary 'London bobby' and who now, having learned his trade, was inspired to work for more stable and consistent trade union activity among his fellow Jewish workers. When he first joined the London Ladies Tailors', Machinists' and Pressers' Trade Union in 1912 there were, as he expressed it later, 'as many unions as workers.'

Fine's own union, which later became known as the United Ladies' Tailors and Mantle Makers Union, gradually absorbed many of those Jewish ladies' tailors and mantle workers who still maintained their solutions and ideas. After acting as secretary of the Friendly Society section he became general secretary of the union in 1918 when it had a membership of some 3,000.

The earlier meetings of the union had been conducted in Yiddish and it was not until younger members complained they could not understand what was going on that records began to be kept in English as well. Only in the 1920s did Yiddish die out as the official language.

The Jewish union presented a curious spectacle of reactionary orthodoxy leavened with a yeast of revolutionary Marxism.

The organisation combined trade union and benefit society activities with the old call-house system. Its offices were in the loft over a stable housing a dozen or so horses which formed part of an old coaching inn at Black Lion Yard in Whitechapel. Climbing the rickety wooden steps members would congregate in the loft, eating black bread, pickled herring and onions and whiling away the time with interminable games of dominoes as they waited for work. Their domino teams were in the championship class.

An employer would enter the yard and shout the number and kind of worker he wanted. A mad stampede down the stairs would bring a jostling crowd of members into the yard surrounding the employer and begging to be taken on. He would often savour his power by humming and hawing, appearing to make up his mind and then changing it, and then make some new proviso which shaved a few pence off the prospective earnings. The unsuccessful would return to the loft and new games of dominoes until the next employer was pleased to present himself and repeat the degrading performance.

In the days of its greatest expansion during the war the Amalgamated Society itself recruited about sixty men working in the East End ladies' tailoring shops, but Gurney Rowlerson as general secretary found their habit of striking without authority so intolerable that he asked Fine to accept them into the rival union. There was some difficulty in that, as members of the Amalgamated Society, they were entitled to higher benefits than they would have received as new recruits to the Jewish union. The Amalgamated Society decided to hand over sufficient funds for the Jewish union to maintain the benefits, rather than keep these turbulent members in its own organisation. So far from meeting the challenge of the rival Tailors' and Garment Workers' Union, the Amalgamated Society was beginning to abandon its own expansionist aims and to withdraw into its own shell.

Pondering the problems of organisation facing him, Fine had no doubts about where the future of his union should lie. There is an old Jewish proverb, 'Better be the tail of a lion than the head of a fox,' and he had long since arrived at the same conclusion as Emmanuel Shinwell, that separate and exclusive Jewish unions could never offer real protection to their members.

It says much for his diplomatic skill and tenacity of purpose that he was able to keep on friendly personal terms with the leaders of the Amalgamated Society, the Tailors' and Garment Workers' and prominent members of the TUC and Labour party like Ben Tillett, Ben Turner and George Lansbury while his own union executive was following a policy of equivocation and delay in the face of strong pressure for a new amalgamation.

Like most others, this Jewish union had prospered during the war years. It had been supported with an advance of £10,000 from the General Federation of Trade Unions in a partially successful strike for an eight-hour day in 1918 and was able to open its own newly built headquarters in Great Garden Street (now Greatorex Street) in 1921, built by the sale of bricks to members and sympathisers at £3 a time.

So long as the Amalgamated Society refused to join with the Tailors and Garment Workers there was some justification for

he Jewish union executive's refusal to lose its own identity by
oining either. This attitude was well understood by the TUC
leaders who allowed the union to affiliate as a separate body on
the understanding that negotiations for a merger between all
three bodies should take place. After three or four years of
fruitless discussion the TUC finally disaffiliated it.

While these moves were taking place, the unions were faced
with serious and disturbing problems as a result of the return
of millions of men from the forces to civilian life. Even during
the boom period union membership fell as women left the
industry. In spite of the new amalgamations with the Scottish
Tailors and the Belfast Shirt Makers, the Tailors' and Garment
Workers' Union had a net loss of 25,000 members between
1919 and the end of 1920.

The losses of the Amalgamated Society were less because its
proportion of women members was so much smaller. The all-
male Jewish union showed a slight increase. Even in conditions
of nationwide boom, the Tailors' and Garment Workers' union
was compelled to redouble its educational and recruiting cam-
paigns, and in spite of this extra effort membership was still
declining. The batches of new younger women coming into the
industry were beneficiaries of the fight for better wages and
conditions which had been waged by their elder sisters and
mothers. They had as yet insufficient industrial experience to
realise the benefits of trade unionism.

The situation was serious rather than desperate. Several
years of patient devotion to organisation were needed to stem
the decline in membership and to rebuild the union's strength.
The trouble was due to the vast redeployment of the country's
labour force in a very short period of time. Andrew Conley as
general secretary and Anne Loughlin as national organiser had
behind them a union which was quite capable of tackling a
problem even of this immense size. Both travelled the country
indefatigably, reconstituting branch and shop committees
which had lost their key members, and encouraging young
girls to take on responsibilities they would never have dreamed
of undertaking on their own initiative.

The economists tell us that between 1918 and 1924 money
wages and the cost of living kept broadly in step, so that there
was no loss in purchasing power. Thereafter wages did not fall
as quickly as the cost of living so that over the whole period

from the end of the first war to the outbreak of the second, there was an increase in real wages of no less than fifteen per cent. These figures were not appreciated at the time by the unemployed trying to live on the dole nor by those in jobs who found their money wages cut while productivity was rising.

When the slump came the trade boards dealing with the clothing industry decided on decreases in the minimum rates. Though the union representatives had fought against any reductions, they were outvoted and the decisions became those of the boards as a whole. However powerful the economic arguments may have been, this cut in money wages after 1921 did not commend itself to the workers on whom it was imposed. Even those who were prepared to distinguish between real wages and money wages saw little point in the argument that since prices were falling, less money would buy the same amount of goods. They did not accept that they had reached an ideal state in 1918 and that their standard of living should be pegged at that level for evermore. On the contrary, they felt justified in seeking a higher standard.

Apart from loss of membership due to unemployment, the unions were now faced with resignations from those still in work who felt themselves betrayed by organisations which had been represented on the body cutting their wages. Being by far the largest union, the Tailors' and Garment Workers' suffered the greatest decline in membership from all these causes. Its peak membership of 102,000 in 1919 had been reduced to 45,000 in 1923. In those four years 9,000 men and 48,000 women were lost.

It was in Leeds, the headquarters of the Tailors' and Garment Workers' Union, that membership fell least and that the best figures for new recruitment were reached. Although London remained the centre for the highest quality clothing and had far more workers engaged in the industry, Leeds managed to provide a sounder and more solid base of operations for a union which had been founded there and had built so successfully on these foundations. There was a latent feeling of tension between the workers in London – citizens of no mean city – and union headquarters in a distant provincial centre which seemed to be suffering less than its fair share of the general misfortune. This was none the less real for being wholly irrational. For historical reasons most of the union's national officers had entered

the industry in Leeds. Conley, Anne Loughlin, Bernard Sullivan, the London district secretary, were all from Leeds and the
London district organiser Sam Elsbury, who had joined the
union in London, was nevertheless an emigré from Leeds.
There was also resentment when Conley introduced the
vital reform after the 1920 amalgamation of centralising the
union funds under the executive in Leeds. The largest proportion of branch dues went direct to headquarters and the national
executive was responsible for appointing and paying the
salaries of all full-time officers down to branch officials.

The long history of frustration, division and defeat which
we have already outlined is sufficient to justify this policy of
central control, and that by a body which was working for the
industry as a whole rather than for any sectional interest. It was
not an easy lesson for the London branches to learn in a flash.
The sub-divisional workers had been used, as a separate Jewish
union, to dealing with their own financial affairs and to appointing their own officers from among themselves. There was a
feeling of resentment at 'outside interference' from a headquarters thought to be dominated by a quite alien religious and
ethnic group in a provincial city. The fact that the Mantle
Makers still had their 'independence' kept the feeling alive.

The union executive had not sat tamely by while wages were
reduced. Unable to hold the line on the trade boards, it had
willingly supported strike action in London and elsewhere in
the years following the war. This was at a time when widespread attacks on wage levels were being met by industrial
action throughout Britain, culminating in the General Strike of
1926.

Clothing workers were not among those called on by the
TUC to 'cease work as and when required by the General Council'. But the union neither could, nor wished to, stand above the
battle. The whole issue of the *Garment Worker* for May 1926 is
devoted to the General Strike with a statement of the miners'
case, the TUC's declarations and the events of the ten days that
shook the country. The executive opened a fund for assistance
for the miners, to which the members responded with their
traditional generosity, and supported the TUC call for every
trade unionist to pay 1d a day to help the miners. By October,
the union had sent well over £7,000 towards the miners' solidarity fund, mainly collected through branches.

The dispute and its aftermath were to cast a long shadow over the labour movement for many years to come, and the tailors, even if not directly implicated, were inevitably affected, as part and parcel of the wider movement.

The union leaders at the time had their own problems to resolve. Strikes were proving costly and a drain on union funds; the prospect of success at a time when the employers were very much on the offensive and gloating over the 'defeat' of the workers in the General Strike was doubtful, to say the least.

If the union continued the policy of aggressive militancy, each new failure would lead to further disappointments among the rank and file and fresh crops of resignations. This would eat into its financial reserves in order to achieve nothing but a reduction in annual income. On the other hand, a policy of conciliation and conservatism, at a time when money wages were being reduced year by year, would equally lead to a loss of membership as the impression grew among the rank and file that the union was doing nothing to protect their interests.

In this dilemma the union adopted the old tactics of the Amalgamated Society, that of the limited strike. Anne Loughlin would set out from Leeds with simple instructions such as 'strike Leicester'. Her arrival in a town during this period was sufficient warning to the employers for them to call an immediate meeting to plan defensive action. More often than not the national organiser was waiting for them as their meeting broke up.

The group of prosperous-looking business men chatting in the lounge of some hotel or the entrance to the assembly rooms would be faced by all five feet of a slight, severely but stylishly dressed woman, with immaculately groomed fair hair, innocent blue eyes and the complexion of a schoolgirl. The more percipient among them would note the rounded but determined chin and the clear incisive way in which she told them precisely what she intended to do. This was to 'clean up' a given number of the worst establishments. The better employers were told that they could best avoid trouble for themselves by bringing pressure on their fellows.

The chronic shortage of factory and other inspectors made it possible for many employers to evade the provisions of the Trade Board Acts and the various Factories Acts. They could often be brought into line by reports to the appropriate authority.

Anne Loughlin's mother had died when she was twelve and her father survived only four more years. She had a knack of inspiring confidence and loyalty among the women with whom she worked. Her dynamic personality and her gift of lucid explanation in the ordinary language of her fellow workers ensured that any place in which she took a job very quickly became a union shop.

Conley, who had become a full-time organiser in 1909, had already marked her out as an exceptionally able organiser by the time war broke out in 1914 – a couple of months after her twentieth birthday. She became the woman organiser in 1915. Much later, in 1948, she succeeded Andrew Conley as general secretary of the union. She had become a Dame of the Order of the British Empire in 1943, and was the first woman ever to preside over the Trades Union Congress – in the same year.

Throughout the difficult period of post-war readjustment and depression, the union remained militant and aggressive. It certainly did not appear to the leaders of the Amalgamated Society to have become respectable and conservative. From this quarter came such descriptions as 'a mob of ignorant agitators' or 'a pack of hotheads who will bring the industry to no good.' On the other hand the less spectacular, though on the whole more successful, tactics adopted did not meet with universal approval. There were those who held that the mere act of striking, irrespective of whether it led to success or failure, was an essential part of the education of the proletariat in the realities of the class struggle.

Chapter Eighteen/*Failure of a Breakaway*

THE NATIONAL MINORITY MOVEMENT; MOND-TURNER TALKS; REGO STRIKE;
LONDON TRADES COUNCIL INTERVENES; ELSBURY EXPELLED; BREAKAWAY
UNION FORMED — INFLATED MEMBERSHIP FIGURES; POLIKOFF STRIKE; DAVE
COHEN LETTER; UNION FIRMNESS; COLLAPSE OF BREAKAWAY

It is against a background of industrial tension and worsening
relations between employers and workers that we must consider the activities of the Communist-led National Minority
movement during the late 1920s. These were to run counter
to all the long and patient negotiations for greater unity by
leading to a breakaway movement in London.

The London organiser, Sam Elsbury, had been brought to
England by his Russian Jewish parents and began work in a
Leeds tailoring shop at the age of thirteen. The early war years
found him working for a time as a coalminer but he eventually settled in London and took up his old trade of tailoring
once more. Joining the sub-divisional branch of the United
Garment Workers, he became successively chairman of the
branch and then London organiser of the Tailors' and Garment Workers' Union. His political beliefs did not bring him
into conflict with the union official leadership in the early part
of the 1920s. In fact he was the subject of a laudatory profile
in the *Garment Worker* as late as August 1926.

Andrew Conley, though a staunch member of the Labour
party which he regarded as the political wing of the TUC, was
neither anti-Communist nor anti-Russian. His interest was in
building up trade union strength both at home and inter-

nationally. He supported the Anglo-Soviet Trade Union Committee, would have liked to have seen the gap between the Social Democrat and Communist Trade Union Internationals bridged, and worked for a single federation of all clothing workers' unions throughout the world. In these aims he had the broad support of the whole of his union.

The rift came soon after the General Strike and was brought to a head when TUC leaders accepted the employers approach for joint talks on how to improve industrial relations. These were the Mond-Turner talks, begun in January 1928, aimed at substituting industrial collaboration for conflict. There was bitter opposition from the left wing and the Communists who had been building up the National Minority movement as an alternative to the official leadership.

Early in 1928 we find the executive board denouncing the National Minority movement's activities in canvassing support for their own candidates for conference delegates. 'The action of this group is directly contrary to the rules and practice of the union, is in opposition to all recognised methods of conducting trade union business and is against the best interests of our union and the membership generally.'

Elsbury attended the annual Trades Union Congress in September of the same year that the results of the Mond-Turner talks – vague and woolly though they were – were overwhelmingly endorsed. He clashed openly with Conley who, as spokesman for the General Council, obtained Congress recognition of four London trades councils which had been officially endorsed as successors to four councils which had been expelled because they were Communist controlled. One of the expelled trades councils was Bethnal Green, and Sam Elsbury among all his other activities had found time to become its chairman.

One of Elsbury's union duties as London organiser was to further the policy of the closed shop. Shortly after the Trades Union Congress in which he had clashed with his general secretary, one of the largest London clothing factories moved out to bigger premises in Edmonton. There one of the girls refused to pay her union dues and in accordance with union policy a special meeting of union members decided not to work with non-union labour.

They were supported by Elsbury who wrote to the general

secretary at Leeds asking the national executive board to sanction a strike. This was in effect an oblique attack on the authority of the general secretary and of the national executive board. The union had opened negotiations with the Wholesale Clothing Manufacturers' Federation for a new agreement, including discussion of the closed shop. It had previously been agreed between the two bodies that no strike would be called against a Federation member while negotiations were in progress.

Elsbury was well aware of these negotiations and knew that Rego Clothiers Limited were a Federation firm. If the union were to honour its agreements it could not strike Rego. This was a plain fact to Conley and the executive board but Elsbury and some of his colleagues disagreed.

Conley was thus in the right in moving cannily as the Rego dispute developed. He called a meeting of the executive board of the union in London to discuss tactics on Sunday 7th October. Five days before the Rego workers had given Monday 8th October as the deadline on which they would cease work. The executive board had to be assembled from all over the country and its meeting was fixed for the evening. Elsbury was able to move more swiftly. He called a meeting of the Rego workers on the Sunday morning consisting of impressionable girls of anything from fifteen to twenty-one. He had no difficulty in playing on their impatience and obtaining an overwhelming vote to stop work the following morning. This was the decision the executive board had to consider when it met later in the day.

Faced with this open ursurpation of its authority (for the executive alone could sanction a strike) the board could not do other than refuse to endorse this irregular action in breach of its own agreements with the employers. There is no reason to believe that the Rego firm, having just opened a new and expensive plant, would have refused to open negotiations about the employment of non-union labour if it had been approached by union officials. Instead the management were faced with the threat of a strike which they knew would not be supported by the union. Hoping that the response would be poor, they made no move to tackle the problem. On Monday 8th October they found their new plant completely idle.

An unofficial strike over one woman whom the shop stewards and London branch officials could not persuade to join their ranks was not one to capture the public imagination or to excite great sympathy. New grievances were raised which had not been discussed with the management. Among them were that the earnings had been reduced by the introduction of more modern machinery in the new plant and that girls who had worked in the old premises now had to spend extra money on fares to Edmonton and in addition pay for a midday meal since there was not time to get home during the lunch break. That the strike had not been called to remedy these and other quite real grievances was quickly forgotten by observers and commentators.

Once the original cause of the dispute had been successfully blurred, the 'image' of the strike could be projected as a struggle by hundreds of cheerful, enthusiastic young girls demanding justice from intolerable oppression. The London Trades Council was persuaded to support them and gave authority to the London committee of the union to receive financial help from all trade union branches affiliated to the council. The girls put on a brave show and won the hearts of the Londoners in a way reminiscent of the great strike of the match girls in 1889. Singing catchy songs and holding high their banners with the strike slogan 'Stick It,' they paraded the streets of London picketing the Rego shops or marching in procession behind the National Unemployed Workers' Movement band. More than £4,000 was raised through the London Trades Council alone. The London tailors imposed a levy of a shilling in the pound on their own earnings and appealed to union branches throughout the country for support.

A new appeal to the executive board to endorse the strike was rejected, and the November 1928 issue of the *Garment Worker* published the executive's statement in full. Andrew Conley wrote a stiff letter to Elsbury after the board's meeting on 13th October. 'The executive board's considered opinion is that to sanction a withdrawal of labour from a federated firm during the period of negotiations with the Federation would inevitably prejudice the prospects of obtaining a new agreement and would be thereby acting contrary to the instructions and intentions of the general conference.'

The union leaders were then subjected to a barrage of scurrilous attacks from the various Communist party organs which accused them of going 'hat in hand' to the employers. 'Cannot someone kick the executive of the Garment Workers into helping the strikers?' wrote the *Daily Worker*. 'Neither Mr Conley nor the General Council of the TUC have lifted a finger to help the workers. The blunt truth is they want to see this strike defeated because some of the leaders in it are members of the minority movement . . . Demand an end to Mondist recognition.' And so on and so on. The London committee refused to distribute the union journal and issued instead their own leaflet accusing the board of acting as strike-breakers.

Ten days after the strike began, the Rego firm offered to negotiate with the union with the proviso that it would not meet the London officials. The London committee insisted that their officials and a deputation of strikers must join in any talks.

Having first tried to break the strike by sacking its workers and opening its gates to all who were willing to work, the Rego firm issued writs against Bernard Sullivan and Sam Elsbury as London secretary and London organiser and against the union itself, claiming damages for conspiracy and intimidation by the pickets. This attempt to invoke the law against pickets touched the clothing workers on one of their tenderest spots. They could hear Druitt, Lawrence, Shorrocks and the rest turning in their graves! The Leeds branch voted to support the Rego strike and opinion hardened in London against the board.

The deadlock was broken when Mr Justice Maugham, before whom the legal case was to be argued, suggested on 20th December that the parties should settle the dispute in the light of the prevailing Christmas spirit. This gave Alfred Wall, secretary of the London Trades Council, who had made several unsuccessful attempts at mediation, a fresh opportunity and he was able to convene a meeting under his own chairmanship the following day. It was attended by representatives of the employers' federation, the Rego firm and the union's executive board together with Sullivan and Elsbury. The meeting agreed to end the dispute with reinstatement of the strikers and the appointment of a committee to discuss grievances. The terms did not include a closed shop. The legal proceedings were dropped and on Christmas Eve Anne Loughlin and Sam Elsbury led a triumphant march of Rego girls on their way back to work.

The London Trades Council afterwards held a careful inquiry which condemned the London officials for their handling of the whole affair. The executive board held its own inquiry into Elsbury's activities. He had already been warned in August 1927 that he must devote all his time to the union and not associate with any group or section not recognised by the union. Despite this, he accepted nomination as prospective Parliamentary candidate for Southwest Bethnal Green by the local Trades Council and Borough Labour party which had been disaffiliated.

Elsbury was carpeted by the executive on 2nd March 1929 and asked, among other things, to explain his association with the publication *The Red Needle* which was full of attacks on the official leadership. There were many counts in the indictment, but they all added up to one thing: he was attempting to discredit and disrupt the leadership of the union. The executive board decided, on 3rd March, that 'they had no alternative but to terminate his services as fulltime official.' Bernard Sullivan, the London secretary, who had joined in defying the executive, was put on probation and issued a statement refusing to support any breakaway movement.

In March, the London members called a mass meeting at which they decided to form a breakaway union, which they called the United Clothing Workers Union. Later the executive board retaliated by expelling three leaders – Dave Cohen, Dave Gershon and Sam Elsbury.

Union leaders' anger at the tactics of the breakaway rebels as 'disciples of disruption' was reflected in the columns of the *Garment Worker* throughout 1929. At the beginning of the year Conley wrote a firm editorial article under the title 'Discipline' recalling his triple experience as a soldier, an athlete and a trade unionist. 'Discipline is an unpopular word. It is also an unfashionable virtue. There are some trade unionists who actually make a virtue of indiscipline. They consider they have the right to organise minority opinion inside the trade union movement . . . Loyalty is the highest form of discipline . . . '

Conley did not confine his attacks to paper, but his efforts to address meetings were repeatedly frustrated and union officials were howled down in the ensuing months. After one such mass meeting had been broken up, the *Daily Worker* reported that 'several touts of the employers who call themselves trade union leaders were shouted down by East End clothing workers . . . Let the workers all over the country follow the example of the London clothing workers and hound the leaders of the Labour party and the reactionary trade unions off the platform,' it concluded.

These were the tactics with which union leaders had to deal. The breakaway leaders put out highly inflated figures to show their success. They claimed a membership of some 10,000, with 5,000 in London, 3,000 in Leeds and 2,000 in Glasgow. But in both the provincial centres, the union acted swiftly by expelling breakaway leaders, and the movement there withered away very rapidly.

The Communist party had miscalculated badly if it expected a big proportion of the national membership to follow Elsbury. In London, the situation was more serious. The mantle workers contained many Communists and Communist sympathisers, and the old jealousy towards Leeds was still a factor. Even in the capital, however, the new body found itself without financial resources to carry out its self-declared policy of ceaseless activity. One of the first acts of the union executive was to obtain a court ruling to the effect that all funds and property in possession of the parent union on 9th March still belonged to it, so that the breakaway union was forced to live on what it could raise by way of subscription or financial support from outside sources.

The TUC condemned the breakaway, and the London Trades Council followed suit at the instigation of Bernard Sullivan, who had remained at his post with the Tailors' and Garment Workers'. The heavy guns were being moved ponderously but surely into position and the whole movement was preparing to defend itself against the attack launched at the Sixth Congress of the Comintern.

The first and decisive trial of strength arose over a dispute at the London firm of Polikoff Limited, where the breakaway leaders sought recognition for their union. Dave Cohen, formerly London member of the executive board, and one of the breakaway leaders, was shop steward for the cutters in this firm, one of the largest in London, employing some 800 workers. Polikoff had an agreement of some years standing with the Tailors' and Garment Workers' and recognised the union and its shop stewards as negotiators. Elsbury was one of the London officers with whom the firm had been used to deal, and Cohen and the other shop stewards were still performing the same functions. It was only natural to recognise the new union.

Trouble began when one or two vacancies occurred for cutters in the factory. Those who applied had remained loyal to the older union and they were told they must join the union recognised by the management. Bernard Sullivan lodged an immediate protest; Polikoff's had an agreement to employ members of the Tailors' and Garment Workers' and this agreement had not been rescinded. At the same time Sullivan managed to get a circular into the hands of the shop stewards explaining the position.

The employers' federation joined in. Just as the Tailors' and Garment Workers' had been under an obligation to honour their agreement with the federation that they would not strike a federated firm while negotiations were in progress, so now the federation appealed to its own member, Polikoff, to honour their side of the agreement that the federation would not recognise unions unless they were affiliated to the TUC. Polikoff now saw this was a rather more complicated question than the free choice of his own employees to join any union they wished. Exclusive recognition of the United Clothing Workers was withdrawn towards the end of April.

Elsbury thereupon struck Polikoff's on 6th May 1929, demanding 'the same facilities for collecting union subscriptions as existed hitherto,' and promising that strike pay would be forthcoming. The Polikoff firm replied with a notice that it was under obligation to recognise only those unions affiliated to the TUC or sanctioned by it.

Dave Cohen found himself torn by a conflict of loyalties and on the eve of the strike he sent an agonised letter to the Polikoff management which was later published in the *Garment Worker*. In it he said, 'After long consideration I have made up my mind to take a serious step and I am leaving the country. I hope you won't think I am doing this because of the various rumours that are floating about with regard to my personal affairs. I can face them all, but there is one thing I cannot face, and that is to be responsible for losing the good conditions which have prevailed in our factory.

'What I mean is that while we were in the Garment Workers' Union we were able to get on amicably, but I can see in the new union any struggle which will take place would be simply a sacrifice of those workers for the sake of the new union.

'To make it quite plain, our factory has up to the present

given as good conditions to the workers as any factory I know
and if it was only fighting for conditions I would still be in your
fight, but I am not going to sacrifice the workers for the sake of
propaganda for the new union. I am sending this letter because
I suppose that I haven't a friend left in the firm to explain this
to the workers. I suppose now they will be calling me traitor
Tell them from me that I have studied them all these years, and
it is I who is sacrificing myself to the last because I see no other
way out for the good of them all.

'I give them all my love and tell them: Don't strike.'

Perhaps 700 of the 800 employed at Polikoff's had responded
to the strike call, but there was an immediate drift back to work.
The claims of the three sides – the firm and the two unions –
are conflicting, but it seems that some 300 were back at work
within a few days. The Tailors' and Garment Workers' had
no dispute with the firm; indeed, the strike was against the
older union rather than the firm. There was no reason therefore why union members should not accept work there in spite
of the cry that they were blacklegging. Completely bewildered
as to where their duty lay, quite a number of members of the
breakaway union simply tore up their cards and decided to
work as non-unionists.

The *Daily Herald* had tried to report this dispute objectively
and it had made little or no comment on the merits of the
dispute. This forbearance was rewarded by a furious attack for
its 'lies and misrepresentations.' The Polikoff pickets sang as
they paraded (to the tune *London Bridge is Falling Down*):

'The *Daily Herald* is no good, is no good, is no good,
The *Daily Herald* is no good, Polikoff's bought it over.'

Not unnaturally the Labour newspaper began to take a more
jaundiced view of the breakaway union and its activities.

The breakaway union still managed to keep the strike limp-
ing along until 23rd May, when the summons against Samuel
Barnett, one of the sixty-seven Polikoff cutters called to court
was tried as a test case. The court found that Barnett had
broken a weekly contract with the firm without proper notice
or reasonable excuse. He was ordered to pay £4 15s damages
and the costs of the case.

Elsbury then had the unenviable task of explaining to a
meeting of his members that there was no strike pay and no

unds to meet the damages and costs which would be awarded
f Mr Polikoff did not withdraw the remaining summonses. An
ugly argument carried out against a background of weeping
girls ended in a decision to finish the strike.

This was the virtual end of the United Clothing Workers
Union. It was no longer a threat, though it remained a diminishing nuisance for several more years. It was also the end
of Sam Elsbury's career with the union. Without him, the
breakaway union lacked any fire it might once have had, and
became just another of the old-fashioned small sectional unions
in the east end of London, with most of its members in small
Jewish sub-divisional workshops. In the factories it was overwhelmed by the Tailors' and Garment Workers' Union. Its
membership declined by about nine-tenths. But it was not for
another five or six years that, following the change in the
Communist line to one of co-operation with the social demo-
crats, its affairs were finally wound up.

Chapter Nineteen/One Big Union At Last

UNION STRENGTHENED; AMALGAMATION MOVES; TUC HELP; MERGER RESULT
AND OBJECTS; UNEMPLOYMENT AND MECHANISATION; CONVEYOR BELT
SYSTEMS AND PAYMENT; LEEDS ORGANISATION; BURTON STRIKE 1936; LONDON
ORGANISATION; MENACE OF FASCISM; UNITED LADIES' TAILORS JOIN

The somewhat unedifying story related in the preceding chapter
shows how the Tailors' and Garment Workers' Union with-
stood the challenge of a breakaway movement. While the
breakaway leaders' own misguided tactics served to discredit
their organisation, the loyalty of union members in the main
clothing centres, together with the firmness of the leadership,
resulted, if anything, in strengthening the organisation.

Within a few months of the Polikoff troubles the general
secretary was able to pen a new year message to the membership: 'We have seen in the last month or two the complete
break-up of the breakaway organisation . . . In their sordid
squabbles they have sacrificed the small handful of the rank
and file who were misguided enough to trust them . . . There
is no room in the union for the mischief-makers or for those who
tried to injure and disrupt our organisation. Their plot against
the union has failed.'

He told the delegate conference that summer, 'The difficult
times through which our union has passed have helped to knit
our organisation closer together and have brought into existence a firmer comradeship, a stronger loyalty and a clearer
perception of the possibilities inherent in our union.'

The way was now open for the final moves for the formation
of a single, all-embracing union for clothing workers.

Both the Tailors' Union and the Amalgamated Society had suffered from the activities of the breakaway leaders in London and had sought to counter these by intensifying their own organisation and recruitment efforts. The competition between the two organisations had become fiercer, but the AST & T in particular was adversely affected by the new production techniques and its more enlightened leaders realised that it was time to bury the old jealousies and forget their traditional exclusiveness.

Negotiations between the two bodies and the London Jewish-based, United Ladies' Tailors opened in November 1929.

The talks were held under the auspices of the TUC, whose representatives, Mr H. V. (later Sir Vincent) Tewson and Mr W. Kean, a member of the general council, steered them through to eventual success. It is significant at a time when there is mounting interest in the reform of union structure that the TUC should have played so decisive a part in the tailors' amalgamation moves.

In October 1930 the *Garment Worker* reported that, in spite of all the difficulties, the prospects of success were brighter than on any previous occasion. In all, eleven meetings were held to thrash out the details, and the discussions were described as protracted and difficult.'

Andrew Conley left his members in no doubt about the issues at stake. In various articles, he argued the case for unity. Weak, irresolute and divided unions are positively a temptation to employers. There is nothing that they respect more than a powerful, closely organised union, with the spirit and will to fight for its members. That is the kind of union we aim to be.'

He deplored the waste in maintaining separate offices, machinery and staffs with the consequent overlapping and confusion. 'Inevitably the two national unions have injured each other in the great task of organising the workers. Much money and time have been wasted in the past in competing against each other, not only in the same town, but in the same workshop and factory, ending in mutual frustration and exasperation.' And, in a phrase, strikingly reminiscent of the words used at Blackpool in 1962, he said 'Our trade union movement has developed for three generations without much conscious guidance or planning. The result is an extraordinarily complex form of organisation. We all recognise the wisdom of simplifying the structure and uniting our forces.'

Separate conferences of the three unions were held in Manchester on 6th August, and jointly the following day. By seventy-three votes to one, the tailors' conference accepted the amalgamation scheme; there was also only one dissentient on the AST & T side. The United Ladies' Tailors however dropped out and refused to sanction the taking of a ballot vote.

The plan provided for continuity of policy and the maintenance of contribution and benefit scales for a transitional period of four years; it protected the administration and branch machinery and the position of full-time officers and organisers. It also promised to safeguard 'all existing trade agreements, trade customs and practices secured by the respective unions, and provided for a gradual transfer so as to 'give time for us to get used to one another's ways of doing business.'

'We are taking a bold and big step, but we are taking it with our eyes open,' proclaimed the union leadership.

The ballot began on 9th November 1931. It was organised through the TUC, which sent out ballot papers and supervised the count. Voting closed on 28th November and the result showed an overwhelming majority among the members of both unions in favour of amalgamation. For the Tailors' Union there was an 81 per cent poll, and a 92.9 per cent vote in favour. For the AST & T, on an 85 per cent poll, 79.4 per cent were in favour and 20 per cent against. The large number of members voting created a record in the history of trade union ballots.

The new union, the National Union of Tailors and Garment Workers, began its official life on 1st January 1932, with its headquarters in Leeds.

One of the factors which precipitated the amalgamation was the worsening of the industrial position. By the beginning of 1931 approximately one in five clothing workers was unemployed and the outlook for them, as for every other section of British labour was black indeed, especially with the election of a government 'dominated by the most reactionary elements in our national life.'

Looking beyond the depression, Conley argued that changing industrial techniques were an additional reason for forging a strong, united organisation. 'Industrial conditions are changing, as science, invention and improved techniques providthose who control capital and the machinery of production with undreamed-of possibilities of exploitation,' he wrote.

For the Amalgamated Society the writing was already on the wall. The late twenties and early thirties brought an acceleration of the trends which emerged after the first war towards bigger units, increasing sub-division of labour in the factories and the decline of traditional craftsmanship.

Gurney Rowlerson, AST secretary, who became the new president (a position he was to hold until 1937) described the changes during his fifty years' connection with the trade, when he made his farewell address at the Blackpool conference in 1937, 'I can remember working in shops where even a sewing machine would not have been tolerated and every stitch had to be done by hand. I have lived long enough to see almost every process usurped by the machine, among them cutting, pressing, seaming, felling, padding, basting, buttonholing and buttoning and with the conveyor belt to carry subdivided portions of the work from one operative to another'.

Some firms had installed the conveyor belt – an invention associated with the name of Henry Ford – as early as 1918, but it was not until the early and mid-thirties that its use became widespread. Its application to clothing manufacture, as opposed to engineering, was of dubious advantage, and it was particularly unsuitable for making up women's clothes, with their frequent changes in fashion and style. But many employers, bewitched by the new machine, pressed ahead with its installation, despite strong protests from the workers.

The speed of the conveyor belt controlled the rate of work, which could be no faster than that of the slowest worker. The fast workers who had been used to higher earnings related to a greater individual output found their earnings reduced. At the other end, the slower workers found their day spent in a frantic battle to keep up with the demands of the inexorable belt. An anonymous 'factory worker' wrote to the *Journal* about the 'cursed conveyor belt . . . The long hours, the high speed, the monotony, the low wages, the inability to move from one's seat until a given signal, the stress and strain makes one feel like a galley slave.' As late as 1937 a resolution was moved by Leeds No 3 at the union's conference, 'condemning the conveyor belt system'.

The union was not, officially, opposed to mechanisation but

it regarded the conveyor belt as unsuitable for garment-making and harmful from the standpoint of the workers' health and welfare. It demanded that the workers should receive their proper share of the advantages of mechanisation. But the union was reluctantly compelled by force of circumstances to accept the conveyor belt system and its various adaptations.

Mechanisation not only radically altered the character of production but brought with it new systems of payment. Until well after the first war, the wages system in the wholesale industry was based on time rates or straight piecework rates. In the bespoke trade, it was on the basis of the log hour and the log statement. With the coming of the conveyor belt on making-up processes, the straight piecework method was increasingly superseded by production bonus methods of payment. The union was able to negotiate agreements with the main employers' organisations in the mid-thirties for a higher rate for women conveyor belt operatives – at 1d an hour above the general minimum time rate. Later an improved agreement was reached with the Co-operative Wholesale Society factories, providing an extra 1½d an hour – the same agreement conceded a forty-five hour week to about 10,000 CWS employees.

Unemployment remained high throughout the first years of the thirties and the union was anxious to safeguard the jobs and skills of its members. In the past time rates had been the recognised method of payment in the cutting room, and were indeed considered as an essential reward for skill. In 1934, the union issued its cutters' bylaws, declaring piecework and bonus production payments in cutting rooms to be 'pernicious'. Despite this the production bonus systems, which the employers regarded as providing a necessary incentive, spread and were introduced into cutting rooms as well as other parts of the clothing factories.

These systems were a perpetual source of friction and the cause of many disputes. Trouble arose especially where premium bonus systems were introduced which allowed the worker only part of the original standard payment for additional work. Thirty years later the union was still pressing for a regulated standard of bonus payments.

It was naturally enough in Leeds, as the biggest centre of the clothing trade, that the effects of mechanisation were most strongly felt. The numbers employed in the industry increased by over 100 per cent between 1921 and 1938, when they reached 50,000. This presented a big potential field for recruitment, and it was in Leeds that the new union had the greatest success. Indeed, the Leeds story during the thirties provides a shining contrast with the frustrations that were met in London during the 1920s. Membership in the city rose from 9,000 in 1933 to 15,000 in 1935 and by the eve of the war had topped the 30,000 mark.

The Leeds tailors were originally divided into two branches – No 1, which developed from the old AUCO, and No 2, from the Jewish tailors, machinists and pressers, under the secretaryship of Percy Johnson and Wolfe Goldberg respectively. They were eventually merged into one central branch.

Moses Sclare, the Russian-born former secretary of the old Jewish union, who became a general organiser in 1926, wrote about the campaign planned for recruitment: 'Our method of organising is the old soap-box method modernised.' The programme included impressive outdoor and canteen meetings and the idea was to concentrate on a small number of factories, involving frequent factory visits. The male cutters in the city became 100 per cent organised, but there was still a big problem to organise the growing number of women.

In 1936 the executive board appointed two extra full-time secretaries in Leeds – Messrs W. Franklin and C. Dawson – and three branches were established. Both had been members of the executive before becoming officials (according to the policy of 'rank and file-ism' adopted in 1926, no full-time officer could serve on the executive). They made a formidable and unusual partnership and their methods which were intensive and often unorthodox, produced results, in terms of increased membership. Franklin was a somewhat unorthodox Jew and Dawson a staunch Roman Catholic. A burly six-footer, with an intimate knowledge of cutting room problems, he expounded his theories with directness and determination. Franklin, stocky, nimble-witted and shrewd, made up for Dawson's lack of subtlety.

Percy Johnson was at that time the Leeds district secretary. He had joined AUCO in 1910 and had been a shop steward and held branch office before becoming full-time branch secretary in 1916. Somewhat dour and 'down to earth' in approach, he was very competent administrator, and was largely responsible for building up the Leeds organisation to a high pitch of efficiency in which factory and branch activities became fully integrated.

Though Leeds was a traditional stronghold of AUCO, the Amalgamated Society was not left out. Its former organiser, Percy Burns, was given a roving commission in the north of England, with permission to make forays into Ireland and Scotland.

Yet, for all the efficiency and energy of its organisers, Leeds had its troubles. An unofficial dispute at Montague Burton's Hudson Road factory in 1936 caused the largest strike in the inter-war period. It lasted three and a half weeks and involved directly and indirectly some 15,000 workers. Despite the ideals of the firm's founder and his desire to be a 'good' employer, the management had not developed the intelligent principles of labour-management relations which are now generally applied there.

Joint consultation was very much in its infancy. (One of its early pioneers was Irving Shuttleworth, managing director of Prices, tailors in Leeds, who encouraged the formation of factory and sectional committees to deal with day to day problems.)

On 20th February 1936 114 Burton fitters stopped work, when their claim for a revision of piece rates for their assistants was rejected, not only by the firm but by the branch committee. In the past, the juniors had been paid out of the earnings of the individual fitters for whom they worked, a vicious system which smacked of all the sub-contracting evils the union had so long been fighting. The Leeds branch committee had been engaged in negotiations with the management for well over a year and had arrived at a settlement which was in fact in operation when the strike began. The fitters rejected the settlement, which involved some reduction in their earnings. They were supported by the shop stewards throughout the factory and all work was stopped.

The executive board sent out immediate telegrams ordering a return to work. Its advice was ignored. In an official statement later it said: 'Unhappily, influences were at work which overruled for the time being the authority of the union.'

It spoke, darkly, of Communist penetration and of the existence of a Communist 'cell' at Burtons. 'Emissaries from outside bodies in no wise connected with our union or with the industry in furtherance of their Communist propaganda appeared upon the scene.'

The strike went on day after day in an atmosphere of mounting acrimony and bitterness. Accusations and counter-accusations were hurled backwards and forwards. As in the Polikoff trouble, union leaders were shouted down when they attempted to put their case. Their reception at a mass meeting at Leeds Town Hall on 6th March was officially described with studied understatement: 'The meeting was less orderly and less amenable to the voice of reason than could have been desired.'

In the end there was a return to work on 16th March which in effect represented a defeat for the strikers. A promise was given of a review of the fitters' claim by the Leeds branch committee, with the assurance that if the fitters found it unsatisfactory they could appeal to the executive board. There was a great deal of bitterness at the end of the strike and allegations of victimisation were made. On investigation, these proved unfounded.

The situation in Leeds calmed down almost as swiftly as it had flared up, and the union went ahead with its job of recruitment and organising. It was in a thoroughly happy atmosphere, with all the bitterness forgotten, that the new office building, Circle House, was formally opened in December 1938.

Though attention during this period was largely focussed on Leeds, good progress in organisation was made in other clothing centres, and the patient work of welding the two unions into a single entity continued. In London calm was again restored under such officials as Bernard Sullivan, still at his old post, A. R. Rollin and Bob Curry. Mr M. Daly, who had been secretary of the West End Branch for many years and was first appointed as an organiser in 1906, had died in 1936 after thirty years' service to the Union.

A particularly happy note was struck when a dinner was held at Polikoffs to celebrate an agreement for 100 per cent unionism. But it was not by any means smooth sailing. Some London firms remained unfavourable to unions. We read in the *Garment Worker* during the late thirties of anti-union trouble at L. Coleman and Company, mantle manufacturers, and at Swears and Wells. In February 1938 a meeting at the East Ham firm of

Messrs Blackman and Conrad was broken up. The report runs: 'Following a rowdy scene in which employers shouted abuse at our organisers and endeavoured in a somewhat undignified way to pull Miss Russell away from the microphone, a radio van meeting called by the union was broken up, with the assistance of the local police.'

A girl who had taken a leading part in organising the factory was sacked, and her two friends were faced with the choice – leave the union or leave the job. (They left the job.) The following month Miss Russell, a woman organiser, and Mr Bob Curry, London organiser, were served with summonses to appear at East Ham police court. (This, be it noted, was in 1938, not in 1866.)

These were typical examples of the difficulties faced by union officials and shop stewards in organising the smaller workshops. The majority of larger clothing manufacturers had recognised the National Union and the sensible ones welcomed and encouraged union organisation in their factories.

While these events were going on in London and Leeds, the political situation inside and outside Britain was getting progressively darker. Trade unionists everywhere found themselves involved in a new and intensive struggle against a more deadly enemy than employers or breakaway movements – Fascism. True to their international traditions the tailors were to the fore in helping the Spanish workers and other victims of aggression, and in denouncing the appeasement of the dictators in Europe.

Conley was among the first to recognise the new menace. As chairman of the TUC in 1934, the year which marked the centenary of the Tolpuddle martyrs, he warned the movement and the nation: 'We are faced with a deliberate and deadly challenge to every ideal and every principle we have inherited . . . Democracy is under attack.'

The year of Munich saw the conclusion of the long-delayed plans for amalgamation with the United Ladies' Tailors, accepted by an overwhelming vote on both sides. A similar vote was recorded in favour of the entry of Waterproof Garment Workers of Manchester, but complications arose which prevented this taking place.

The merger with the United Ladies Tailors was acclaimed in March 1939. Conley commented: 'A new chapter in the history of trade unionism in the garment-making industry thus begins. The objective I have held steadily in view since I became active in working class organisation has been attained.'

Chapter Twenty/'Union Work Must Go On'

OUTBREAK OF WAR; UNION'S DOUBLE AIMS; 'SQUANDERING OF MANPOWER' ATTACKED DURING PHONEY WAR; UTILITY AND CONCENTRATION; WAR PROBLEMS AND ACHIEVEMENTS; KEEPING IN TOUCH WITH MEMBERSHIP; 1945 ELECTION

It had long been apparent to the more far-seeing leaders of the Labour movement that the Chamberlain policy of appeasement could only have one outcome and that Hitler would sooner or later be bound to plunge the world into total war. It is thus somewhat surprising to find that at the union's biennial conference which met in London in July 1939, delegates made hardly any reference to defence preparations or to the possible effects of a war on their industry and their union. The conference was mainly concerned with internal domestic issues such as alterations of rules and changes in the composition of the executive board.

Yet, when the storm broke in those early days of September, the union showed that it was capable of rapid adjustment to a crisis situation – far more so indeed than the Government and most of the population. Andrew Conley lost no time in putting the issues squarely before the membership. Back from the Trades Union Congress at Bridlington, he penned an editorial letter with a twofold message – First, 'This is a war against Fascism and tyranny and it is the duty of everybody to throw all they have into the fight.' Secondly, there must be no weakening of the trade unions. On the contrary it was more than ever important to build up their strength. 'Come what may, trade unionism will survive and will not only survive, but grow.'

'Our own task as a union,' he wrote, 'is to defend the interests of our membership and to concentrate our efforts, along with the unions with which we are affiliated in the fellowship of the Trades Union Congress, to assist the national effort until the Nazi government in Germany is overthrown and peace is restored, on a basis of justice and fair play.'

The union's organisation, he promised, would continue to function normally as far as possible. Its officers would remain at their posts and would be available to the membership as always for advice, counsel and help.

To this end circulars and letters were sent out to all branches, emphasising the need for carrying on union activities with regular branch and committee meetings, and for officials in every area to keep in touch with the members. The slogan was set, 'Union work must go on.'

Conley's message set the tone for all the union's actions and attitudes during the long war years. Month by month in the union journal, the *Garment Worker*, his balanced and informative articles, clearly and cogently written, kept the members fully in the picture. He told them frankly how they would be affected by various government schemes and what the union was doing both to protect their interests and to further the war effort. Even in the darkest days his messages brought comfort and inspiration.

Throughout the whole period of the war he kept a persistent watch, prodding this department and that, stirring the handful of recalcitrant employers who refused to co-operate with the union and its officials, insisting on their right to be consulted at every level. His criticisms were constructive, not carping, and he threw himself into the struggle with the same energy and dynamism that he brought to bear in the campaign to form one big union. He realised that the war situation presented a challenge to organised labour and that the unions were moving from the stage of agitation into that of responsibility. They must prove their fitness to participate in national policy-making.

Though it was clear from the outset that a gigantic switch-over from production of civilian clothing to that of uniforms and equipment for the armed forces would be involved, progress was slow and halting in the first months of the war. Unemployment rose steeply in the clothing industry and six

months after the outbreak one in ten garment workers were
still jobless. It took a long time for increased military orders to
offset the slump in ordinary civilian demand.

In those days of the 'phoney' war, Conley kept up a constant
barrage of criticism, aimed at those in high places. He criticised
the 'squandering' of manpower, and condemned the government's inefficiency on the economic front. He also criticised
'favouritism or unfair discrimination', in placing government
orders, and called for planned and coordinated control over
the whole industry to ensure a more rational allocation of
contracts and fairer distribution.

He was also constantly irritated at the employers' failure to
make consultation effective. This was all the more disappointing
because early in the war the clothing industry had set up a
joint committee to deal with all wartime problems (such as
government contracts and rates of pay, displacement of labour,
overtime payment, payment for loss of time through air-raids,
and reinstatement). The industry had been commendably
quick off the mark in establishing a joint body, but despite its
brave start the committee made little impact. Conley complained that the employers were only paying lip-service to the
idea of joint co-operation. 'The position is far from being a
satisfactory one,' he wrote. 'Proper discussion and reasonable
consideration of the questions raised have proved impossible.'
At meetings union delegates were usually treated to long rig-
maroles to the effect that the employers were very busy men,
who had suffered considerable inconvenience at having to
attend; they must finish in time to let them catch their trains.
Yet the difficulties were just as great for the union representatives. They too were busy men; they too had trains to catch, but
they took the committee seriously and made it a point of honour
to attend.

The 'phoney' war came to an end abruptly. Hitler invaded
Norway and the Low Countries, France fell and a coalition
government under Churchill took over in Britain. Labour party
leaders, who had refused to serve under Chamberlain, played
a dominant part in the new government and took over many
key positions. After the 'nine months of incredibly shortsighted
lethargy' the union welcomed the evidence of a new sense of
direction and purpose at the top, and in particular applauded
Ernest Bevin's appointment as Minister of Labour.

Bevin, in accepting Churchill's invitation, insisted that the ministry should be strengthened, given real teeth to contribute to the organisation of the production drive, and should not just be a sausage-machine for supplying the personnel. Looking further ahead, he foresaw that his department could have the biggest say, next to the Foreign Office, in shaping the peace and the economic pattern of the future.

He lost no time in making his presence felt, though it inevitably took time before the full machinery of mobilisation could move into top gear. One of his first acts was to appoint a board to advise him on the whole field of industrial welfare, including hours, canteens, rest breaks and working conditions. Anne Loughlin became an invaluable member of this board, whose importance and usefulness increased as the war situation developed. The vast human and social problems involved in transferring hundreds of thousands of women and girls from civilian industry to munitions, the difficulties created by the air-raids, the blackout, long hours, domestic upheavals and transport difficulties were the concern of the Minister and his advisers.

The government's plans to place clothing, along with other civilian industries, on a wartime footing took shape gradually. The whole paraphernalia of controls and austerity, which became so familiar a feature of the war and postwar years, was introduced in stages. Clothes rationing was brought in in June 1941 and by the summer of 1942 the utility production scheme was in operation.

At first utility applied to about fifty per cent of the industry, but later it was extended to cover about eighty per cent of the cloth supplied. In the union's view it should have been 100 per cent. With utility went price control and austerity restrictions for both men's and women's clothes. These make strange reading, after twenty years, at a time of intensive competition to woo the customers.

The regulations cut down the use of trimmings, and specified the maximum width and length of skirts and the number of pleats: they restricted the number of styles and fixed minimum standards of make. The restrictions on men's clothing included a ban on double-breasted waistcoats and jackets; they did away with slits and buttons on cuffs and limited jacket pockets to three; trouser bottoms must not be wider than nineteen inches, and turnups were out. Austerity was complete when the Foreign Office announced that even diplomats would have to forego their turnups!

An important instrument of control on the production side was the concentration scheme. This was originally announced in May 1941 and according to Conley the news 'fell like a bombshell'. While the union leaders had no quarrel with the purpose of the proposed measure, they resented the peremptory manner in which the decision was taken, without proper consultation with the trade. The concentration scheme was not put into effect until July 1942, when a plan was announced for Leeds, main centre of clothing production and a 'scarlet' area on the Ministry of Labour map. Similar schemes were later applied in the North-West and Midlands, and very much later to London.

The objective of concentration was to save factory space for storage of munitions, to economise in materials and to release manpower for service and war needs. A limited number of firms were 'designated' for clothing production; they were given regular allocations of priority cloth and had their workers protected under the Essential Work Orders. (This meant that no employer could sack a worker and no worker could leave his job without permission of the Ministry. It also ensured work at recognised wages and conditions and provided a guaranteed week.)

By and large, the manufacturers whose firms were designated found many advantages in the control. The union itself accepted the scheme, as evidence that the home economic front was at last being effectively mobilised. When concentration was brought in Conley wrote: 'We cannot help it – it is a policy dictated by stern necessity,' and he told his members bluntly 'Wartime service imposes the same obligations on you as on your fellow workers in the fighting services.' He was just as angry with workers who did not pull their weight, and were habitual absentees or latecomers, as he was with the minority of employers who were 'throwing grit in the machinery' by refusing to recognise the union or allow its officers facilities in their workshops. Yet, while accepting concentration as inevitable, the union throughout insisted that there should be full and genuine consultation in the planning of the transfers from clothing to munitions.

At one stage Conley warned that the industry was 'getting perilously near the edge of such a morass as the cotton industry foundered into before it was safeguarded under the Essential Work Scheme.' He also stressed the need for proper training of garment workers for engineering work, and made the point that the industry should not be denuded of its labour force without thought for the future clothing needs of the population.

Altogether the clothing industry lost over one-third of its manpower during the war. By 1945 there were only 65,000 men and 284,000 women engaged in garment making. Yet, even with its depleted labour force, it achieved spectacular production figures and made more than 409 million uniforms and other garments for the armed forces and other war services.

The smooth working of the clothing control system and the industry's output record was in no small measure due to the efforts of the union. Hugh Dalton, when he was President of the Board of Trade, paid public tribute to the union's work and organisation, and to its general secretary. The tribute was well-deserved, for the years of war were difficult and arduous ones for all union officers and stewards. They had the dual task of both seeking to ensure maximum efficiency and output in the clothing factories and workshops, and also of looking after the interests of the members, in accordance with the maxim laid down early on: 'Union work must go on.'

The sheer physical difficulties of carrying on the union job imposed a tremendous strain. One London officer described graphically the way in which union work was carried on even at the height of the blitz: 'With the roof of our meeting-hall blown off; with our club room windows shattered by Hitler's blasted bombs; with the extended blackout and the danger by day and by night, it would have been unreasonable to expect that those of our members who remained in town should come to the union. Therefore we had to go to the members.' The branch officers sought out their members in workshops, in their homes or, if necessary, in local shelters, tubes or rest centres. As a result of their initiative, a drop of eighty-five per cent in branch revenue reported at the end of September 1940 was reduced to about thirty per cent by the end of November.

In the factories and workshops, stewards and union representatives on joint committees carried on a tireless battle to

improve efficiency, cut costs, combat absenteeism and help ease
the shopping and other domestic problems of the married
women who flocked into the factories. Sometimes they had full
cooperation from the employers: elsewhere they met with a
negative, or at the best grudging, response and the feeling that
they were invading the field of management responsibilities

The union executive, early on, made arrangements with a
number of other unions, such as the National Union of General
and Municipal Workers and the Transport Workers' Union
for the recognition of Garment Workers' cards. This was an
important step to safeguard membership and to ensure the
return of ex-workers to the trade and the union after the war.

Union officers were also actively engaged in recruiting members and winning over the 'nons'. As soon as the Essential Work
Order was applied to the industry, the executive board
launched a drive among the designated firms to win 100 per
cent membership.

The biennial conferences were held, without interruption,
throughout the war, and the main difference compared with
pre-war conferences lay in the increased number of women
delegates.

The union succeeded during the war in negotiating wage
increases, in order to keep pace with rising prices and match
the increases in other industries. There were settlements in
1940, 1941, 1942 and 1944, when men received 6s a week on
each occasion and women 3s, 4s, 4s and 5s. The 1944 settlement
was reached after many months of foot-dragging by the employers and the union had reported the deadlock to the Ministry of Labour. A joint meeting was held at 8 St James's
Square, where the two sides were kept in separate rooms, while
the Ministry's chief conciliation official Mr (now Sir) Robert
Gould moved patiently between them until they agreed on a
figure. This was an early example of the 'padding the corridors'
technique adopted, usually with success, in the post-war years,
by the Ministry's industrial peacemakers – Sir Wilfred Neden
who succeeded Sir Robert and Mr St John Wilson who took
over in 1958.

In all, wartime increases totalled 24s a week for men and
16s for women. 'This,' declared Conley later, 'is a considerable
achievement.' It showed that despite all the difficulties and
loss of membership, the union had been able 'to forge ahead'

nd 'testified to the continuous concern for the workers' welfare
nd the vitality of our organisation.'

What better reason, he asked, could there be for non-
members to join? 'There is no reason on earth why every
worker in these trades should not be unionised. That is our
ask. Let us go to it with goodwill.'

The 1945 conference, meeting at Blackpool, resolved to
launch a campaign to raise membership to the quarter million
mark by December 1946. It was the year of victory in two
enses – the national victory over Hitler and the Labour party's
lection triumph over the Conservatives. The *Garment Worker*
ommented: 'The serried ranks of the Labour members are
living witness to the peaceful revolution which has taken place
n our midst . . . Social democracy is given another chance, and
. much better chance than ever before, to prove its worth.'

Chapter Twenty-One/*Brave New World*

AUSTERITY CONTINUES; HIGH HOPES FOR FUTURE; POST-WAR RECONSTRUCTION PLANS; THE CRIPPS WORKING PARTY; DAME ANNE BECOMES GENERAL SECRETARY; FORTY-FOUR-HOUR WEEK; RECRUITMENT DRIVE; EMPLOYERS OPPOSE DEVELOPMENT COUNCIL; DEBATE IN PARLIAMENT; WILSON GOES AHEAD

Peace brought no relief to the hard-pressed clothing industry. On the contrary, the end of hostilities in Europe coincided with a crisis in production and accentuated the acute difficulties of materials and manpower. It was even feared at one stage that it would not be possible to honour the clothes ration. Some months before VE day, Conley was appealing to members not to slacken their efforts or to allow their 'understandable weariness' to get the upper hand. There were still heavy demands from the service departments – the war against Japan, it was thought, would last a long time – and the massive programme of supplying 'demob' suits was in hand. The scheme had been prepared by the Board of Trade backroom staff and was aimed at so equipping returning soldiers that 'when a man steps out of the depot, clothed in civilian garments, he will pass among the civilian population as well dressed as any, and better dressed than most.' This claim was perhaps not foolhardy. After years of rationing, austerity and doing without, most people's clothes had fallen into an extremely shabby, down-at-heel condition.

The situation looked so serious that the government issued an official statement, saying, 'The Board of Trade are well aware that after five years of war stocks of clothing have fallen

John Newton

A float used in the 1962 campaign for shorter hours

and it is only natural that, on the eve of victory, they should be at a low level.' There would be a considerable time-lag, it warned, before any increased supplies could be expected to reach the shops. *The Times* carried a lengthy correspondence in which many employers blamed the shortage on the government's utility scheme. This, the union warned members, was part of a concerted attack on Mr Dalton and the government's whole conception of control over production, prices and profits. The minority who attacked utility were not however typical of the whole body of employers. Most manufacturers agreed that the utility scheme had been necessary and should be continued so long as there were shortages of materials and manpower.

An article appeared in the *Drapers' Record* in January 1946: 'Why is it that some producers appear keen on the retention of some measure of control? The reason is that the trade as a whole has never been so prosperous as it has been during the past six years.'

This attitude confirmed the views expressed in a letter to *Women's Wear News* the previous year: 'In the good old, bad old days pre-1939, the clothing industry was hardly a healthy specimen . . . What a change today! What an amazing return to health! Buyer respects seller and no one passes the twentieth of the month owing a farthing and such a thing as cancelling an order is unheard of.'

The shortage of clothing workers was part of the national pattern – civilian industries were said to be four million workers below their prewar strength. The clothing trade alone was nearly 200,000 below normal.

As part of the massive process of switching back from a war to a peace economy, steps were immediately taken to boost the industry's manpower. This time, there was complete consultation with the union, which pledged its full support in the campaign to get clothing workers back to their old trade. Union leaders realised that this would not be an easy task. An article in the *Garment Worker* referred to the 'clear evidence of the unwillingness of garment workers to return to the industry under present conditions.' Wages were lower than in many wartime industries and welfare arrangements were 'woefully behind the times.' 'Sanitary accommodation is, in many places, a disgrace. Such necessary amenities as proper medical and health facilities are largely non-existent. Even structurally, workshops and factories, with very few modern exceptions, are gloomy, dark, ill-ventilated and chaotic in their lay-out.' It was small wonder that workers who had for four or five years worked in 'modern well-equipped and relatively comfortable conditions were strongly disinclined to go back.'

Another big drawback was the clothing trade's record of fluctuating employment and under-employment. Before the war men only worked on the average thirty-eight weeks out of fifty-two and women only thirty-two.

The union offered the only possible solution – the activities of the industry must be planned and placed on a stable and regular footing. It must be made more attractive and offer better wages and conditions if it was to compete successfully with other industries which were scrambling for workers. The lessons of planning and control learned in the war must be applied in peacetime.

When victory came in sight everybody (or nearly everybody) in Britain had begun to think about the future. The Beveridge Report on social security had blazed the trail for the achievement of one of the four freedoms – freedom from want. The coalition government had declared its determination to achieve freedom from idleness with plans for maintaining full employment. The Trades Union Congress had published its own broad plan for postwar reconstruction, and called on every individual union to draw up detailed schemes for their own industries.

The Garment Workers' was one of the first unions to respond. The executive board issued its own plan for post-war reconstruction, which was adopted at the 1945 Trades Union Congress. Its central proposal was for the setting up of a national board, consisting of employers, union and government representatives, to organise the industry's activities so as to eliminate seasonal fluctuations and ensure full employment, and to safeguard the public interest. (The union's emphasis on a central board is important, in the light of the subsequent history of the efforts to set up such a body for the industry.) The board's proposed responsibilities were defined in an eight-point programme as being (1) planning of production and distribution on the basis of the needs of the people; (2) bulk purchase of raw materials; (3) control over prices; (4) no production or distribution except under licence; (5) extension of utility to a

wider range and improvements in the quality of cheaper ranges;
(6) encouragement of scientific technique; (7) progressive
abolition of rationing and control; (8) maintenance of the
guaranteed week.

A resolution on these lines was carried at the Trades Union
Congress at Blackpool in September 1945, where it was moved
by John Newton, a member of the executive board, who was
later to become general secretary of the Tailors' and Garment
Workers' Union.

The union's own conference, also held at Blackpool, was an
extremely important one. As well as formulating plans for their
own industry, the delegates called for major developments in
the union's organisation, and for improvements in wages and
conditions. The conference urged, among other things, a forty-
hour week, the abolition of overtime, two weeks' paid holiday,
equal pay for equal work, a guaranteed week, and a charter to
secure adequate welfare and conditions in clothing factories
and workshops. It also called attention to the need for proper
training for young entrants and the returning men and women
from the services and munitions.

This may seem a formidable shopping list for a trade union
to present to employers. But in the heady atmosphere of the
months that followed VE day there seemed no limit to the
advances that could be won, and organised workers everywhere were determined to see that the patience and sacrifices
of the war years met their just reward.

The 1945 conference was presided over by Edith Maycock,
the first woman ever to hold the office of chairman in the union.
Ten years later she was again in the chair – the conference was
again held at Blackpool – and commented on the contrast.
Throughout our discussions that week in July 1945, there was
a note of enthusiasm and optimism. Every delegate felt that
great opportunities were just round the corner. We looked
forward to better times for the industry . . . ' (We shall see in
the next chapter why the high hopes of 1945 were frustrated.)

Edith Maycock has been described as 'among the foremost
of the women trade unionists of the twentieth century.' She was
a lifelong member of the old Amalgamated Society, and battled
hard for the rights of women. She was born in Kettering
and did much to build up the union's strength in the area. In
her youth, she used to walk for four miles to and from work,

and cycled all round the villages in the area giving out
leaflets and propaganda. 'We organised for the love of
organising,' she later recalled.

Miss Maycock was elected to the executive in 1927 and
remained a member until her death in 1961. She played a
prominent part in the moves leading to the amalgamation of
the AST & T with the Tailors' and Garment Workers' Union
and represented the union on the heavy clothing working party
and the productivity team which visited America. Slight, be-
spectacled and shy, she never sought the limelight, but as
John Newton wrote after her death, 'The union . . . was her
life. It was a life given unselfishly and without material reward.'

The election of a Labour government in 1945, a government
'of our own people,' had raised hopes that ministers meant
business when they talked about planning and about giving
the union a real say in determining future policy. The appointment of Sir Stafford Cripps as President of the Board of Trade
where he would be responsible for carrying out industrial
policies, was warmly welcomed. He was 'not only a minister
of very great ability but a man of high social ideals.' Trade
unionists recalled his brilliant advocacy on behalf of the
miners: others remembered his scientific as well as his forensic
skill – altogether he seemed the right man to tackle the hercu-
lean task of re-establishing national production on a sound basis.

At the very first meeting with the new President, the executive board were assured of a sympathetic hearing for their post-
war plan, and very soon after, Cripps announced his policy for
setting up tripartite working parties to guide every major
consumer industry on the post-war path to prosperity. His
initiative was warmly commended by the unions for his
policies were very much on the lines they themselves had advocated.

In February 1946 the appointment of a working party for
the heavy clothing section of the industry was announced
appropriately enough in Leeds. The employers' representatives
asked for time to consider the plan, but the unions accepted
on the spot and named their six representatives (Messrs Cor-
ley, T. G. Jones, J. McCorkell, J. E. Newton, Dame Ann
Loughlin and Miss Edith Maycock). Six employers were
eventually nominated, and five independent members, under
the chairmanship of Sir Cecil Weir, made up the team.

The working party lost no time in getting down to its detailed analysis of the industry and drawing up recommendations for its future. Its report, published in March 1947, covers every aspect of the industry's organisation, production and distribution methods.

The working party's main recommendation was for the setting up of a central body to carry out common services for the industry, to act as a link with the government and with other industries, and to become the 'voice' of the clothing industry. The organisation, it suggested, should be (like the working party itself) on a tripartite basis, with equal numbers of employers and unionists and with independent members, and it should be free from government control.

Apart from wages and conditions, which were specifically excluded, it would cover the whole range of industrial activities; it would investigate the causes of seasonal fluctuations and suggest remedies; it would establish a central information and a design centre, arrange for the collection of up-to-date statistics and keep a register of all firms. To promote efficiency, the report suggested that more attention be paid to the training of higher management and foremen, and to time and motion study. There should be closer links between clothing manufacturers and machine-makers, and the Factories Acts should be strengthened. It called for improvements in workshop layout and design and for higher standards of welfare and amenities, and while refusing to restrict entry into the trade, stipulated that any new firm must conform to the recognised standards.

The report was hailed by the union; and the 1947 conference passed a resolution backing its recommendations. The conference chairman described it 'as a solid foundation upon which we believe a sound, prosperous and thriving industry can be built up.'

Parallel working parties had been set up for the light clothing and rubber garment sections. Their reports which appeared about the same time covered much the same ground – both recommended the establishment of some central body for the industry.

The urgent need for some action to guide the industry was underlined by the continued shortage of workers and the difficulties experienced in re-absorbing former clothing operatives. Their return was slow and gradual. Between June 1945 and

June 1946 only about 22,000 workers returned, and by 1947 the total number was more than 100,000 below the pre-war level. This, together with the shortage of cloth, due in its turn to the shortage of workers in the textile industries, meant that all the wartime restrictions had to be retained. (Clothes rationing in fact was kept until March 1949.) With the drive for exports, the home consumer came very low in the list. Sir Stafford, addressing the union's conference in 1947, said quite frankly that there was no prospect of any easement. 'We can afford better to do without more clothes than without enough food and raw materials,' he said. In a rare burst of whimsicality he added that if husbands spent more on their own clothes and less on their wives, this might have helped to right the balance – that is if they dared.

About this time, Dior's New Look was sweeping Europe. Its graceful long skirts and fitted waists attracted women everywhere who were sick and tired of austerity fashions and straight and short skirts. Dame Anne Loughlin condemned the spread of this fashion. 'I take the same view as Sir Stafford Cripps about the absurdity of introducing this new fashion into this country,' she wrote in the *Garment Worker*. 'It seems to be utterly stupid and irresponsible that time, labour, material and money should be wasted upon these fashionable imbecilities.'

Dame Anne, who succeeded Andrew Conley as general secretary in the New Year 1948, took over at a difficult time for the union and the industry. The halcyon days of co-operation for a common purpose were fading, and many employers were growing restive under the continued restrictions. The Labour government was losing popularity and had suffered two severe blows to its policy and prestige in the fuel crisis of the spring of 1947 and the balance of payments crisis of the summer. Abroad the warm glow of comradeship and international goodwill had been succeeded by the icy blasts of cold war. In her first message to the members the new general secretary lamented: 'The world we live in is topsy-turvy. Every day we seem as a nation to wake up to some new crisis.'

In the immediate post-war period the union itself had been able to chalk up some notable achievements in negotiation and was one of the first unions to announce success in the campaign for shorter hours. An agreement on a forty-four hour week, coupled with increases in the minimum rates (representing 7s for men and 9s for women) was announced in February 1946. It would, the union said, 'provide a solid basis for our hopes for a better deal for garment workers in the post-war years.' Another, earlier advance, which the union welcomed, was the ending of the old trade boards and the change in their name to wages councils. This action by Bevin, when he was Minister of Labour, was described in the *Garment Worker* as 'the most important proposal of its kind since 1909,' which would provide a 'more satisfactory permanent basis for orderly wage negotiations, and helped to prevent unorganised sections from slipping back into sweated conditions.'

Despite these advances, which should have stimulated the 'nons' into joining the union, the efforts to recruit more members did not meet with the success hoped when the 250,000 target was launched in the heady air of Blackpool in 1945. 'We are not going to make the grade,' the *Garment Worker* sadly admitted, though it paid tribute to the successful efforts in some areas in enrolling new members.

To the employers' accusations that it was not representative of the workers in the trade the union retorted: 'We do not deny that we are badly organised in some sections, but we do claim to represent the workers in the industry.'

An underground current of opposition began as soon as the first proposals for a central council for the industry were mooted, and the union noted that tendentious statements against the scheme were floated in the trade press and elsewhere. Dame Anne wrote: 'Why there should be opposition is very difficult to understand.' She recalled that the working parties had agreed to the idea of a central body and had accepted 'the claims of the workers to a voice in the counsels of the industry and in the framing of its broad policies.'

Dame Anne's comment was, 'It is now more than ever necessary, no matter what it costs, to organise the industry, women and girls particularly, and to unite all our forces to help return the Labour government.' It was quite evident, she said, that 'the help of the Tory party has been invoked to defeat the establishment of a development council. Our industry has to reckon with reactionary political forces as well as the opposition of the employers' organisations.'

Indeed, to read the Hansard report of the debate on the

Order on 1st November 1949, one might think oneself back in the House when the Trade Boards Acts were debated forty years earlier. Sir Frederick Banbury, who led the employers' opposition then, might have been present in person.

Sir Peter Bennett, a Birmingham industrialist, argued that clothing was not a single industry, but a group of industries.

'There are about 201 associations connected with this industry,' he said. 'They say that to have one council and one organisation to handle everything from ladies' corsets to waterproofed overcoats, from machine-made clothing to bespoke tailoring, from all the small pretty-pretties which ladies use to the big heavy overcoats which men wear, is an absurdity.'

Lord Hinchingbrooke (Dorset) feared that the council would be the thin end of the wedge. 'When the fowl has been properly dressed and trussed . . . the Lord President will come down to the House and say the industry is ripe for nationalisation.'

It was Mr Sidney Shephard of Newark, whose connections with the trade dated back thirty years, who vigorously opposed the scheme. He described the council's proposed functions as 'complete eyewash'. 'It will serve no useful purpose. It will impose an additional cost on the industry . . . It will divert the activities of busy men from their own duties and it will add a few more to that ever-growing number of civil servants,' he declared. 'I am certain that it will not further the efficiency of the industry.'

Mr Shephard roused Labour MPs to a further pitch of fury when he declared, 'The employers have said that they will not co-operate, but I dare say there will be a few quislings prepared to do the dirty work.'

Harold Wilson was more than a match for the Tories on the opposite side of the House. Coolly, lucidly and drily, he demolished their arguments one by one and explained why the government had taken its decision. He recalled that the employers had co-operated in the working party policy and recommendations, and had inexplicably changed their views. The existence of so many small firms and the diffuse nature of the industry was an argument for, and not against, setting up the council. Not all the employers were against the scheme, but those who were had never produced any reasoned case or suggested any constructive alternative.

'I am regretfully forced to the conclusion that the employers' objections are purely political, just as the opposition to this order is purely political,' he concluded. Hansard reports: Question put. The House divided. Ayes: 196 – Noes 77.

Though routed in Parliament by a more than two to one majority, some employers did not let the matter drop. Six clothing manufacturers, in a last-ditch attempt to put the clock back, took the unwonted step of issuing a writ challenging the legality of the order and asking for a declaration that it was void. Their move failed ignominiously and was dismissed in the High Court after a brilliant appearance for the Board of Trade by Sir Hartley Shawcross, then Attorney-General.

The Board of Trade went ahead and early in 1950 the members of the Council were announced. There were six union members (the original names were Dame Anne Loughlin, Mr Maurice Barr, Miss Edith Maycock, Mr J. McCorkell and Mr Frank Mulligan with Mr F. C. Henry from the Waterproof Garment Workers' Union). Five of the six employers were directors of manufacturing companies (three from the heavy and two from the light clothing sections), with a representative of the cws on the proofed garments side. Two members represented technical and distribution interests and there were three independent members. Captain J. Fox Williams, an industrialist, who had been a member of the heavy clothing working party, was appointed chairman.

Its official purpose was defined: 'The Council shall exercise their functions in such a manner as appears to them to increase as much as possible efficiency and productivity in the industry, to improve and develop the service that it renders to the community and to enable it to render that service more economically.'

The union welcomed the long overdue establishment of the Council, but was in no doubt about the difficulties ahead. 'Its creation is a challenge to the industry,' Anne Loughlin wrote in the *Garment Worker*. 'It is particularly a challenge to the workers and above all to the organised workers . . . It can only be successful if the workers give it enthusiastic backing.'

Chapter Twenty-Two/The Frustrating Fifties

DISMANTLING OF CONTROLS; SPECTRE OF UNEMPLOYMENT; SABOTAGE OF DEVELOPMENT COUNCIL — AND JOINT CLOTHING COUNCIL; JOHN NEWTON NOW GENERAL SECRETARY; SEEKS NEW WAGE STRUCTURE; THE 1956 DEADLOCK; UNION VICTORY AND 'LESSONS'; TRAINING SCHEME; NEW TRENDS IN THE INDUSTRY; TOWARDS A FORTY-HOUR-WEEK

The opening of the second half of the twentieth century was generally, and quite irrationally, hailed in the popular press as heralding a new era of prosperity and adventure for the British people. But for the clothing industry in general, and the union in particular, the year 1950 did not hold out any promise of dramatic improvement. It is true that the development council, for which union leaders had battled so long and tirelessly, had at last been established. But, born as it was in the teeth of opposition from leading employers, the infant seemed foredoomed to a short and stunted life. The defeat of the Labour government in the autumn of 1951 marked the beginning of a long era of Conservative rule and the gradual return to a *laissez-faire* economy. This had profound effects on conditions in the clothing industry.

Pledged to 'set the people free,' the new government lost no time in dismantling the carefully built-up structure of controls, and utility was an early casualty. The union was one of its chief mourners. The executive board expressed 'deep concern' at the decision to drop a scheme 'which had served a most useful purpose, not only to the industry but to the consumer public,' and urged that it should be retained.

From then on there came a gradual reversion to many of the pre-war conditions which the union had hoped were a thing of the past. With the end of controls, new firms were free to enter the industry and the ups and downs of fashion again became a dominant factor. Moves to eliminate seasonal fluctuations by advance planning and the allocation of contracts went by the board and the unemployment figures steadily mounted. John Newton, then northern regional organiser, wrote in mid-1952 that the past two years 'demonstrated the instability and vexations to which the industry is now apparently subject,' and noted: 'The spectre of unemployment is with us once again.'

One spark of comfort clothing workers gleaned in those bleak days was the news that the two-piece bathing suit designed with high back and apron skirt was ousting the bikini in popular favour!

Faced with a worsening situation, the union did all it could to support the efforts of the Development Council to bring some order and method into the industry.

Dame Anne wrote in the *Garment Worker*, 'We want to see our industry healthy and efficient, and one to which everyone, employers and employed, can rightly be proud to belong.' To the union's co-operation must, indeed, be largely attributed such successes as the Council was able to achieve during its brief life.

As soon as it was appointed, the Development Council announced a bold programme of work and study. It set up a sub-committee, with Dame Anne as its chairman, to study the causes of seasonal unemployment, and suggest cures. It issued a report urging better working conditions, with suggestions for bringing more light and colour into gloomy workshops. It started an investigation into women's measurements, to try and establish some sort of order in the prevailing jungle of women's wear sizes. It established a library and information service, arranged film shows, meetings and fashion parades, started an industrial consultancy service and, in general, set about giving the industry its own new look.

Its director, Mr David Loweth, declared, 'The final and best answer to its critics is solid accomplishment. The industry must have value for money and the Council and I are determined that that is what it will get.' (The Council was financed on the basis of a compulsory levy of 7s per £1,000 turnover, subsequently reduced to 4s.)

The second and, as it turned out final, report, issued in the autumn of 1952, bore witness to the hard and devoted work of the staff. A team of senior technicians, including experts on production engineering and modern management techniques, was operating a useful consultancy service, which was becoming increasingly popular with manufacturers and retailers. The Council drew up a scheme for training and apprenticeship and to open an office in America to promote the sales of British wear. It set about collecting more reliable statistics (especially from government departments and public authorities) as an essential basis for plans to spread contracts between good and bad seasons. It was speaking and acting as the recognised central voice of the industry and its authority was growing.

Dame Anne commented on the report that the Council was 'laying good foundations for the future,' and agreed with the assessment of a recent editorial in *The Times:* 'It would certainly be unfortunate if it were not allowed to continue when it was showing such practical promise.'

The Development Council, however, could not withstand the growing tide of resentment and opposition – sabotage would perhaps not be too strong a word to use. The new President of the Board of Trade, Mr Peter Thorneycroft, in December 1952, decided to wind up the Council, after less than two years' existence. He had given union leaders a firm assurance that the employers would co-operate in a voluntary body, so in its place a new Joint Clothing Council was set up.

The voluntary council had much the same terms of reference as the Development Council, but there were two important differences – the new forty-strong body consisted only of members of the two sides of the industry and the whole idea of independent representation was dropped. So was the system of a compulsory levy, which was the employers' fundamental objection to the scheme.

The union bitterly deplored the passing of the Development Council but decided to make the best of a bad job and give the new body a chance. John Newton wrote: 'We shall work honestly and diligently to make it a success.'

Newton had been elected general secretary at the end of 1952, and had succeeded Dame Anne Loughlin, who had been compelled to retire because of ill-health. He took over his duties as general secretary at the beginning of March 1953. A Yorkshireman born and bred, he needed all his native doggedness and tenacity in the job ahead.

Like its predecessor, the Joint Clothing Council, which started its activities in February 1953, made a brave start and announced a programme on the lines already laid down. But it, too, was doomed. In the autumn of 1954, two employers' organisations, the Wholesale Clothing Manufacturers' Federation and the British Mantle Manufacturers' Association, announced their 'irrevocable' decision to withdraw. On 7th December the council decided to dissolve itself and an official liquidator was appointed.

Their decision arose from their objections to the proposal to raise a levy to finance the work of the Council. The Council had inherited the funds of the old Development Council on its dissolution, but it transpired that it could only raise a levy under the headings of scientific research, promotion of exports and improvement of design. This definition the leaders of the Council felt was too narrow and the Board of Trade agreed to bring in a bill to amend the relevant section of the Industrial Organisation and Development Act of 1947, under which the old Council had been established, so as to strengthen the new body's financial position. The bill had its first reading in January 1954. The largest and most influential employers' organisations demanded its withdrawal, and others sought deferment. The President of the Board of Trade bowed to the storm and the bill never had its second reading.

In fairness, it must be said that the President, Mr Thorneycroft, was personally in favour of a central organisation for the industry, and had tried to persuade the employers to co-operate. He himself admitted that he felt there were still substantial arguments for some central organisation. He realised however that it was no good having one that was not supported by the employers.

The statement the Wholesale Clothing Manufacturers' Federation issued for public consumption to explain why they were withdrawing from the Joint Council did not reveal the whole story. It was laconic, evasive and full of platitudes about how hard they had tried to make it a success. They said that it had been of no practical benefit to the industry generally, bearing in mind the expenditure of time and money involved, nor did the proposed programme for the next two years hold out any hope that new services of real value to their section would be provided by the council which, in any event, had proved to be much too unwieldy and cumbersome . . . their arguments against the Development Council also applied to the new council and would indeed have been fundamental in relation to any similar type of body. In other words, they were against any and every form of central organisation. It went on to say that new machinery of that kind was unnecessary, trotting out the old familiar argument about the diversity of the clothing industry and the belief that existing organisations could fulfil the same purpose.

Finally the employers declared that the Federation wished to meet the union with a view to establishing . . . joint machinery for the discussion of matters regarding research and the improvement of productivity and any other matters of mutual interest.

This may have been intended as an olive branch or a gesture to allay the indignation of the union. If so, it was a singularly empty one. No approach was ever made to the union on these lines.

Thus ended any and every attempt to establish a central organisation for the whole clothing industry. Comment in the trade press was unfavourable, though the tendency was to blame events rather than individuals. According to the *Maker-up*, both councils had been 'a mixture of faith, hope and politics . . . the hard truth is that the whole project was mistimed. Had it been started in 1945 or 1946, it would have stood a pretty good chance of success.' The *Merchant Tailors' Journal* described the liquidation as 'a bitter disappointment,' and said there was evidence that the bespoke trade would have received 'considerable and lasting benefit' from the council.

The union was justifiably incensed. Its leaders felt that they had been led up the garden path and that their long and loyal co-operation in the work, first of the working parties and later of the councils, had been set at naught. The general secretary wrote that the winding up of the Council illustrated the unsatisfactory nature of the relations with some of the leading employers' organisations. 'This is no fault of ours . . . Many of us worked very hard indeed to promote a central organisation, and we have often showed a degree of tolerance and patience which it may not always be possible to repeat.'

Relations with the employers at this time were about as bad as at any time since before the war, although it is only fair to say that in many individual firms there were excellent relations. But it is hardly surprising to find that for some time after the death of the clothing council, the union tended to turn its main efforts inwards, and concentrate even more on building up its bargaining strength.

As a first step the union sought a revision of the basis of the national agreement, introduced as long ago as 1919. It suggested the setting up of a Joint Industrial Council with wider terms than the Wages Council which would wipe out the remaining vestiges of the trade boards' stigma. Union leaders complained of the 'deplorable and out-moded' attitude of many employers, who thought their obligations began and ended with the Wages Councils. The proposal for a change was resisted by the employers who suggested instead a purely advisory joint consultative council. Yet even this modest reform took three years to accomplish. It was not till May 1958 that the establishment of a Joint Consultative Council, to discuss matters of mutual interest at regular meetings was announced. But it has largely remained a paper organisation.

'This was the nearest approach that the union's representatives could obtain towards the establishment of a Joint Industrial Council,' commented the *Garment Worker*.

The union had long been calling for a revision of the whole wage basis to replace the existing cumbersome, untidy and obsolete system. The 1951 conference appointed a special committee to investigate wage-fixing methods and union leaders lost no opportunity, in the *Garment Worker* and elsewhere, of pressing their case. Indeed it was highly illogical and historically absurd that whereas the Garment Workers' was a national union, representing the vast majority of clothing workers, the employers were still organised in separate and often competing groups. This meant that the union had to submit separate claims and conduct time-consuming negotiations with a multiplicity of bodies, a procedure which led to long delays and frustrations for the membership.

Dame Anne had written in 1951 that the synchronisation of claims and increases was highly desirable and was indeed the ultimate goal, but 'it is not as simple as it looks.

Negotiations with the Wholesale Clothing Manufacturers
Federation normally set the pattern and are followed by
separate negotiations with the Shirt, Collar and Tie Manu
facturers' Federation, the Corset Trade Association, the British
Rainwear Manufacturers' Association, the Overall Manufac
turers, the Merchant Tailors' Federation as well as with
parallel bodies in Ireland and Scotland. Even after direc
negotiations have resulted in some settlement, the proposal
on minimum rates have to be submitted to all the Wages Coun
cils, and have to be approved by the Minister of Labour.

This complicated procedural minuet was danced in practi
cally every year during the fifties. Continual rises in the cost o
living and advances in other industries compelled the unio
to table almost annual claims – to keep running, like the Re
Queen, in order to be able to stay in the same place. Thes
claims met with varying degrees of success.

A major concession was secured in 1956, when the employers
albeit reluctantly, agreed to grant increases irrespective c
earnings, instead of just on the minimum rates. But there wa
small progress made towards winning equal pay for equa
work, a scandal in an industry where four-fifths of the em
ployees were women, although some progress was made to
wards narrowing the gap.

Methods of incentive payment provided a constant and un
resolved source of friction, But on balance the union coul
point to substantial advance. Looking back on the decade, th
Garment Worker recorded in 1960 that though the fifties 'wer
not happy years,' they were years of 'continuous progress
Men's wages were increased by £2 16s and women's b
£2 5s 10d.

It is worth pausing to take a closer look at the negotiations c
1956, which were particularly crucial for the union and th
whole trade union movement. These were conducted at a tim
when employers in every industry were getting 'tough', i
accordance with the government's policy of income restrain
Mr Macmillan was attacked at the Brighton Trades Unio
Congress in September, and the TUC was committed to nor
co-operation on wages. The union actually anticipated th
TUC decision. In February the executive board had put in
claim for 5d an hour on the minimum for men and women, wit

Union members today

Threading the needle

a 4d an hour increase over and above earnings. It was based on the cost of living, the profitability of the industry (which had just had one of its best post-war years' trading) and the need to prevent clothing workers drifting to jobs in better-paid and more attractive industries.

The employers offered 2d for men and 1½d for women merely on the minimum rates. This, their 'final' offer, was rejected as utterly inadequate, and the union summoned a special emergency conference at the Leeds headquarters on 7th July. The 200 delegates unanimously pledged full support for the executive's policy and authorised it to take strike action as and when necessary. The evidence of firmness and solidarity caused a change of front. The executive board was invited to a meeting ten days later at the Queen's Hotel. Leeds. After eight hours, agreement was reached on the basis of a new offer of a 2½d an hour increase for men and women irrespective of earnings, and increases in the national minimum rates of 4d for men and 3d for women.

During the long and stormy meeting, the employers heard some plain speaking from the general secretary. Declaring 'The black blot of a sweated industry is still with us,' he pointed to the Wages Council's near-starvation rates of £6 19s 4d for men and £4 11s 8d for women. These compared with a minimum rate of £7 2s 4d for a labourer in engineering, £7 13s for a roadsweeper and £8 0s 6d for a colliery labourer.

'We ask you to recognise the fact that we live in the year 1956, not 1910,' Newton said. 'We say that we have the right to live as well as those we clothe and we are determined to do so.'

Even though the amount granted was not as great as the original claim, the fact that the employers were forced to go beyond their 'final' offer was an important victory for the union. The chairman at the next year's conference pointed out: 'The lesson is plain for everyone to see. It is not a new lesson. It is the lesson that workers in every industry have learned, over and over again, in thousands of struggles over the years. It is that if you want a fair deal, if you want decent wages and working conditions, you must organise and organise again.' The conference there and then decided to launch a special recruitment campaign, particularly designed to convince the 'nons' about the advantages and benefits of belonging to the union.

Such special membership drives were only one facet of the continuing and steady efforts of officials and stewards in every region to bring in more members. It was often an uphill task, especially in the workshops making women's light clothing.

The large proportion of married women among clothing workers and the high turnover in many factories added to the difficulties, and presented problems such as union officers in shipyards and mines have never had to cope with. The aim was not only to enrol more members, but to make them take an active part in union life. As John Newton put it, soon after he took over, numerical strength was only half the battle. 'I would rather have ten enlightened and voluntary members than twenty who grudgingly pay their dues.'

He later made a point of praising the voluntary work of the union's 2,000 shop stewards, 'the backbone of the union,' at a time when shop stewards generally were getting a bad press and being blamed for all the current industrial troubles.

The union was also deeply concerned with improving the efficiency of its internal administration and training its officers. To expand the training and education programme and to keep pace with the increasing costs of administration, contributions, which had been 1s 5d per week for men and 9d for women, were raised in 1956. More money was spent on presentation and propaganda. Indeed the Tailors were to the fore among unions in harnessing modern techniques to aid recruitment, using not only leaflets and posters, but display advertisements, strip cartoons and, in the late fifties, a popular calypso record 'Come on Gal'.

This was particularly aimed at young factory workers to show that to join the union was, in modern idiom, to 'get with it.' The *Garment Worker* appeared in the autumn of 1958 in a new and brighter format, and carried articles of general interest John Williamson would have been startled at the change since his day, but he would surely have approved.

Preoccupation with internal affairs did not prevent the union from continuing its efforts to make the clothing industry more efficient, even though there was no longer any central council to give a lead. The union's basic attitude was summed up in this phrase: 'We as a union have never been opposed to new methods leading to increased efficiency, provided management fully takes us into their confidence and discusses and con sults with us, and we obtain our rightful share of increased production.'

The clothing industry as a whole, despite an annual turnover of nearly £1,000 million, had lagged behind many other industries. It had no research centre and, until May 1958, no national training scheme. The voluntary scheme then agreed despite its limitations was welcomed by the union, in the wholesale clothing trade, but it was regretted that it applied only to boys, and not to girls.

Despite the new scheme, many firms were reluctant to change their habits and we find the *Manufacturing Clothier* in 1960 criticising employers for their apathy and failure to support 'beat the bulge' conferences. It warned: 'The best of these youngsters will not be coming in unless something is done to make prospects more attractive . . . There was a time when a young girl would enter because she knew she would learn how to make clothes. But she will be fortunate if she is shown how to perform more than two or three operations.'

A few progressive firms provided excellent facilities for training at every level, while some of the new factories in the development areas set up special training bays under skilled instructors.

Working conditions in the new, light and airy factories on the trading estates in the old depressed areas were a far cry from the old sweatshops of London's East End, and should have been a model for the whole trade. This makes it all the more disturbing to read reports as recently as 1956 about the spread of homework.

Though there were no revolutionary innovations in production methods, comparable with the introduction of the sewing machine one hundred years before, there was a growing tendency for machines to replace hand work, especially on finishing processes. There were developments in production engineering technique, while new man-made fibres replaced many of the traditional materials.

The general speed-up in the tempo of production and the desire to lead a fuller life stimulated the trade unions in their campaign for a shorter working week during the latter part of the decade. Shorter hours had long been given priority among the tailors' demands, and in common with other organisations the union made a determined effort to achieve a reduction in the working week. Declaring 'the forty-four-hour-week is as dead in the garment industry in 1960 as the forty-eight-hour-week was in 1946,' the union proceeded to demand a staged reduction with a cut of two hours in 1959-60, and a further hour in 1961 and 1962 until the forty-hour-week was achieved.

In the spring of 1960, the employers agreed to introduce a forty-two-hour-week without loss of pay. This was a major landmark for the union. Though its dream of a forty-hour-week was not realised, the settlement was a step in the right direction. Incidentally it provided an immediate fillip to recruitment.

The National Union of Tailors and Garment Workers was one of the first to win an annual holiday with pay – that was in 1939 – and payment for statutory holidays a few years later. It negotiated an agreement for holiday pay at average earnings in 1952. The cut in working hours was thus a logical development of its long struggle to improve the lot of men and women in the industry.

That struggle continues. Faithful to its traditions and historical objectives, the union is ceaselessly striving to build up its resources to provide better protection and give an improved service to its members, as well as meeting the needs of the general public. The garment workers have established the only comprehensive national organisation in the clothing industry, and speak with one voice for its workers, whereas the employers are still divided among themselves in many different organisations. As Andrew Conley forecast in 1930, the National Union of Tailors and Garment Workers has proved to be 'a powerful, closely organised union with the spirit and will to fight for its members'.

Index